Magic Lantern Guides

KONICA
MINOLTA
MAXXUM 5 D
DYNAX

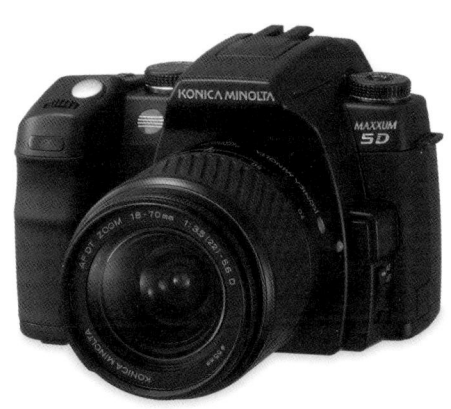

Peter K. Burian

LARK BOOKS
A Division of Sterling Publishing,Co., Inc.
New York

Book Design and Layout: Michael Robertson
Cover Design: Barbara Zaretsky
Associate Art Director: Shannon Yokeley

Library of Congress Cataloging-in-Publication Data

Burian, Peter K.
  Konica Minolta Maxxum 5D/Dynax 5D / Peter K. Burian.-- 1st ed.
     p. cm. -- (Magic lantern guides)
  Includes index.
  ISBN 1-57990-866-7 (pbk.)
 1. Konica camera--Handbooks, manuals, etc. 2. Minolta camera--Handbooks,
manuals, etc. 3. Digital cameras--Handbooks, manuals, etc. 4.
Photography--Digital techniques--Handbooks, manuals, etc. I. Title. II.
Series.
TR263.K55B87 2006
771.3'3--dc22

                                            2005030782

10 9 8 7 6 5 4 3 2 1
First Edition

Published by Lark Books, A Division of Sterling Publishing Co., Inc.
387 Park Avenue South, New York, N.Y. 10016

© 2006, Peter K. Burian
Photography © Peter K. Burian unless otherwise specified

Distributed in Canada by Sterling Publishing,
c/o Canadian Manda Group, 165 Dufferin Street
Toronto, Ontario, Canada M6K 3H6

Distributed in the United Kingdom by GMC Distribution Services,
Castle Place, 166 High Street, Lewes, East Sussex, England BN7 1XU

Distributed in Australia by Capricorn Link (Australia) Pty Ltd.,
P.O. Box 704, Windsor, NSW 2756 Australia

This book is not sponsored by Konica Minolta Holdings, Inc. The written instructions, photographs, designs, patterns, and projects in this volume are intended for the personal use of the reader and may be reproduced for that purpose only. Any other use, especially commercial use, is forbidden under law without written permission of the publisher. The works represented are the original creations of the contributing artists. All artists retain copyrights on their individual works, except as noted.

Minolta, Dynax, Anti-Shake, and other Konica Minolta product names or terminology are trademarks of Konica Minolta Holdings, Inc. Other trademarks are recognized as belonging to their respective owners.

Every effort has been made to ensure that all the information in this book is accurate. However, due to differing conditions, tools, and individual skills, the publisher cannot be responsible for any injuries, losses, and other damages that may result from the use of the information in this book. Because specifications may be changed by the manufacturer without notice, the contents of this book may not necessarily agree with software and equipment changes made after publication.

If you have questions or comments about this book, please contact:
Lark Books
67 Broadway
Asheville, NC 28801
(828) 253-0467

Printed in China

ISBN 13: 978-1-57990-866-9
ISBN 10: 1-57990-866-7

For information about custom editions, special sales, premium and corporate purchases, please contact Sterling Special Sales Department at 800-805-5489 or specialsales@sterlingpub.com.

Contents

10

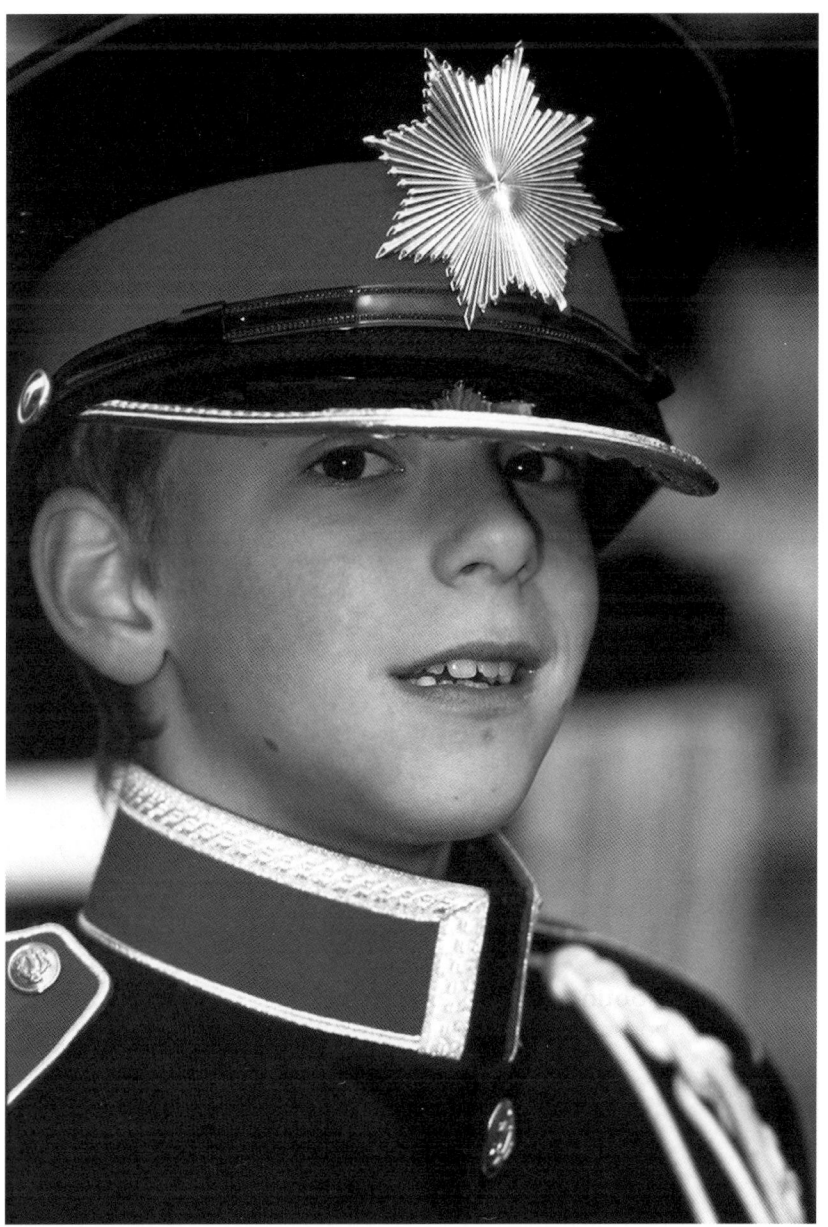

13

Introduction

The Maxxum 5D/Dynax 5D, announced in July 2005, is an affordable second entry in Konica Minolta's lineup of digital SLRs. Like the Maxxum 7D/Dynax 7D, the 5D incorporates the unique Anti-Shake (A/S) system that provides image stabilization with Maxxum/Dynax lenses. Using this system that shifts the entire CCD sensor module, the camera allows you the advantage to make sharp photos at fairly long shutter speeds.

As a matter of convenience, I will often refer to the newer model as the 5D and the older model as the 7D. Though a number of differences become apparent when comparing these two cameras, it is also clear that the 5D incorporates many of the benefits of the 7D, including the same autofocus, metering, and sensor technology. It also inherited all essential 7D capabilities and is just as fast in Continuous Advance mode, shooting at 3 frames per second (although it records fewer shots per burst).

The 5D is smaller than the 7D and weighs 6 ounces (170g) less. It employs a lower resolution LCD monitor (115,000 pixels for the 5D compared to 207,000 for the 7D) and has fewer options associated with its camera functions. It does not accept a vertical grip accessory and the PC cord socket (for connecting studio flash systems) has been omitted (but the same function can be added with an optional PCT-100 adapter).

↶ *The Maxxum 5D/Dynax 5D is a versatile and reliable camera that helps you create beautiful images, making digital photography enjoyable and rewarding.*

15

However, the 5D is not a "stripped down" model. For one thing, it offers several benefits over its older sibling, including faster start-up time (1 vs. 2 seconds). The Maxxum 5D/ Dynax 5D is a fast and convenient digital SLR that's easy to use in point-and-shoot modes but is highly suitable for serious photography due to its remarkable versatility.

About This Book

When the terms "right" and "left" are used, it is assumed that you are holding the camera in the horizontal shooting position. Also, the term "single lens reflex" will usually be abbreviated to "SLR."

In order to get the most from your 5D, it is helpful to become intimately familiar with the camera and its many conventional and digital features. This book is intended to assist you in achieving that aim. I'll go well beyond simple instructions detailing which button to push or which dial to turn. My goal is to help you turn this high-tech device into a great picture-taking tool, maximizing its performance to achieve exactly the intended effects. I'll provide many explanations, hints, and recommendations as to how, when, and why you might want to use—or not use—each feature. Although you may want to read this book page by page from front to back, you can also jump around from one chapter to another as you wish, or use it as a reference to quickly find information or tips on specific topics.

After testing nearly a hundred film and digital SLR cameras for photographic magazines, I know that the key to satisfaction is a full appreciation of all the features, and how and why each one is best used. Consequently, this book provides a great deal of information intended to enable full appreciation of the Maxxum 5D/Dynax 5D.

Be sure to have your camera close at hand as you read; try each feature until you can easily remember how it is accessed. Skip to different chapters, if necessary, to find

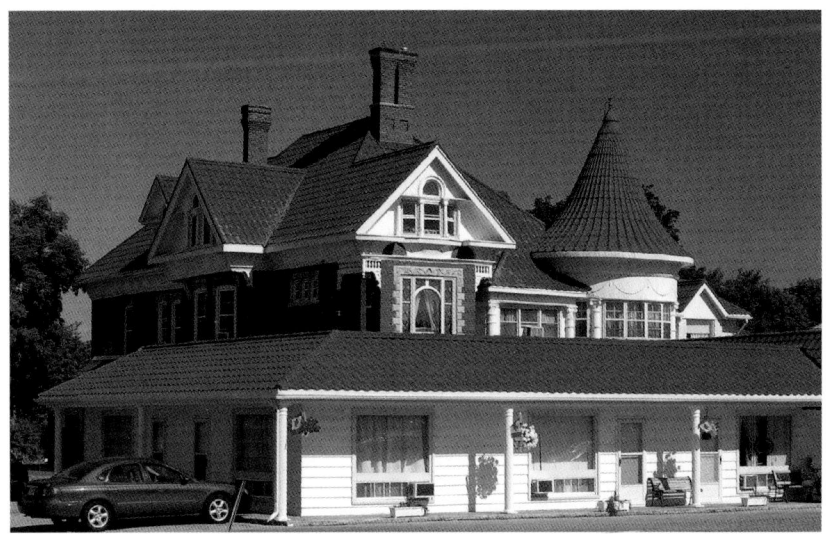

information that you need immediately. Later, when you have more time, pull out the book again and read about other features that might also be useful to you. And don't forget to put the handy Quick Reference Card in your wallet so it will be with you whenever you need it.

Peter K. Burian
Toronto, Canada

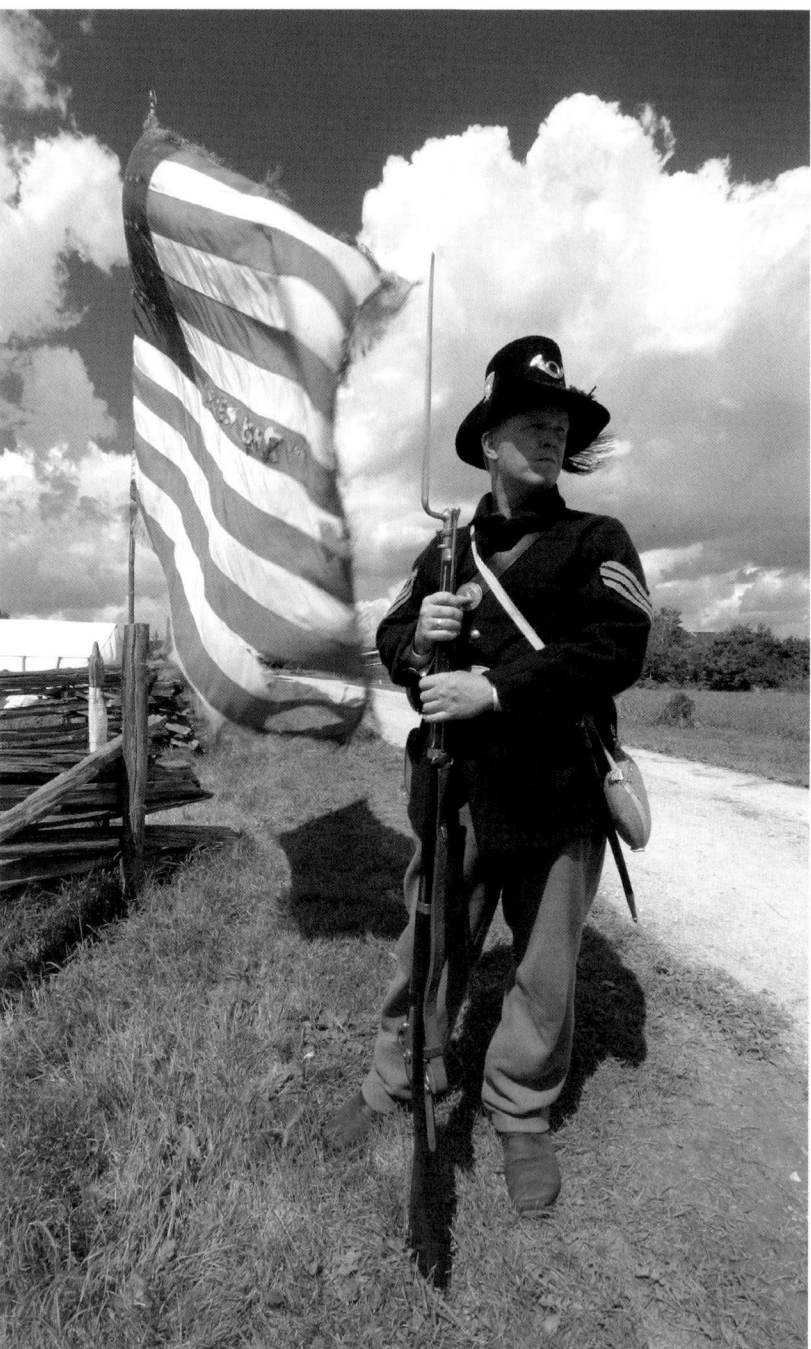

Understanding
Digital Photography

Digital photography has helped people become more interested than ever in creating images and preserving memories. One thing is certain—owning a digital camera is a sure way to discover new excitement and enthusiasm for photography. When compared to some other brands of entry-level digital SLR's, the Konica Minolta Maxxum 5D/Dynax 5D is one of the most full-featured, and should enhance your continued enjoyment of shooting great photos.

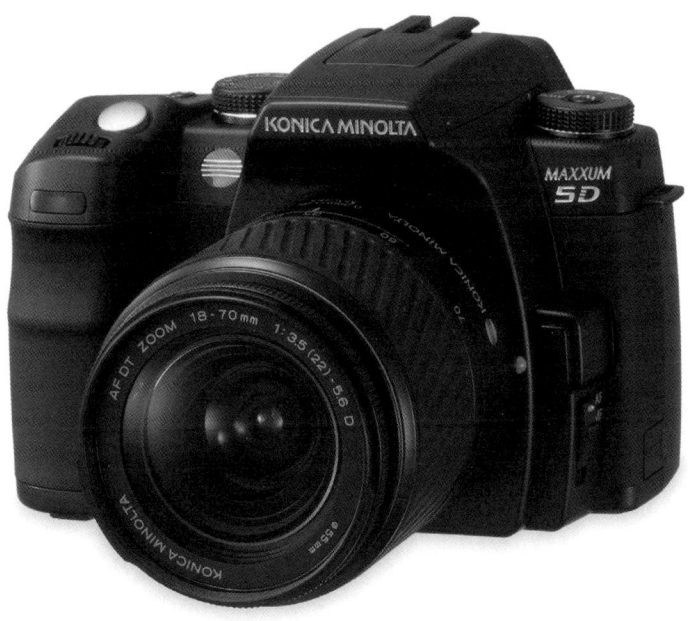

Even in its fully automatic modes—Portrait program with auto flash in this case— the 5D can produce technically pleasing images.

Before looking at the specific operations of this camera, we will outline some important digital concepts to serve as a quick refresher, especially with regard to how they differ from concepts in film photography.

A Note About Digital Cameras

There are some special things that digital cameras do differently than traditional film cameras that make them exciting and fun to use. However, some of these differences may seem complicated or confusing at first. Though most of the features and controls found on 35mm film cameras are also available on the 5D, there are many new controls and operations. Some are unique to digital photography, while others have been added to increase the camera's versatility for different shooting styles and requirements. This doesn't mean you have to master them all. It is important to remember that, with today's automated, full-feature cameras, it is not necessary to be an expert to get great results. The goal of this book is to help you understand how the camera operates so that you can choose the techniques that work best for you and for your style of photography.

Differences Between Digital and Film Photography

It wasn't long ago that you could easily tell the difference between photos taken with a digital camera and those shot with a traditional film camera. This was because pictures from digital cameras didn't measure up in quality. However, this is no longer true. With the 5D, you can make pictures 8 x 10 inches (A4) or larger that will look as good, or better, than an enlargement from a 35mm negative. When made from your technically best images, even 13 x 19-inch (Super B format) prints can be suitable for framing.

While there are differences between digital and film photography, there are also many similarities. Whether digital or

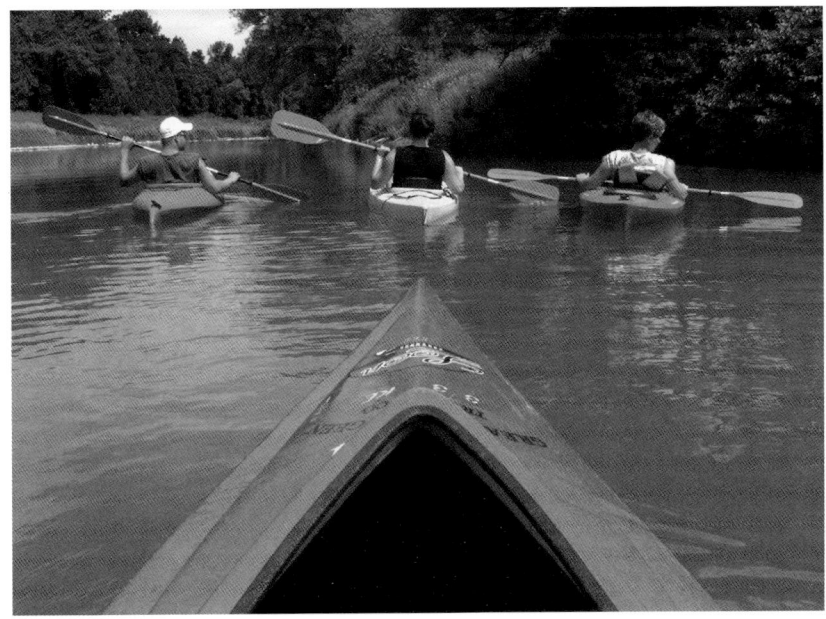

*Both 35mm and digital cameras were designed for the same pur-
pose, and the picture-taking process is similar in many respects. But
digital employs entirely different technology and offers several benefits, including instant image review on the LCD monitor. These make
digital preferable for both family snapshots and serious photography.*

film-based, a camera is basically a light-tight box that holds
a lens to focus the image. You regulate the amount of light
entering this box to strike the light-sensitive medium (film or
sensor) by adjusting the f/stop or the shutter speed.

The difference, of course, is that in traditional photography, the image is recorded on film and later developed
with chemicals, whereas in digital photography the camera converts the light to an electronic image. A digital
camera processes this image internally, but a film camera
simply stores the exposed film. While many exposure
techniques remain the same, understanding what's different about digital photography will help you take advantage of the many enjoyable and creative possibilities of
this new technology.

Film vs. the Digital Sensor

Both film and digital cameras expose pictures using virtually identical technologies. The light measuring (metering) systems are the same, both work with ISO-based systems, and the shutter and aperture mechanisms controlling the amount of light admitted into the camera are the same. These similarities exist because both film and digital cameras share the same goal: to deliver the appropriate amount of light required by the film or sensor to create a good picture.

Not surprisingly, however, digital sensors respond differently to light than film does. From dark areas (such as navy blue blazers, asphalt, and shadows) to midtones (blue sky and green grass) to bright areas (such as white houses and sand beaches), a digital sensor responds to the full range of light equally, or linearly. Film, however, responds linearly only to midtones (those blue skies and green fairways). Therefore, negative film blends tones very well in highlight areas and slide film blends tones well in shadow areas, whereas digital sensors often cut out the bright tones. Digital responds to highlights like slide film and to shadows like negative film.

With both film and digital cameras, many things happen between the time that you take the picture and the time you see it. And, although film reacts chemically to light and a digital sensor reacts electronically, the end result is similar. So similar, in fact, that most people would be hard pressed to tell the difference between a digital snapshot and a film snapshot.

The LCD Monitor

In conventional photography, you are never really sure your picture is a success until the film is developed. You must wait to find out if the exposure was correct or if something happened to spoil the results, such as the blurring of a moving subject or unwanted stray reflections from an on-camera flash.

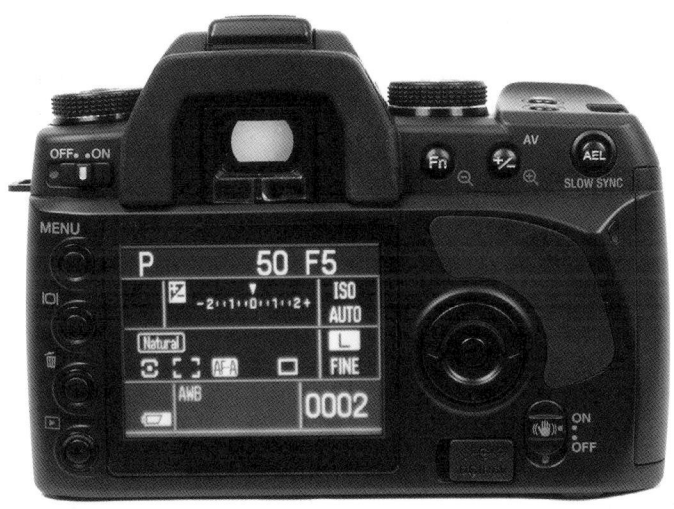

In addition to displaying images after they are taken, the oversized LCD monitor provides information on the camera modes and settings in use.

When using a digital SLR, however, you can see an image on the LCD monitor almost immediately after taking a picture. Admittedly, you cannot see all the details that you would see in a print, but this ability means that you can evaluate the picture you have just shot. If the exposure, lighting, or composition is not quite right, simply re-shoot on the spot. This feature is especially useful in flash photography. In addition to confirming correct exposure, the LCD monitor allows you to check for any excessively bright highlight areas or dark backgrounds, as well as allowing you to evaluate other factors, such as the effect produced by multiple flash units and/or reflectors.

Exposure and the Histogram
Digital cameras do not offer magic tricks that let you beat the laws of physics, so incorrect exposure will still cause problems. Too little light makes dark images; too much light makes overly bright images. Granted, you can correct digital

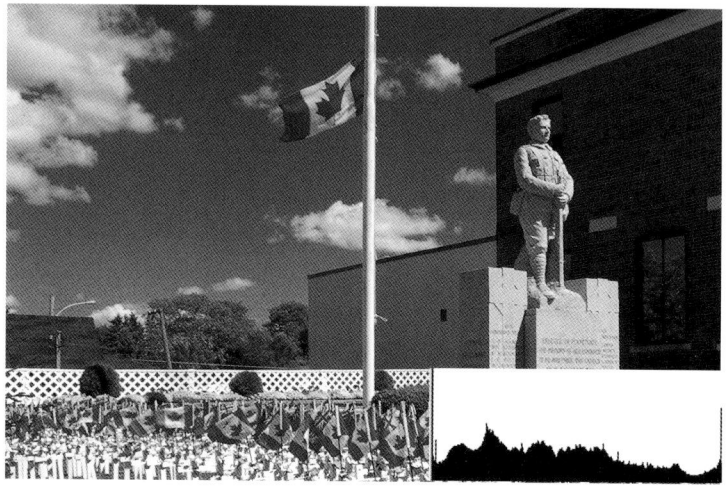

It's well worth learning to interpret the camera's histogram because this feature guides you to create exposures that perfectly satisfy your technical or aesthetic intentions.

images to a certain extent afterwards by using software in a computer, but programs can't add blown details to overexposed images. Getting the correct exposure in-camera can save you a great deal of post processing work.

After you shoot a digital image, a quick glance at the LCD monitor will indicate whether the exposure (image brightness) is close to accurate. Better yet, you can also access two features found in digital photography that give a more scientific evaluation of brightness values: the histogram scale and the highlight/shadow warning, which in the 5D is called a Luminance Limit Display (see page 162 for details). Because you are able to check exposure using these tools, there is less need to bracket (shoot a series of images at different exposure levels) when using the 5D than with a traditional film camera.

Memory Cards vs. Film

Memory cards are necessary to store images captured by a digital camera. These removable, reusable cards offer several advantages over film:

More Photos/More ISOs: Standard 35mm film cassettes are available in either 24 or 36 exposures. Memory cards come in a wide range of capacities, and all but the smallest are capable of holding more exposures than a roll of film (depending on the selected file size). Also, a single card can record different ISO settings on a picture-by-picture basis—much simpler than switching rolls of film.

Reusable: Once you make an exposure with film, the emulsion layer is permanently changed and thus, the film cannot be reused. With a memory card, you can erase photos at any time, removing the ones you don't want, creating space for additional photos. This simplifies the process of dealing with and organizing your final set of images. Once images are transferred to your computer (or other storage medium, such as a CD or DVD), images can be erased or the card can be reformatted and reused.

Durability: Memory cards are much more durable than film. They can be removed from the camera in virtually any conditions without the risk of ruined pictures. They are less susceptible to heat damage and can even be taken through the airport carry-on x-ray inspection machines without suffering damage. (However, the cards are susceptible to magnetic fields so keep them away from stereo speakers and other devices containing powerful magnets.)

Small Size: In the space taken up by just a couple of rolls of film, you can store or tote multiple memory cards that will hold hundreds of images.

Greater Image Permanence: The latent image (exposed but undeveloped film) is susceptible to degradation from atmospheric conditions such as heat and humidity. And new security monitors for packed and carry-on luggage can also damage film. Traveling photographers find that digital photography allows them much more peace of mind. Not only are memory cards more durable, but their images can also be easily downloaded into storage devices or laptops. No more concerns over what to do with precious exposed film!

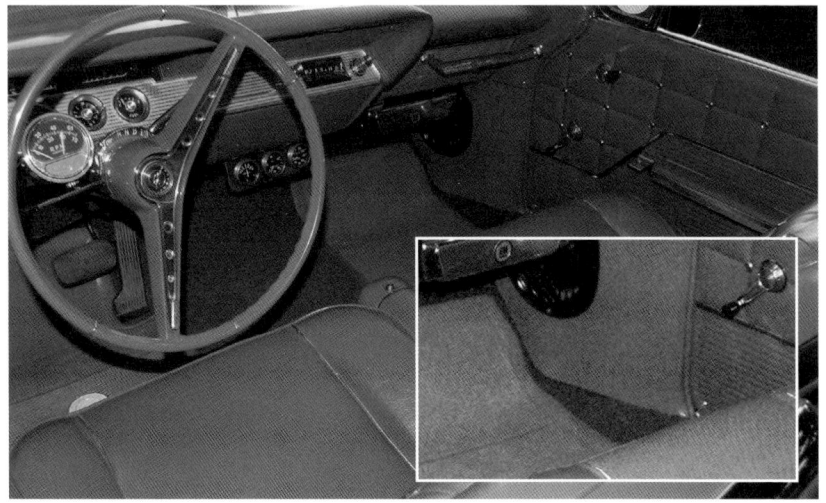

High ISO settings (1600 in this example) as well as long exposures are two factors that can generate noise in your picture, as illustrated by the blotchy specks in the inset above.

Noise/Grain

Grain in film appears as an irregular, sand-like texture that, if large, can be unsightly and, if small, is essentially invisible. (A textured look is sometimes desirable for certain creative effects.) It occurs due to the chemical structure of the light sensitive materials and is most prominent in fast films, such as ISO 1600.

The equivalent in digital photography is known as noise, which often occurs as colored specks most visible in dark or evenly colored areas. Digital noise occurs for several reasons: sensor noise (caused by heat from the electronics and optics), digital artifacts (when digital technology cannot deal with fine tonalities such as sky gradations), and JPEG artifacts (caused by image compression). Sensor noise is the most common.

Digital noise is most prominent in images made at high ISO settings (often higher than 400), and will increase as the ISO increases. The colored specks are even more obvious in images that are underexposed, especially when lightened afterward in image processing software. You can buy after-market software for noise reduction, but it's best to use ISO 400 or lower whenever practical for optimal image quality.

Sensor noise may also be increased with long exposures under low-light conditions, as in night photography. In most situations, the 5D produces images with little digital noise at ISO settings up to 800. It also includes a feature that moderates digital noise during very long exposures.

ISO (Sensitivity)
Digital sensors don't have a true ISO. However, their sensitivity has been adjusted electronically to mimic film ISOs. Hence, you can set the ISO to 100 for average daylight shooting, 800 for faster shutter speed's or smaller apertures in less bright situations, or 1600 for lowlight photography. With a digital camera, you can change ISO from picture to picture, without changing memory cards. It's like changing film at the touch of a button! This provides certain benefits, such as the ability to first shoot indoors without flash at ISO 800, then follow your subject outside into bright sun and optimize image quality by switching immediately to ISO 100. It's like changing film at the touch of a button!

File Formats
A digital camera converts analog image information to digital data and records to a digital file. The 5D offers two distinct file formats: JPEG and RAW. It also offers another option: RAW+, which records each photo in both the RAW and the JPEG (Fine quality) formats simultaneously.

JPEG: Joint Photographic Experts Group, the most common format in digital photography, is actually a standard for compression of images rather than a true file format. Digital cameras use JPEG because its compression reduces file size, allowing more pictures to fit on a memory card.

RAW: A generic term for a format that has little or no internal processing applied by the camera. Most camera manufacturers have developed proprietary versions of RAW, and the 5D's RAW files are noted by the suffix "MRW" (but I will often refer to MRW files as RAW).

Many, if not most, digital cameras give you choices about how many of the sensor's pixels to use when shooting pictures. You do not always need to utilize the camera's maximum resolution. Your memory card will hold more images when the camera is set to record at lower resolutions, but it will not capture as much data; and the more digital information (higher resolution), the bigger print it is possible to make.

White Balance
Most pros who have shot film over the years can tell you about the challenges they've faced when balancing their light source with the film's response to the color of light. For example, daylight-balanced (outdoor) film used indoors under tungsten household lamps will produce pictures with an orange cast. Accurate color reproduction in this instance would require the use of a blue color correction filter.

The color of light also varies in other circumstances, though our eyes and brain make natural adjustments so we do not notice this variation. Light is quite blue on an overcast day, even bluer in a shady area, green under fluorescent lighting, orange under tungsten lamps, and so on. In film photography, filters attached to the front of a lens can correct for the color cast by altering the color of the light so our subjects are rendered as we normally see them.

With digital cameras, all this has changed. Color correction is managed by the white balance function, an internal setting built into all digital cameras. The camera can automatically check the light, calculate the proper setting for its color temperature, and make the necessary modification. This automated system is programmed to produce the following: whites should be white in the final image; all other tones should be accurate as well, without a blue, yellow, green, etc., color cast.

Cost of Shooting

While film cameras generally cost less than digital cameras, the cost of shooting digital is lower. A couple of reusable memory cards are much less expensive than a large supply of film, and there's no need to pay for processing or for printing every image on a roll of film. The more pictures you take, the sooner you will recoup the difference in the cost of a 5D versus the cost of a comparable 35mm film camera.

More importantly perhaps, you may become a better photographer when using a digital camera. Since you won't need to worry about the cost of film and processing, you'll be more likely to really "work" a subject, exploring it from various angles and trying a variety of creative photographic approaches. This can be liberating because it encourages greater creativity. Any shots that don't work out can simply be deleted.

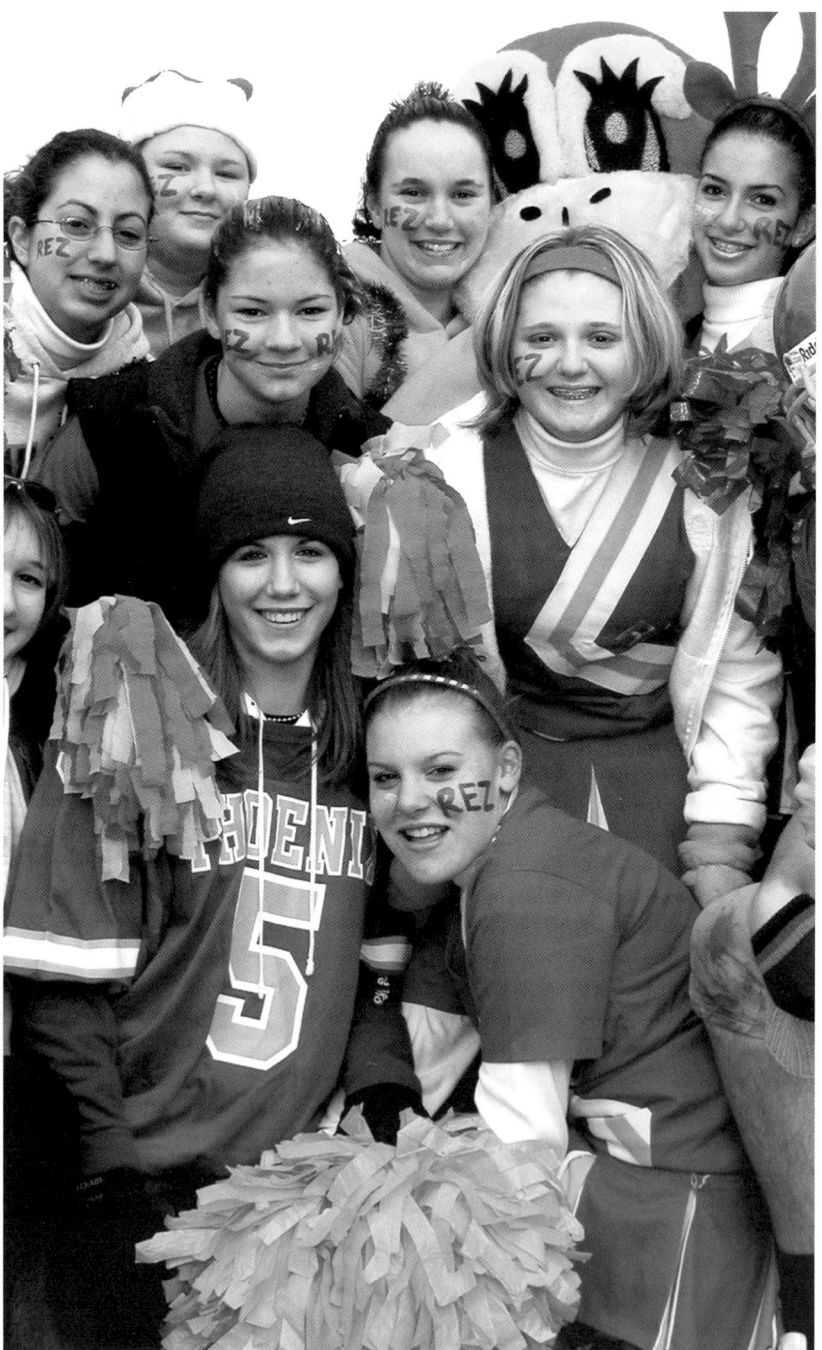

Getting Started Quickly

This chapter will help you start shooting digital snapshots immediately, before learning the full scope of control possible with your Maxxum 5D/Dynax 5D. In time (and with the help of this book), you will want to understand how to utilize this camera to its fullest capacity. But first, you may follow this quick guide that outlines basic operations. Anyone with 35mm SLR experience will find a number of these steps familiar.

Attach the neck strap before starting to use the camera and adjust the strap to fit your body. The strap should always be used to prevent damage caused by accidentally dropping the camera.

Insert the Battery

Although the NP-400 battery supplied with the camera may be partially charged, it will offer better performance if fully charged. Use only the supplied charger. The process takes 90 minutes or less and is finished when the lamp on the charger is extinguished. After charging, remove the battery from the charger and unplug the accessory from the wall socket.

⟲ *The white balance feature sets the camera for the type of available light. Not available in film photography, this control is one of the advantages of using a digital SLR such as the 5D.*

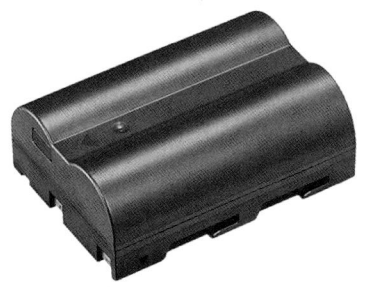

A NP-400 battery is supplied with the 5D, but we recommend you buy a second so that you will have a spare battery fully charged and ready for shooting. Photo © Konica Minolta.

Make sure the main (power) switch is OFF. Open the battery chamber door on the bottom of the camera and insert the battery with contacts first. When the small latch clicks in, close the chamber door. Turn the main switch ON. Check the battery level indicator at the bottom left corner of the LCD monitor (located on the back of the camera) to make sure it is indeed fully charged.

Set the Date and Time

Press the MENU button (on the back upper left of the camera) and follow the instructions provided in the monitor. Use your thumb to control navigation of the arrow keys (up, down, right, left) on the outside ring of the four-way controller (on the back of the camera to the right of the LCD monitor—it has arrow keys that point in four directions). When finished, press the AF button in the center of the controller to confirm your choices. (Think of the AF button as an OK button since you'll use it for that purpose often.)

Don't worry, the camera will not print the date/time on your images as some 35mm film cameras do. The data will be included in the shooting information recorded by the camera and can be accessed with image processing software such as any of the Adobe Photoshop programs. In future, you'll appreciate this reminder.

Mount a Lens

Make sure the camera is turned OFF to prevent any electronic fault whenever mounting or removing a lens. Remove the body cap on the camera and the rear cap from any Maxxum/Dynax lens. Line up the red index indicators on the lens and body. Insert the lens into the camera mount and rotate the barrel clockwise until you hear a click confirming that it's locked in.

Caution: Do not touch anything inside the camera body. Work quickly to minimize the risk of particles such as dust, sand, or pollen entering the camera. For the same reason, always use the body cap and lens caps when the lens is not mounted.

Adjust the Eyepiece

Set the diopter adjustment dial (on the back of the camera to the right of the eyepiece cup) to suit your specific eyesight, whether you wear eyeglasses or not. To do so, look through the viewfinder when the camera is on. Turn the dial until the large circle on the viewing screen appears sharpest to your eye.

Load a Memory Card

In most countries, the 5D is sold without a memory card, so you'll need to buy one in order to begin using the camera. It will accept the Type I and thicker Type II CompactFlash cards of any capacity, as well as Microdrive memory, a miniature hard drive resembling a CompactFlash card.

Think twice about buying a Microdrive. Unlike Compact-Flash cards, this device contains moving parts that can be damaged should you drop it. Buy a CompactFlash card with at least a capacity of 256 megabytes (MB). The cost per megabyte of memory goes down with higher capacities, so you may find that a 512MB card is not much more expensive than a 256 MB card.

CompactFlash cards come in a variety of capacities. A 6-megapixel camera, like the 5D, can quickly fill a card holding 256 MB of memory, so carry extra cards. It is usually wise to buy several medium-size cards rather than one big one. Photo©DayMen Photo Marketing.

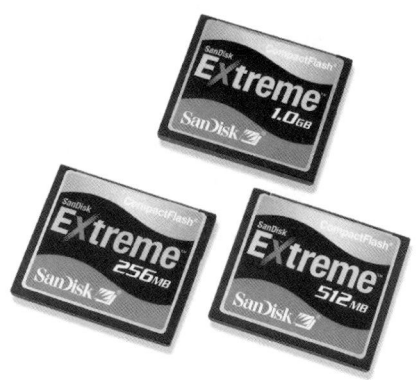

To load a memory card make sure the camera is OFF. Open the door for the card slot on the right side of the camera, and insert your card so it is facing toward the front of the camera with the electronic contact points pointing downward into the slot. It will not fit smoothly any other way, but use care not to force the card into position. After inserting the card, close the card-slot door. Now you can turn the camera ON.

If you already own some of the thin SD or MMC format memory cards required by some other cameras, you can also use them in the 5D. Simply buy a Konica Minolta SD-CF 1 adapter. Similar accessories may be available in other brands, but may not be compatible with your camera. Consult your Konica Minolta dealer to make sure you buy the appropriate device.

Format the Memory Card

You need to format your memory card in the camera when you first insert it in order to insure the most reliable performance. Make sure you have already downloaded any existing image files from your memory card to your computer.

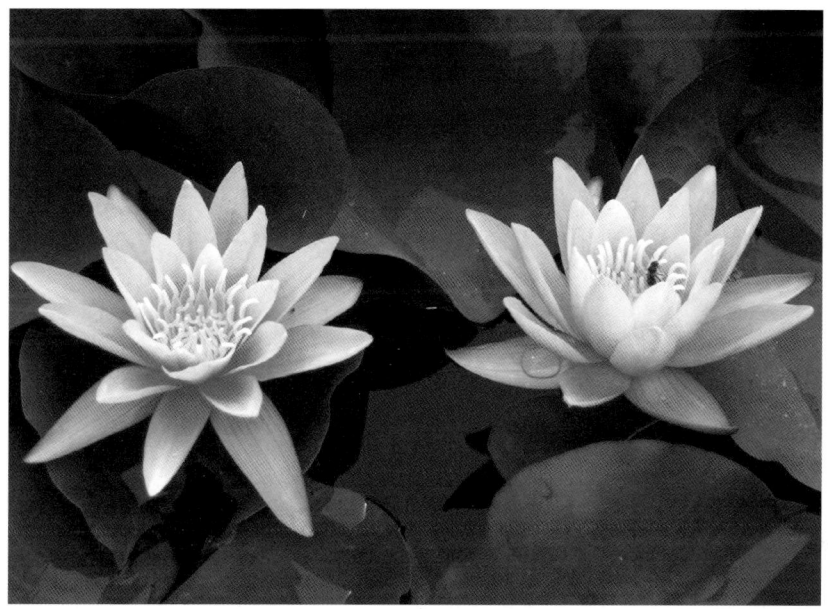

*To make sure you are ready for the next great photo opportunity, for-
mat your memory card in the camera immediately after downloading
images. Remember however, that formatting permanently deletes all
image data on the card.*

Once the card is inserted and the camera is turned ON,
press the camera's playback button ▶ (on the back of the
camera in the bottom left corner). Now, press the MENU
button. A list of options will appear in the LCD monitor,
including Format (the second item in Playback menu 1.)
Scroll to that option using the up/down arrow keys on the
controller, then press the right key until Enter appears in the
monitor. Next, press the AF button in the center of the controller. Now, using the left or right key, scroll to the Yes
option. Press the AF button, and formatting will commence.
Apply light pressure to the camera's shutter release button to
return to normal operation.

Sometimes an error message may appear in the LCD monitor
when you insert your memory card (Unable to use card, Format?). If this occurs, it is likely the card was previously used in

another camera. In this case, use the right/left arrow keys on the controller to select Yes in the LCD monitor, and press the AF button in the center of the controller to confirm your selection.

It's wise to format a card every time you are finished shooting and have downloaded the images to a computer. It takes only a short time. In addition to deleting all of the existing images and resetting the card's memory to full capacity, this step will minimize the risk of communication problems between card and camera. A small lamp on the back of the camera glows red while the formatting is taking place.

Caution: Formatting a card will permanently erase any images on the card. Before doing so, be sure that you want to proceed. Never format the card in a computer because computers use different file structures than digital cameras; this can make the card unreadable for the camera.

Take Your First Shots!

At this stage you're ready to start taking photos with your 5D using the default settings provided by Konica Minolta and the fully automatic exposure mode called AUTO. Be certain that the camera is ON. To make sure that camera operation will be fully automatic, follow these steps.

1. Select AUTO on the exposure mode dial (on the top right of the camera) to use the 5D as a basic point-and-shoot camera. All functions (exposure, JPEG size/quality, flash, ISO, and so on) are at the factory-set default settings.

2. Set the AF/MF switch (for auto and manual focus, on the left front of the camera) to AF.

3. Rotate the white balance dial (on the top left of the camera) to AWB.

4. Turn the Anti-Shake system (A/S) on; the control is on the lower right back of the camera.

The Maxxum 5D/Dynax 5D will use the following settings:

- A "smart" light metering system called a 14-segment honey-comb pattern.

- Autofocus with Wide Focus Area that allows for quick focus even on an off-center subject. The Automatic AF mode (AF-A) will be used, with automatic switching into Continuous AF mode (AF-C) should your subject begin to move.

- Auto ISO will automatically adjust the sensitivity to light.

- Noise reduction On for moderating digital noise (colored specks) that can occur in images made at exposures of one second or longer.

- Auto White Balance AWB for good color balance in all types of light.

- Single-frame Advance drive mode.

- JPEG file format; Large image size (3008 x 2000 pixels—the highest level); and Fine image quality (the middle level file compression).

- If the shutter speed indicated in the viewfinder is below 1/60 second, raise the flash. In low light, the focus assist pre-flash will be activated to aid the AF system in acquiring focus quickly.

- The A/S system will compensate for any camera shake.

Aim and Shoot

Hold the camera steady with your right hand on the grip and left hand cradling the lens. Aim the camera at a subject, perhaps a person. Partially depress the shutter release button to activate the light meter and autofocus systems. The circular indicator displayed along the bottom of the viewfinder screen will confirm focus. One of the AF area points on the viewing screen will light to show which area of the image will be in sharpest focus. Fully depress the shutter release button to take the picture. After shooting, you can view the image you have made on the LCD monitor. If you're not happy with the composition, or a person's expression, re-shoot the image.

Use the LCD Monitor

Slight pressure on the shutter release button also activates the data display in the LCD monitor on the back of the camera (unless the LCD monitor has been turned off to conserve battery power). A great deal of information is presented about camera settings, though not all of the data is visible at all times (see pages 59 and 94).

You cannot use the LCD monitor for viewing your picture before shooting, as you can with point-and-shoot digital cameras. However, the monitor does display an image for two seconds after it is recorded; that time period can be extended to 5 seconds or 10 seconds, with a feature in Recording Menu 1 (see page 101).

You can also use the LCD monitor to review images in Playback mode after shooting your pictures. Along with the image, you can choose to display or not display a great deal of information about settings that were used to make each photo. This is helpful to determine whether or not you have captured an acceptable image.

Review your pictures in Playback mode by pressing the playback button ▶ located on the back left of the camera.

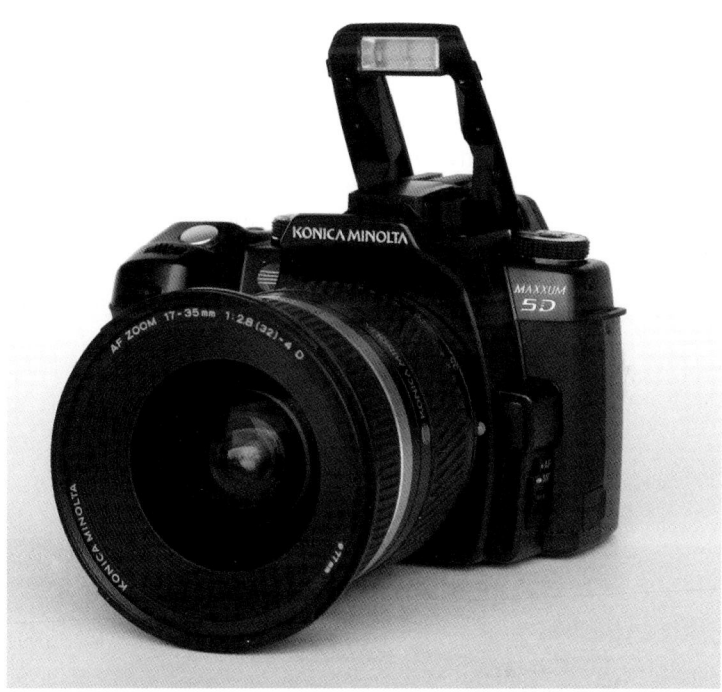

Though not extremely powerful, the built-in flash is remarkably convenient. Plan to use it often, especially for filling in shadows in outdoor photography.

Scroll through all of the images on a memory card using either the control dial (on top of the camera, in front of the shutter release) or the left/right keys on the controller. Rotate images if desired, using the down key. (Automatic vertical image rotation can be set in Custom Menu 2; see page 114.)

The Built-In Flash

A burst of extra light can often improve certain images, especially people or other nearby subjects, whether indoors or out. For example, flash is great for filling in shadows cast over a person's face by their bangs or the bill of a cap. If you think you need added illumination, manually lift the built-in flash using the small tabs on either side of the unit. Flash will then fire for every shot, whether you're shooting in low light or in brilliant sunshine. After taking an image, examine it on the LCD monitor. If you are not happy with the effect produced by flash in outdoor photography, press the built-in flash back into place and take the shot again.

Hint: The built-in flash is not as powerful as accessory flash units, so do not use it for distant subjects. The actual range of the flash varies depending on the ISO that has been set. If you use ISO 100, expect a maximum flash range of about 7 feet when shooting indoors. At ISO 400, the maximum flash range is about 14 feet. (ISO is discussed in subsequent chapters.) Outdoors, on bright days, when flash is required only to fill in shadows, the effective range is about 25% greater.

Remove the Memory Card

To remove the memory card, first turn the camera OFF. Open the card-slot door and find the small card-eject lever; press the lever to extend it. Now press it again to cause it to eject the card so you can pull it out easily. Push the lever back into place and close the door.

Caution: Be certain that the camera is OFF and that the green lamp above and to the right of the controller is not illuminated, confirming that the camera is not writing data to the card. Removing a card while data is being recorded can damage the card and cause a permanent loss of image data.

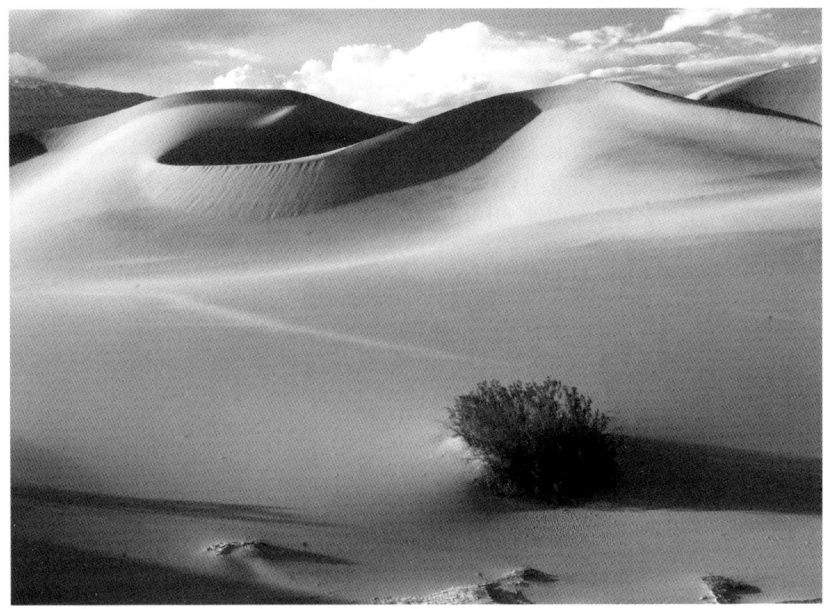

Although the 5D was designed for use in various outdoor conditions, it requires protection from the elements such as rain, wet snow, blowing sand, and salt water spray.

Camera Care and Cleaning

Keep your 5D and all lenses clean and well protected when not shooting. Do not expose the camera or lens to water, dust, sand, or salt. A camera bag and a clean, dry storage environment should prevent dust and dirt buildup. Always keep the body cap on the 5D when a lens is not mounted; this will prevent dust and contaminants from getting inside the body and settling on the sensor. Keep the front and rear caps on your lenses as well. When you set the camera down, be sure that the lens is not pointing toward the sun, to prevent damage to the CCD sensor.

Always switch the camera OFF before mounting or removing a lens. This will minimize static electricity, reducing the amount of dust that will be attracted to the CCD sensor. When shooting in a location with a great deal of sand or dust, do your best to change lenses quickly in a protected spot. Hold the camera pointing downward when changing lenses.

In addition, do not leave the camera in hot locations, such as the interior of an automobile parked in the sun. Try to minimize exposure to extreme humidity. In such conditions, keep the camera/lens in a camera bag when not in use.

When storing the camera for more than a week, remove the battery and the memory card. It is a good idea to protect the memory card as well as the camera. In order to minimize the risk of lost data, do not place the card near a magnet (as in audio speakers) or near any appliance that produces high static electricity discharge. And keep your camera bag immaculately clean; use a vacuum cleaner to remove dust and other contaminants from the bag, on a regular basis.

All of this is more important with a digital camera than it is with a film camera because small amounts of dust can settle on the image sensor and show up in your images as specks, most visible in the sky or other evenly toned area. Dust on a sensor can be difficult to remove.

Put together a basic camera care kit, including two microfiber cloths and photographic lens cleaning solution, plus a large blower bulb for blowing dust out of the camera interior. All such accessories are available from photo retail stores. Also carry a soft, absorbent cotton cloth (an old T-shirt perhaps) to dry of the exterior or the camera and lens when working in damp conditions. (Do not shoot in rain or snow unless the camera and lens are well protected.)

Dedicate a microfiber cloth for the purpose of cleaning your lenses; do not use it for other purposes, such as cleaning a smudged LCD monitor (use a cloth of a different color for that). In most cases, a gentle breath of warm air on the front element plus a quick wipe with the microfiber cloth is all you do to clean your lens. To remove stubborn smears or fingerprints, use a photographic lens cleaner solution. Do not use solutions designed for other purposes such as cleaning eyeglass lenses. Apply a drop of solution to a small part of the microfiber cloth; do not pour it onto the front or rear element of the lens because liquid may seep into the optics. Wipe away any of the solution using a dry part of the microfiber cloth.

Cleaning the CCD Sensor
Prevention of dust accumulation is definitely preferable to cleaning when it comes to the CCD sensor. You'll know if the sensor does become dusty because spots will appear in your images. In that case, you may decide to clean the sensor. The exact method for doing so is a bit complicated; the process requires the use of the camera's electronic menu (see page 120).

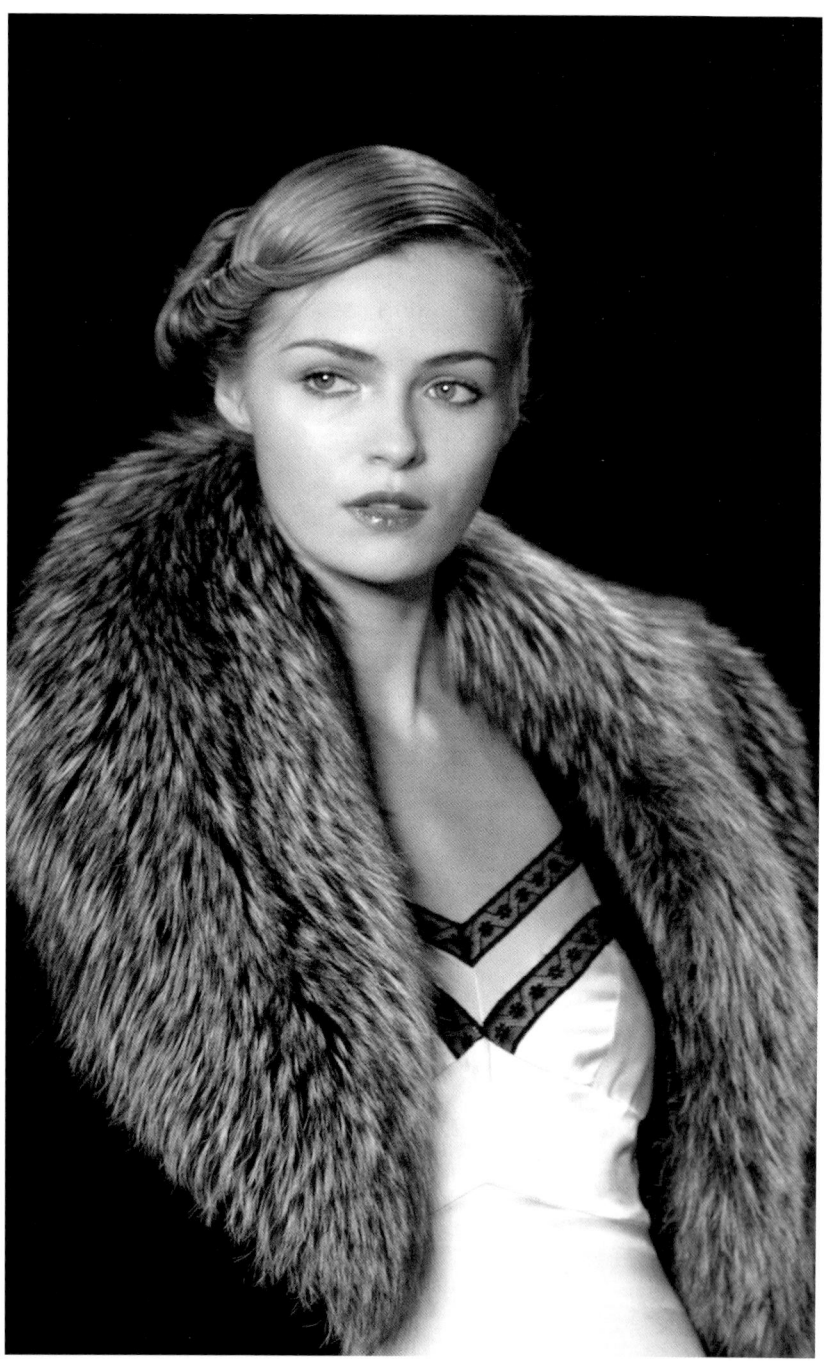

Features and Functions

Although priced to compete with entry-level digital single-lens-reflex (D-SLR) cameras, the Maxxum 5D/Dynax 5D is a remarkably versatile model and possesses some technology not available in other cameras in the same class. While it's easy to use for those new to digital SLRs, the 5D will also satisfy experienced photographers thanks to its many advanced capabilities.

Design

A fairly compact camera made of rugged material, the 5D features a big, convenient rubberized handgrip as well as large, easy-to-manipulate external controls. Its 115,000-pixel 2.5-inch color LCD monitor is larger than the LCDs on many other cameras. This screen displays the necessary options during menu navigation as well as current settings while shooting. It also displays recorded images.

In after-shot viewing or in Playback mode, full shooting data—plus a histogram display—is available for each image. Simply press the up key on the controller if you wish to see that information while viewing any image.

The 5D sports fewer analog controls than the 7D, so it's less likely to intimidate a first time digital SLR buyer, but offers a vast range of functions that are accessed electronically: with the full menu or the smaller Function sub-menu (accessed with the Fn button located on the upper right back of the camera).

Although suitable for professional applications, the 5D is designed for photo enthusiasts who want a camera with ease of use, high resolution, and great versatility.

Minolta Maxxum 5D/Dynax 5D – Front View

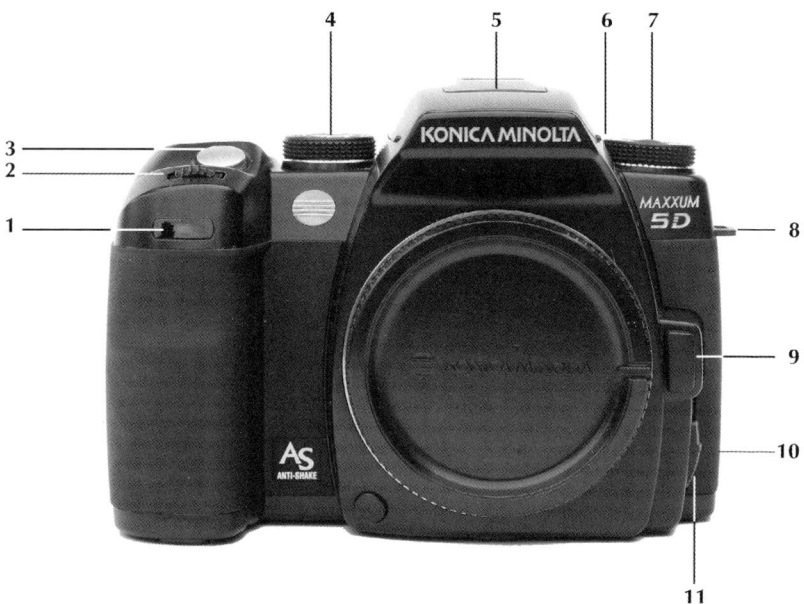

1. Self-timer lamp
2. Control dial
3. Shutter-release button
4. Exposure-mode dial
5. Flash
6. White balance (WB) dial
7. White balance (WB) button
8. Strap eyelet
9. Lens release
10. Remote-control terminal
11. AF/MF switch

Minolta Maxxum 5D/Dynax 5D – Back View

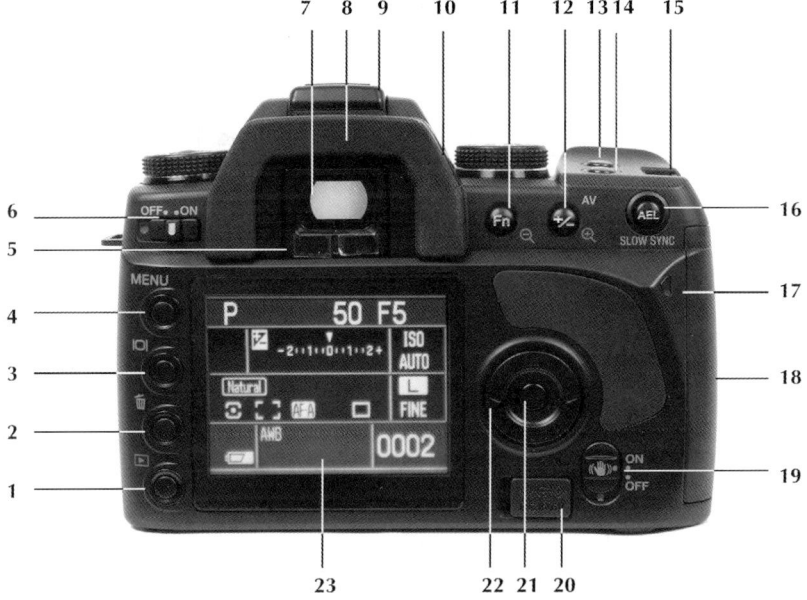

1. Playback button
2. Delete button
3. Display button
4. Menu button
5. Eyepiece sensors
6. Main switch
7. Viewfinder
8. Eyepiece cup
9. Accessory shoe
10. Diopter-adjustment dial
11. Function button (Fn)
12. Exposure compensation button
13. Drive mode button
14. Camera sensitivity (ISO) button
15. Strap eyelet
16. AE lock button (AEL)
17. Access lamp
18. Card-slot/USB port/Video-out terminal door
19. Anti-Shake switch
20. DC terminal
21. AF Button
22. Controller
23. LCD monitor

Minolta Maxxum 5D/Dynax 5D – Top View

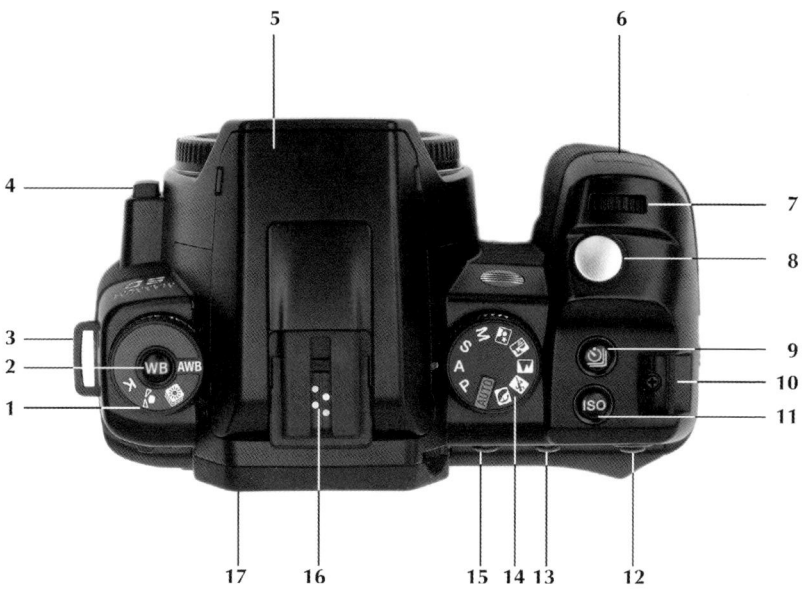

1. White balance (WB) dial
2. White balance (WB) button
3. Strap eyelet
4. Lens release
5. Flash
6. Self-timer lamp
7. Control dial
8. Shutter release button
9. Drive mode button
10. Strap eyelet
11. Camera sensitivity (ISO) button
12. AE lock button (AEL)
13. Exposure compensation button
14. Exposure mode dial
15. Function button (Fn)
16. Accessory shoe
17. Eyepiece cup

This is an autofocus camera, but it allows for manual focus fine-tuning in AF mode using the focus ring if Direct Manual Focus (DMF) is selected with the function (Fn) button. Naturally, the camera can be set for manual focus mode as well. Although it is not compatible with older Minolta manual-focus lenses (MD and MC), the camera accepts all Konica Minolta AF lenses made since 1985.

The 5D also features Konica Minolta's latest image processor, CxProcess III, for high-definition, natural-looking images and pleasing skin tones. The processor's Advanced LSI engine assures great speed and responsiveness, while a high-capacity buffer (temporary image storage bank) allows for shooting a series of images at up to 3 frames per second. The 5D is surprisingly lightweight for a high performance digital camera, but rugged enough to withstand extensive uses.

Spend time with your camera getting to know it well. Become familiar with each of the controls. Many of the abbreviations and icons used to denote the various features are common to numerous other cameras, so they may already be familiar. Some are intuitive; for example, WB stands for white balance, Fn denotes Function, AEL stands for autoexposure lock, and so on.

Specifications

The 5D includes a wide range of features.

Image Sensor: 23.5 x 15.7 mm CCD sensor with RGB filter array; 6.1 million effective pixels.

Field of View Crop: 1.5x. (See pages 55 and 191).

Recording: RAW (12-bit), JPEG and RAW+JPEG formats. (See pages 67-77).

Image Sizes: In pixels: 3008 x 2000 RAW; 3008 x 2000, 2256 x 1495, and 1504 x 1000 selectable in JPEG.

JPEG Quality: Standard, Fine, Extra Fine.

White Balance: Auto, Preset (Daylight, Shade, Cloudy, Tungsten, Fluorescent, and Flash with selectable warm or cool biasing in high or low increments), Custom, and Color Temperature (Kelvin) with selectable Magenta/Green compensation for fluorescent adjustment. Also white balance bracketing. (See page 84).

Color Mode: sRGB options: Natural, Natural Plus, Black & White, Portrait, Landscape, Sunset, Night View, and Night Portrait. Also Adobe RGB and Embedded adobe RGB (See pages 85-88).

Image Adjustments: User selectable contrast, color saturation, and sharpness in -2 to +2 levels. (See pages 89-90).

Noise Reduction: Available with one second and longer exposures. (See page 90).

Menus:	User selectable electronic menu system includes Recording menu (2 tabs, or pages), Playback menu (2 tabs), Custom menu (2 tabs), Setup menu (3 tabs). (See pages 98-121).
Viewfinder:	Fixed eye-level roof-mirror pentaprism, 95% field of view, 0.83x magnification, Spherical Acute Matte (G-type) focusing screen, eye relief, 20mm from eye-piece; diopter correction -2.5 to +1, removable eyepiece cup.
LCD Monitor:	115,000-pixel 2.5-inch (63.5mm) TFT color.
Playback:	Single or multiple image display, magnification up to 4.7x, slideshow, data and histogram display with Luminance Limit display selectable.
Anti-Shake:	CCD-Shift system with LED indicator scale in viewfinder. (See pages 124-127).
Autofocus System:	Nine selectable AF areas including a cross-hatched central AF area. (See pages 130-132).
Focus Modes:	Autofocus modes: Single-shot AF (AF-S), Continuous AF (AF-C, with predictive focus control), Automatic AF (AF-A selects automatically between AF-S and AF-C), and Direct Manual Focus (DMF), available after focus confirmation. (See pages 128-130). Also, focus lock and focus-assist with pre-flash (1 meter to 5 meter range). Manual focus.

Drive: Single-frame Advance, Continuous Advance up to 3 frames per second (fps), Self-timer with 2- or 10-second delay. (See pages 133-135).

Shutter Speeds: 30 to 1/4000 second plus Bulb; top flash sync speed 1/160, 1/125 with the Anti-Shake system ON.

Sensitivity: Auto ISO as well as ISO 100 to 3200; Lo 80 and Hi 200 also available for zone matching low key and high key subjects (see pages 138-140).

Exposure Modes: AUTO (fully automatic), Program with Program shift, Aperture Priority, Shutter Priority, Manual Exposure (fully manual) modes. Also five Digital Subject Programs: Portrait, Sports Action, Landscape, Sunset, and Night Portrait. (See pages 140-143).

Metering Modes: 14-segment Honeycomb pattern (evaluative), center weighted, and spot metering. Also, autoexposure lock (AEL), exposure compensation, and exposure bracketing. (See pages 155-158).

Flash: Built-in with Advanced Distance Integration (ADI) with D-type lenses; pre-flash TTL and manual control; GN 39/12 in feet/meters at ISO 100; fill flash, flash cancel, red-eye reduction, flash exposure compensation and bracketing, Slow sync and Rear curtain sync selectable; high speed sync and wireless off-camera flash possible with HS(D)-series accessory flash units. (See chapter 171-176).

Accessory Flash:	Compatible with Program Flash units 5600HS(D), 3600HS(D), and 2500(D). Also compatible with Macro flashes with optional MFC-1000 control unit; limited compatibility when adapter is used with some older flash units. (See pages 174-189).
Other Features:	Depth of field preview, optional automatic rotation of vertical images.
Video Output:	NTSC or PAL selectable.
Connectivity:	USB 2.0 Full-Speed and Video Out.
Printing Output Control:	EXIF Print, PRINT Image Matching and PictBridge compliant.
Power:	One NP-400 lithium-ion battery; optional AC adapter.
Dimensions:	5.2 x 3.7 x 2.6 inches; 130.5 x 92.5 x 66.5 mm.
Weight:	20.8 oz; 590 g.
Compatible Computer Operating Systems:	Windows 98/ME/2000/XP; MAC OS 9.0 and higher.
Optional Accessories:	AC adapter AC-11, Anglefinder and Magnifier Vn, diopter adjustment 1000, remote cord RC-1000S and RC-1000L, Flash Adapter FS-1100, PC Flash Adapter PCT-100, Maxxum/Dynax AF lenses, DiMAGE Master 1.1 (or higher version) software.

The CCD Imaging Sensor

While the sensor in the 5D records images in full color, its individual pixels are actually not able to record color values at all. They are only able to record the intensity of the light. Therefore, filters are placed in front of the pixels so each can only record one of the three primary colors (red, green, and blue) of light. These filters are arranged in a specific order, most commonly using the Bayer pattern, where there are twice as many green pixels as there are red and blue.

When the light projected by the lens comes into contact with the imaging sensor during exposure, the light-sensitive pixels accumulate an electrical charge. More light striking a particular pixel translates into a stronger electrical charge. The electrical charge for each pixel is converted into a specific value based on the strength of the charge so that the camera can actually process the data.

Because each pixel on the sensor only records the value of one of the primary colors, full color must be interpolated based on information from adjacent pixels. The final image data is then written to the camera's memory card as an image file. An exception to this would be the RAW capture format. Images made in this capture mode consist of raw data (actual pixel values) from the sensor stored in a file format (MRW) that needs to be processed using special software for conversion to a universal image format.

In addition to the Bayer pattern filter, a low pass anti-aliasing filter is located in front of the sensor. This reduces the wavy colors and rippled surface patterns (moiré) that can occur when we photograph small, patterned areas with a camera that uses a high-resolution sensor.

The Sensor and Effective Focal Lengths

As with the vast majority of digital cameras, the 5D's sensor is smaller than a 35mm film frame, which measures 24 x 36 mm. Because of the smaller size, the focal length of any lens appears to be longer than it would appear in 35mm photography. Many seasoned photographers like to think in 35mm SLR terms, so they often describe lenses on digital SLRs by their "effective focal lengths." To calculate this effective focal length, multiply by 1.5. For example, a 28–75mm zoom becomes equivalent to a 42–112.5mm zoom in the 35mm format. The smaller sensor reduces the wide-angle capability of the lens, but increases its capacity for telephoto zoom.

This 1.5x factor for effective focal length, or "focal length magnification," is actually a field-of-view crop. In other words, the focal length is not actually increased. The apparent magnification occurs because the small sensor records a smaller portion of the scene than a larger 35mm film frame would. Consequently, the image appears as if it had been taken with a longer lens, one with a narrower field of view that encompasses less of any scene.

This factor is certainly useful in wildlife and sports photography as it reduces the need to use super telephoto lenses (i.e., 500mm or greater) for tight shots of a distant subject—a moderate telephoto lens (such as the long end of a 100-300mm zoom) will often do the job. But in wide-angle photography, the effective focal length magnification is a drawback because we need extremely short focal lengths to create images with a true ultra-wide effect. That's why Konica Minolta is making shorter, or wider, lenses, such as the 11–18mm zoom; at its short end, this lens provides the ultra wide field of view that we would expect from a 16.5mm lens on a 35mm camera.

File Formats

The 5D records images either in a compressed JPEG format or as RAW data in a proprietary format called MRW. The camera also includes an option to record a RAW image and a Fine quality JPEG image simultaneously. These various file formats are discussed in detail on pages 67-77. JPEG is the most common file format for capturing images. With the 5D, you can select any of three different file sizes and also any of three quality levels.

White Balance Controls

Though our eyes naturally adjust, the color of light varies throughout the day, especially with different types of light sources. A digital camera must make corrections to produce images that appear natural without strong color casts. This feature is called white balance control.

The 5D offers a wide range of options for white balance, ranging from Automatic White Balance to WB Bracketing and Color Temperature (Kelvin) selections with an available Magenta/Green "filter" for fine tuning settings with difficult fluorescent lighting.

The Menu System

Although the 5D includes external (analog) controls for frequently used functions, several features are available in a sub-menu accessed with the function (Fn) button. Numerous additional features can be found in the full electronic menus (accessed by pressing the MENU button on the left back of the camera). Some of the most important menu options include: image size and quality, flash mode, exposure bracketing levels, digital noise reduction, plus Digital Effects Control (DEC), a feature that controls settings for contrast, sharpness and color saturation levels. (See pages 98-121, for more about the menu systems.)

Viewfinder Display

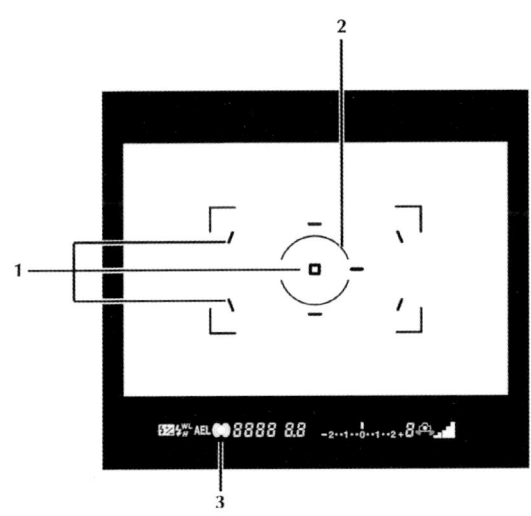

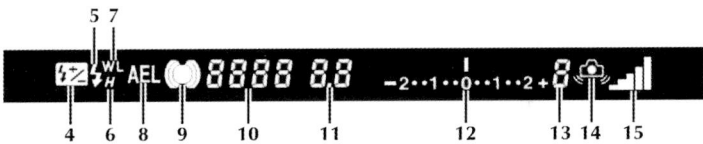

1. AF area points (9 points)
2. Spot metering area
3. Viewfinder display panel
4. Flash compensation indicator
5. Flash signal
6. High speed sync indicator
7. Wireless/remote flash indicator
8. AE lock indicator
9. Focus signal
10. Shutter speed display
11. Aperture display
12. EV scale
13. Frames remaining
14. Anti-shake warning
15. Anti-shake scale

The Viewfinder

The 5D uses a bright, eye-level viewfinder with a fixed roof-mirror "pentaprism" that's lighter in weight than the all-glass pentaprism used in the 7D. The finder shows 95% of the image area at 0.83x magnification when using a 50mm lens focused at infinity. That level of magnification is about average in the affordable D-SLR category. The eyepoint is 20mm, indicating that you can see the entire image area when holding the camera as far as 20mm from your eye or 16mm from the rubber eyecup when that accessory is in place. This is beneficial for those who wear eyeglasses when shooting, and are unable to hold the eyepiece closer to their eyes.

You may find that it's not necessary to wear your corrective lenses because the viewfinder eyepiece allows for a -2.5 to +1 diopter adjustment. Adjustments are made using the small diopter adjustment dial on the right side of the rubber eyepiece cup on the back of the camera. If you normally wear eyeglasses, try this feature to determine whether it's adequate to allow you to shoot effectively without your corrective lenses. If not, then make the adjustment while wearing your eyeglasses or ask your retailer about the optional Konica Minolta Eyepiece Corrector Series 1000—these accessories are available in higher strengths than the diopter that is built into the camera.

Just below the viewing screen, when looking through the viewfinder, there's a data display panel that shows information about camera settings. Keep in mind that not all of the available data is displayed at one time. The stair graph at the right end of the data display denotes the level of camera shake compensation that is occurring at any time, from low to high.

The nine AF area points and the spot metering circle are etched on the viewfinder's ground glass screen. When using the camera in autofocus, one or more of the AF area points light up briefly to indicate the point of focus.

LCD Monitor Display (Recording Mode)

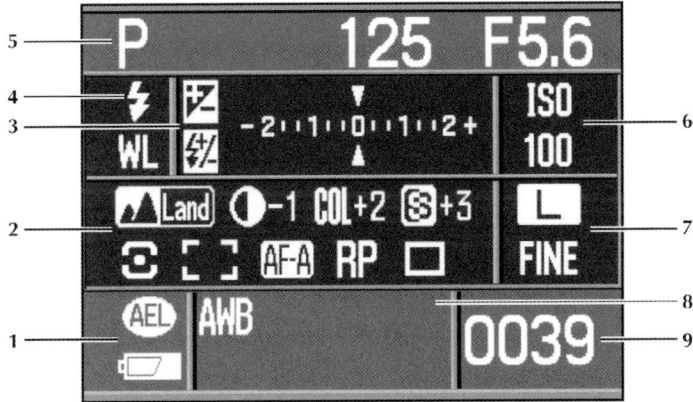

1. *AE lock/battery condition panel*
2. *Color mode/Digital Effects Control/Metering/AF area/ AF mode/Release priority/ Drive mode panel*
3. *Ev scale*
4. *Flash panel*
5. *Exposure mode/Exposure panel*
6. *Camera-sensitivity/Zone Matching panel*
7. *Image size/quality panel*
8. *White balance panel*
9. *Frame counter*

The LCD Monitor

The 5D employs a single LCD screen that displays images after they are taken. Photographers who have worked with a point-and-shoot digital camera are often disappointed when they find that digital SLR monitors, including this one, cannot be used for composing an image.

In addition to playing back images for review, the LCD monitor also displays all types of shooting data as well as menu options. For a more complete description of the LCD monitor, see pages 93-97.

The Anti-Shake (A/S) Device

The 5D features Konica Minolta's proprietary Anti-Shake (A/S) system that shifts the CCD image sensor module to compensate for camera shake, producing sharper pictures in hand-held photography. This feature is compatible with every Konica Minolta AF lens except for the AF 16mm Fish Eye and Macro Zoom 3x–1x. Hence, there's no need to buy expensive new lenses to take advantage of image stabilization.

Autofocus

Although Konica Minolta Maxxum Dynax lenses can be manually focused if desired when using the 5D, you'll probably want to take advantage of the reliable autofocus (AF) system. It's effective in both bright light and low light, but will not be reliable in extremely dark situations. In that case, raise the built-in flash; it will fire a pre-flash burst to brighten the subject and help the AF system to find focus. Or, use one of the accessory Maxxum/Dynax Program Flash units with an AF-assist beam projector feature.

Three autofocus selections are available by using the Function (Fn) button. The system is activated when you press the shutter release button partway down:

- *Single-shot AF* (AF-S) is used for static subjects.
- *Continuous AF* (AF-C) is used to follow a moving subject.
- *Automatic AF* (AF-A) switches between AF-S and AF-C, depending on the movement of the subject. This is the default setting for the 5D.

See pages 128-129 for more detailed information about the use of these modes.

The 5D also allows you to select from nine different focus-area points. There is also a feature called Direct Manual Focus (DMF, see page 130) that allows you to fine-tune your focus manually without leaving the AF mode.

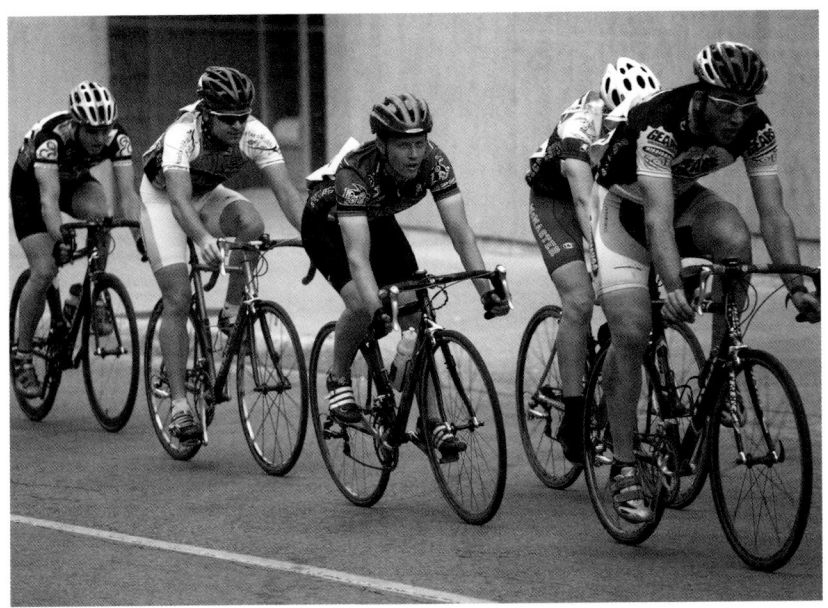

When using the 5D for action photography, select Continuous AF (for tracking subject motion) plus the Continuous Advance drive mode (for shooting bursts at 3 frames per second). Practice using this combination and you will soon be able to make some very effective images.

The Drive System

Since a digital camera does not use film, it does not technically have a drive system to move film through the body. Even so, the frame advance system is often called a drive system and is selected with the drive mode button 🖳 . You can select Single-frame Advance (one shot each time you press the shutter release button) or Continuous Advance (up to 3 frames per second for a series of images). The number of frames that you can shoot in a single burst depends on the image capture mode as well as the JPEG size and quality settings that you've selected.

Note: The control for selecting a drive mode includes options for single-shot and continuous exposure bracketing (see pages 159-160) as well as white balance bracketing (see page 84). Unless you want to vary the exposure or white balance for each frame that you shoot, do not select either of these options.

There are also two self-timer settings: a 2-second delay, or a 10-second delay. Refer to pages 133-135 for more information about the 5D's drive system.

Sensitivity (ISO) Settings

Use the ISO button to choose from several settings for light sensitivity. The settings are based on film ISO ratings. The options include AUTO (automatic selection of ISO based on subject conditions) and six different user selectable levels from ISO 100 to 3200, plus two other options: Lo 80 and Hi 200. All of these are discussed on pages 138-140.

Exposure Modes

The 5D offers several modes for automatic and manual exposure control. You can select the exposure mode by using the exposure mode dial. Choose AUTO, Program, Aperture Priority, Shutter Priority, Manual exposure, or one of the five Digital Subject Programs (see pages 140-154).

Metering Modes

The Maxxum 5D/Dynax 5D offers three exposure metering options (selected with the Fn button) that will be familiar to anyone who has used a high-tech 35mm SLR camera.

The 14-segment honeycomb pattern (evaluative) metering is the standard, default option. A microcomputer considers the brightness in 14 honeycomb-shaped areas of a scene and

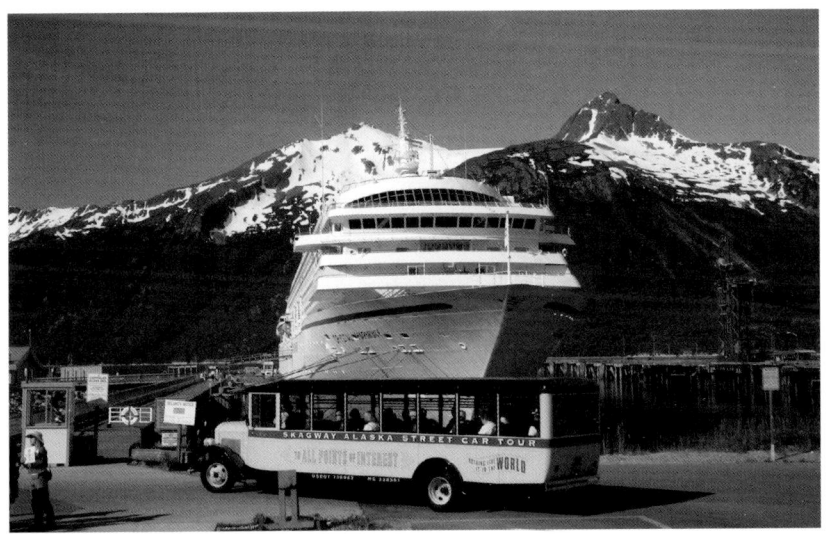

The sophisticated honeycomb pattern metering system often produces accurate exposures with scenes that include large light-toned subjects. To fine tune exposures even further, you may need to use exposure compensation, such as +0.7 used for this image.

makes calculations to provide the best overall exposure based on that evaluation. This sophisticated system works well in most exposure situations.

Center weighted metering averages the light values over the entire scene, but gives extra emphasis to the central region. This is a low-tech approach to exposure metering common in most older SLR cameras.

Spot metering measures brightness only within the circular area etched into the viewing screen, and is intended for use by photographers with expertise in light metering.

Exposure Adjustment Options

Several features are available for fine tuning the exposure, for subjects with unusual reflectance, or to optimize a specific area of a scene. The options include exposure compensation, flash exposure compensation, autoexposure lock (AEL), and exposure bracketing.

The Built-In Flash

The camera incorporates a flash unit hidden at the top of the pentaprism. When you want to use flash, raise the unit by pulling upward using the small tabs on each side. Should you not want to use flash, press it down until the unit locks into place. It will never pop up automatically (as it does with some cameras), preventing annoyance when you do not want to shoot with flash. However, if you do raise the flash unit, it will always fire, even in very bright light. That feature can be useful for filling shadows cast by a hat over a person's face, for example.

   The built-in flash can be used in any of the 5D's exposure modes. When it's charged and ready to fire, a small lightning bolt symbol ⚡ appears in the data panel at the bottom of the viewing screen. After you take a flash photo, the signal will blink in confirmation if a correct flash exposure was made. If it does not blink, move closer to the subject and/or select a higher ISO setting and take the shot again. Don't take a subsequent shot until the flash is recycled, a process that usually takes about three seconds.

External Ports

The camera features several covered terminals for attaching accessories. On the back, you will find a port for the optional AC Adapter AC-11 and the remote control terminal. The optional remote cords RC-1000S and RC-1000L can be used to remotely trigger the shutter, which helps to eliminate camera vibration during long exposures.

On the right side of the camera body you will find the card-slot door covering the memory card slot and the USB port/Video Out terminal. The USB cable included in the 5D camera kit connects the camera to a computer's USB port for downloading image files, or to some recent PictBridge compatible printers for printing directly from the camera (see pages 226-228 for more information). The USB port also accepts the second cable included in the kit. This is used for connecting the camera to a television monitor's video-in port for showing images on a large screen.

Power Sources

A single proprietary NP-400 rechargeable lithium-ion (Li-ion) battery (included with the camera) will power the 5D for about 500 frames per charge (with occasional flash use and occasional use of the LCD monitor). You'll get fewer shots per charge if you frequently use the built-in flash or the image playback feature. The number of shots per charge is also dependent on the temperature; in bitter cold, it can drop substantially. Recharging time for a dead battery is about 150 minutes.

Note: The 5D is programmed to turn off the LCD monitor and most other functions when the camera is not in use in order to conserve battery power. To turn them back on, just press any camera button. You can set the period of time for "LCD off" from 5 to 60 seconds in Setup Menu 3 (see page 119).

The camera does not accept universally available batteries, such as AAs, so it is wise to carry a spare NP-400, especially on long outings. The camera can also be plugged into household power using the optional 6-volt Adapter AC-11 with the correct power cord for your region. This option is useful for preventing battery drain if you download images directly from the camera to a computer, or plan to print directly from the camera while it's connected to a printer with a USB cable.

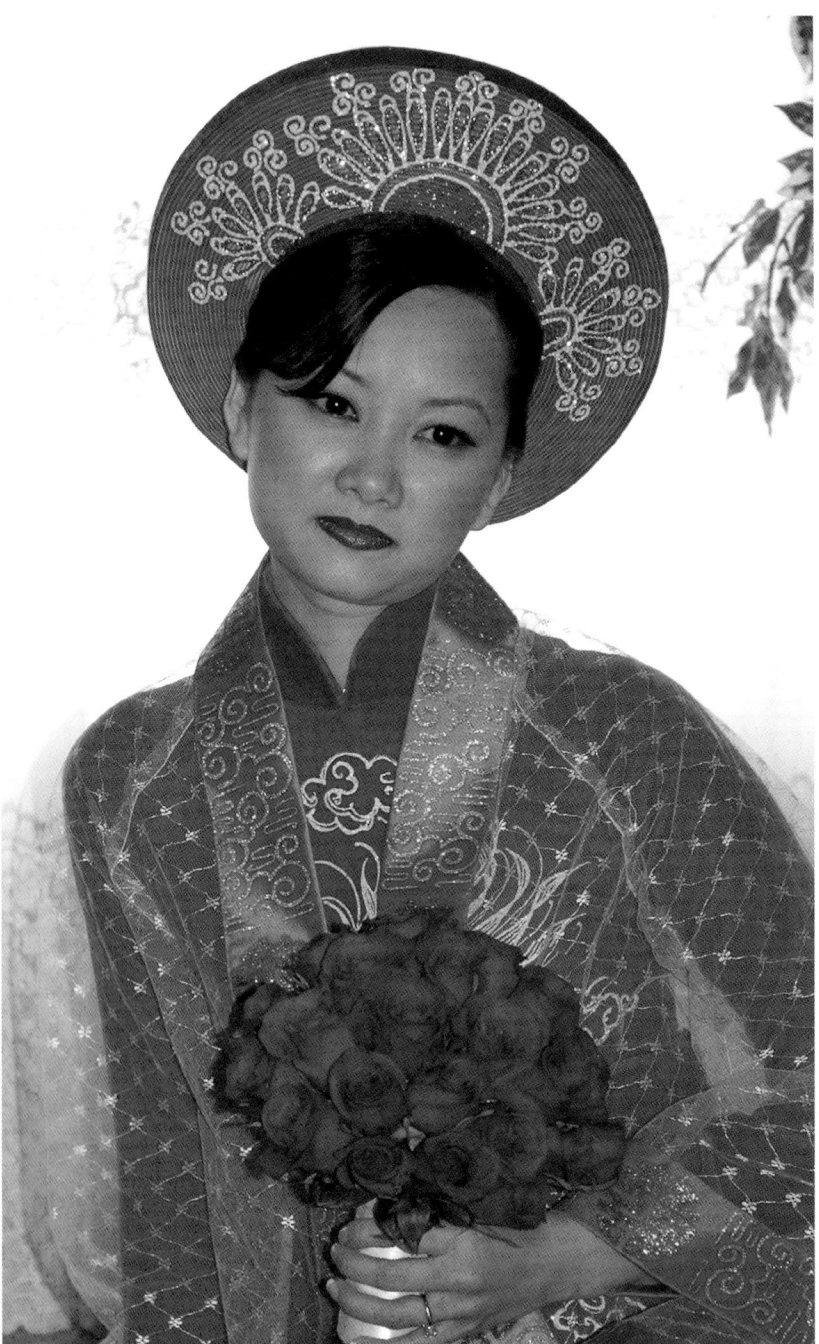

Digital Recording and In-Camera Processing

File Formats

A digital camera processes analog image information from its sensor and converts it to digital data. Typically, the conversion results in 8- or12-bit color data for each of three different color channels: red, green, and blue. A bit is the smallest piece of information that a computer uses—an acronym for binary digit (0 or 1, off or on).

One great feature of the 5D is its ability to capture a RAW file. Konica Minolta calls this proprietary RAW file its MRW format. What sets RAW files apart is that they have undergone little or no internal processing by the camera. These files also contain 12-bit color information, which is considerably more data than some other file types. Also, when you work with the RAW file in your computer you have greater artistic control over the image because you are starting with more complete data than other file types can offer (i.e. JPEG). However, you must use editing software that is compatible with this particular RAW format. Konica Minolta bundles just such a program with the camera: DiMAGE MasterLite.

JPEG, which is really an international standard for the compression of images, is the most common file type created by digital cameras. Digital cameras use it because it reduces the size of the file, allowing more pictures to fit on a memory card. That's because the compressed JPEG's 8-bit file uses less memory than 12-bit RAW files.

The 5D's sensor has an effective resolution of 6.1 million pixels. This means that a picture can be printed at 7 x 10 inches (17.8 x 25.4 cm) if you use a setting of 300 ppi (pixels per inch) in your image-processing program. You can make much larger prints by setting lower ppi levels or increasing file sizes.

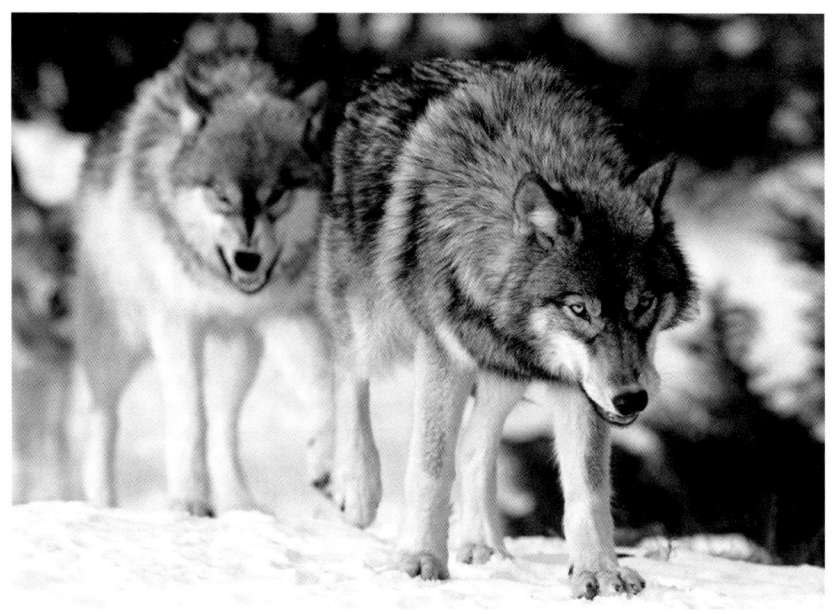

While shooting hundreds of images at a game farm for photographers, I used JPEG instead of RAW because that format allowed me to capture a longer series of pictures in a single burst. This factor, as well as the amount of computer time required for RAW conversion and enhancement, is important when deciding whether to use RAW or JPEG.

When a photo is recorded in JPEG form, proprietary processing takes effect. It evaluates the captured 12-bit image, makes adjustments to maximize the data, and then compresses the image as a JPEG with a reduced color depth of 8-bit. Because this process discards what it deems "redundant" data, JPEGs are referred to as a "lossy" compression. Keep in mind, however, that when the file is opened in a computer, the lost data is rebuilt quite well, especially when the amount of compression is low (i.e. the picture was taken using high quality settings). In addition, quality is maintained by not reusing a JPEG format in the computer. In other words, once downloaded and opened, the file should be saved in TIFF format or in the image-editing software's native format (such as PhotoShop's psd).

Both RAW and JPEG files can give excellent results. The unprocessed data of a RAW file (which can be converted to 16-bit color depth using a RAW converter software program) can be helpful when faced with tough exposure situations, but the small size of the JPEG file is faster and easier to deal with.

For most purposes it usually doesn't matter whether an image originated as a RAW or high-quality JPEG file. What matters most to professional art directors, clients, or friends and relatives is the appearance of the image; how it communicates and how well it fulfills its purpose as a snapshot, a framed piece of art, an email attachment, or a magazine photo. You don't have to shoot in one particular format or the other on order to create publishable files. Both work extremely well.

The most important factor in deciding which format will work best for you is your own personal shooting and working style. If you want to shoot quickly and spend less time in front of the computer, JPEG might be the best file for you. If you loved working in the darkroom and processing film, then RAW is a great continuation of that process. If you are dealing with problematic lighting, RAW may give you the best results. If you have tons of images to deal with, JPEG may be the most efficient.

JPEG or RAW formats are as much reflections of your photographic style as they are formats for capturing images (JPEG is technically a compression scheme and not a true format, but it is effectively used as a format). The key is to be aware of how you like to work and what results you need. You have to test the formats for yourself with your camera and its software to see if you gain anything using one over the other.

Resolution

When we talk about resolution in film, we are simply referring to the detail that the film can see, or "ascertain." Resolution in a lens (the detail a lens can resolve) generally doesn't change. Unfortunately, resolution is not as simple a concept when it comes to digital photography.

Resolution in the digital world is expressed in different ways depending on where you are in the digital process. For example, in the case of digital cameras, resolution indicates how many individual pixels are contained on the imaging sensor. This is usually expressed in megapixels. Each pixel captures a portion of the total light falling on the sensor. And it is from these pixels that the image is created. Thus, a 6-megapixel camera has 6-million pixels covering the sensor. On the other hand, when it comes to inkjet printing, the usual rating of resolution is in dots-per-inch (dpi), which describes how many individual dots of ink exist per inch of paper area.

The resolution capacity for each image captured by your camera is usually expressed in terms of megapixels, or millions of pixels. The Maxxum 5D/Dynax 5D offers different resolution settings (detailed on pages 72-73) so that you don't always have to utilize the camera's maximum resolution, but generally it is best to use the highest setting available (i.e. take the most finely detailed pictures possible with your camera). You can always reduce resolution in the computer, but you cannot create higher resolution if you never captured the data to begin with. Keep in mind that you paid for the megapixels in your camera! The lower the resolution you are shooting with, the less detail your picture will have. This is particularly noticeable when making enlargements.

There are situations where it may be preferable to shoot at a resolution that is less than maximum capacity. For example, if you know you will only be using the photo for emailing or web page purposes, you probably don't want a large file size. Lower resolution image files will also save storage space and processing time. You can fit more low-resolution

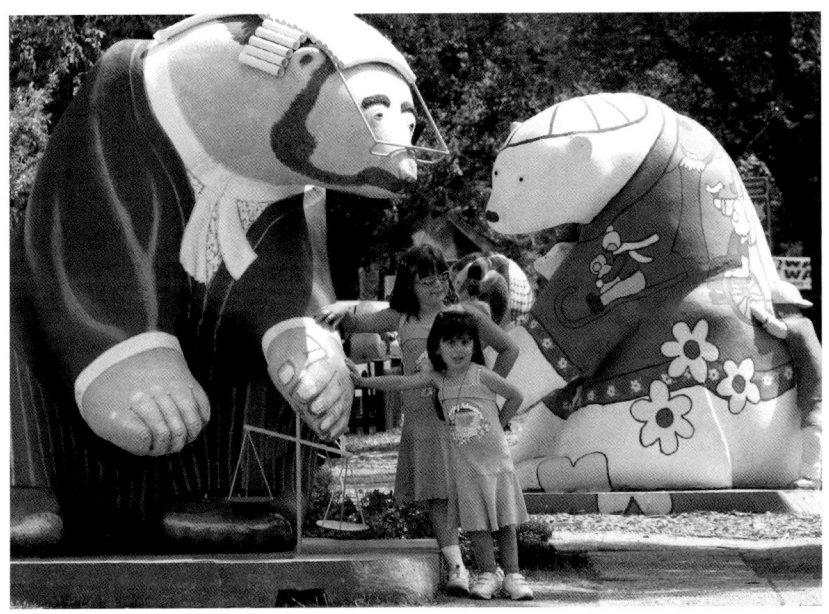

If you want pictures strictly for a family web page or for sending via e-mail, the smallest JPEG size and a modest quality level may suit your purpose. But if large prints are important, it's best to shoot with the highest size/quality combination. You can always downsize photos to screen resolution (72 dpi) in your computer for the Internet and re-name them so they don't over-write the original "master files."

images on your memory card than those captured using higher resolution settings. These small files (starting at about 640 x 480 pixels) are easier to transport. (File sizes, when listed in pixels, appear as a larger number multiplied by a smaller number.) To determine how large a print you can make (with acceptable resolution quality) simply divide each of the pixel equation numbers by 200 (the 200 refers to a linear print resolution of 200 dpi). The resulting numbers will give the size in inches. (A file recorded at 640 x 480 pixels, for example, would only produce a sharp image up to the size 3.2 x 2.4 inches!)

Digital camera files generally enlarge very well in pro-grams like Photoshop, especially if you shot them in RAW format first (because there is more data in that format to work with). The higher the original shooting resolution, the larger the print you can make. Again, if the photos are specifically for email or web page use, you do not need to shoot with a high resolution in order for the images to look good on screen.

JPEG Settings

When shooting JPEGs, you must set the amount of compres-sion you want to use. The more you compress, the smaller your file will be. This allows more images to fit on a mem-ory card and makes file transfer quicker. However, the qual-ity of the file is negatively affected by increased compres-sion. When data is restored later in image-processing soft-ware, some "artifacts," such as jagged subject edges, may appear if too much compression has been applied to the file.

To set the image quality, use Recording Menu 1 ⚊1 and choose from the following options (see pages 99-100 details on how to set image quality):

- **MRW (RAW):** no compression.
- **MRW and JPEG (RAW+):** no RAW compression, middle amount of JPEG compression.
- **Extra fine (X.FIN):** the least amount of JPEG compression.
- **Fine (FINE):** the middle amount of JPEG compression.
- **Standard (STD):** the highest amount of JPEG compression.

The sensor on the 5D can record images as large as 6 mil-lion pixels (3008 pixels wide x 2000 pixels high), but when shooting JPEGs, the camera can convert and store image files at three different sizes:

- **Large (L):** 3008 x 2000 pixels (6 megapixels), the default.
- **Medium (M):** 2256 x 1496 pixels (3.4 megapixels).
- **Small (S):** 1504 x 2000 pixels (3 megapixels).

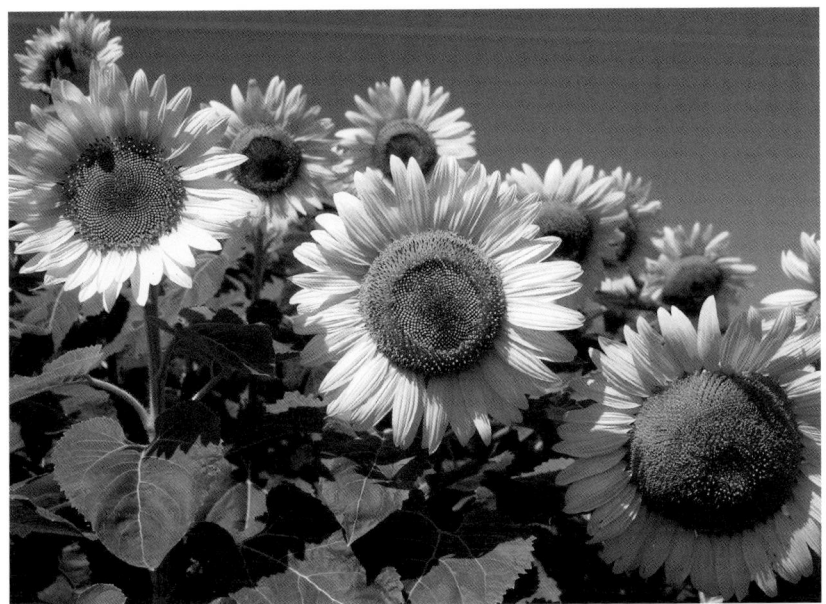

While RAW can produce superlative image quality, the largest/finest JPEG combination also generates exceptional images with great definition of intricate detail, as in this photo.

Use Recording Menu 1 to select image size (see page 101).

Your choices of size, and quality depend on your shooting circumstances and how you want to use your images. Choose a lower JPEG resolution and/or lower quality (higher compression) if you plan to only email images, display them on the Internet, or make small prints (e.g. 6 x 4 inches—15 x 10 cm—or less). In these cases, small to medium sized JPEGs may suit your purposes. The same goes if you have a memory card with a capacity of only 256 or 512 megabytes (MB).

In most cases, however, it's best to use Large resolution (L) and extra fine quality (X.FIN) to capture the most information possible. You can always reduce resolution with your image-processing software after downloading to your computer, but you cannot add detail that you never captured in the first place.

MRW RAW Files

These files undergo very little in-camera processing and they contain more color and tone information than JPEGs, plus they are always created at the camera's maximum resolution. Consequently, they are significantly larger and use more memory in both your card and your computer. I recommend a high capacity memory card (at least 512MB, but preferably 1 gigabyte (GB) or more) if you plan to frequently shoot in RAW capture mode.

The MRW files created in RAW capture offer greater dynamic range (latitude) than JPEGs, as well as more flexibility in computer processing to affect exposure and color temperature. Since MRW files give you more data, you have more options about how to process and use that information than you do with JPEGs.

Because the MRW format is not compatible with all image-processing programs (especially older ones), special software must be used to convert these files to a format (such as TIFF) that is recognized by standard image-processing programs. DiMAGE MasterLite will work, as well as programs such as DiMAGE Master, Adobe Photoshop CS2, and Elements 3.0 and 4.0, among others.

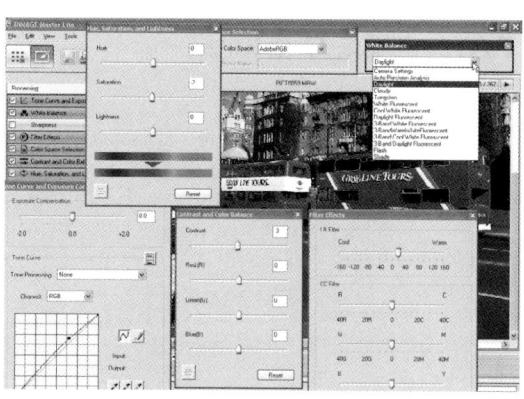

Software like DiMAGE Master Lite and DiMAGE Master (pictured) is required to convert MRW files to a format that is compatible with many image-processing programs.

Approximate File Sizes

The chart below shows how large the files are in megabytes (MB) with the various format and resolution options offered by the 5D:

Quality	Large (3008 x 2000 pixels)	Medium (2256 x 1496 pixels)	Small (1504 x 1000 pixels)
MRW (RAW)	8.8 MB	N/A	N/A
Extra Fine JPEG	5.9 MB	3.3 MB	1.6 MB
Fine JPEG	3 MB	1.7 MB	0.85 MB
Standard JPEG	1.8 MB	1 MB	0.55 MB

For best results, keep your Maxxum 5D/Dynax 5D set to the Large/Extra fine JPEG combination, or use the RAW capture mode. If your memory card has limited remaining capacity, switch to the JPEG Large/Fine combination for smaller JPEG files that will retain high quality. A better option, however, is to carry extra memory cards.

RAW+JPEG Capture

The 5D gives you the option to shoot with both MRW and JPEG files at the same time. This feature can be useful when you want quick, small JPEGs to email to friends or send to a client for FPO (for position only) purposes, and RAW for more critical in-computer processing at a later time. This can be useful as long as your memory card is adequate to handle the large amount of data generated by using this option.

To select this option, again use Recording Menu 1 **◘1** (see page 100).

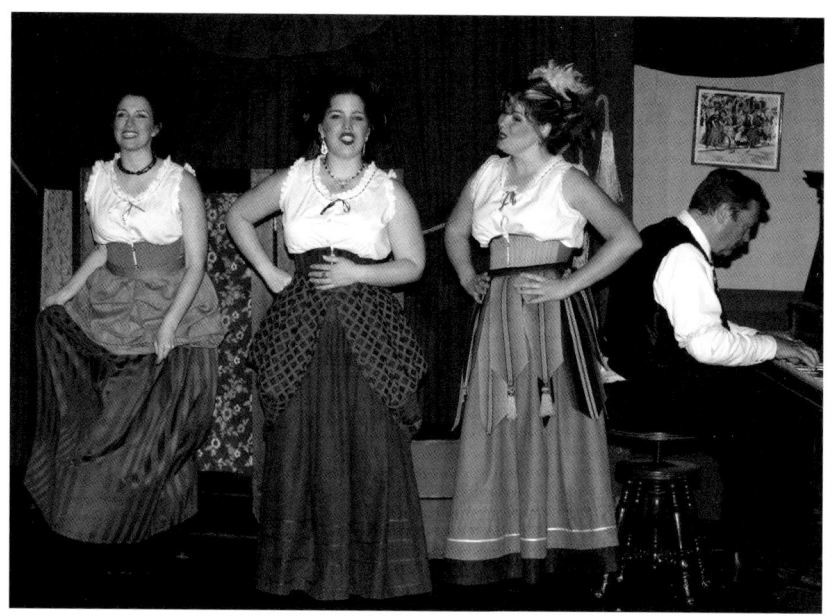

Select the RAW+JPEG option in difficult lighting conditions. The 5D will generate an MRW file that is suitable for correction as needed, along with a JPEG that you can use for quickly making small prints to hand out at an event.

Though the camera automatically selects a quality of FINE (the middle amount of compression) for the JPEG portion of this combination, you can choose the JPEG resolution—S, M, or L—by scrolling to *Image size* in Recording Menu 1 and making your selection.

The size of the RAW+JPEG files is large—8.8 MB for the RAW file, plus the size of the JPEG (see the chart on the previous page). The 5D will save both the RAW file and the JPEG with the same name, but will use an .mrw and a .jpg suffix, respectively. I suggest selecting the RAW+JPEG Small option for most purposes.

Both JPEG and RAW files include data about all camera settings in compliance with EXIF 2.2 (EXIF stands for Exchangeable Image File Format). This allows you to check shooting data when viewing an image in-camera and also in a computer. The EXIF data is also employed by some printers when printing directly from the camera via a USB cable.

RAW vs. JPEG

You can adjust and correct images made in either JPEG or RAW formats by using a compatible image-processing software program. However, RAW files will allow more adjustment for color, white balance, contrast, and exposure without the file degradation, which may occur with JPEGs from over processing in the computer. Since a RAW file contains significantly more information than a JPEG, it offers greater latitude for correcting technical problems. Generally you can also expect more pleasing prints at larger sizes (e.g. 13 x 19 inches—33 x 48 cm) from files originally shot in RAW.

Let's say you are shooting inside a stadium under sodium-vapor lighting and you forget to change from Automatic White Balance. At the end of the day you notice all your images exhibit a strong color cast. Or, perhaps your exposure was a bit off for some of the shots at one end of the field. You'll usually have better results correcting these types of problems if you were shooting in RAW capture mode.

Note: While no software can work miracles with a grossly over or underexposed image, you should be able to correct moderate exposure errors (plus or minus one stop or EV) without giving the RAW image an artificial look.

Yet working with RAW does have certain drawbacks. The larger RAW files consume more space on a memory card than JPEGS. In addition, converting and adjusting MRW format files usually involves more post-processing time than working with JPEGs.

Frankly, most photo enthusiasts use Large/Extra Fine JPEG as their primary recording format, and that certainly makes sense. Use RAW capture for once-in-a-lifetime moments, for images that you plan to print in extra large sizes, and in situations where it's tough to get a perfect exposure and white balance.

White Balance

Unlike the film used in conventional cameras, the sensors in digital cameras can be adjusted for the different color temperatures of light. In other words, we can cause the camera to produce a natural-looking image, rendering whites as pure white in various types of lighting. When the whites are accurate, other tones are accurate as well, without a strong color cast.

White Balance—How it Works

Every light source emits a different range of wavelengths, varying from primarily short (appearing blue) to primarily long wavelengths (appearing red.) Even the light from the sun can vary. It is cooler (bluer) than normal on overcast days, and warm (reddish) during a sunrise or sunset. While our brain adjusts for these differences, reducing our perception of them, photographic film and digital sensors record them more objectively.

The color of light is defined numerically using the Kelvin color temperature scale. Lower Kelvin temperatures denote the warm, reddish light produced by a bonfire, an incandescent lamp, and the sun when it is low in the sky. Higher Kelvin temperatures denote the cool, bluish light at twilight, on heavily overcast days, or in a shady area.

On the Kelvin scale, full sunlight (mid day) is typically around 5100K to 5500K. The light on an overcast day is usually between 5500K and 6500K. In full shade, the light is even bluer: typically between 7000K and 8000K. The range provided for these different types of light is quite broad because it's affected by the exact time of day, the extent of the clouds that filter the light from the sun, the time of year, and atmospheric factors such as haze, smog, fog, or dust particles in the air.

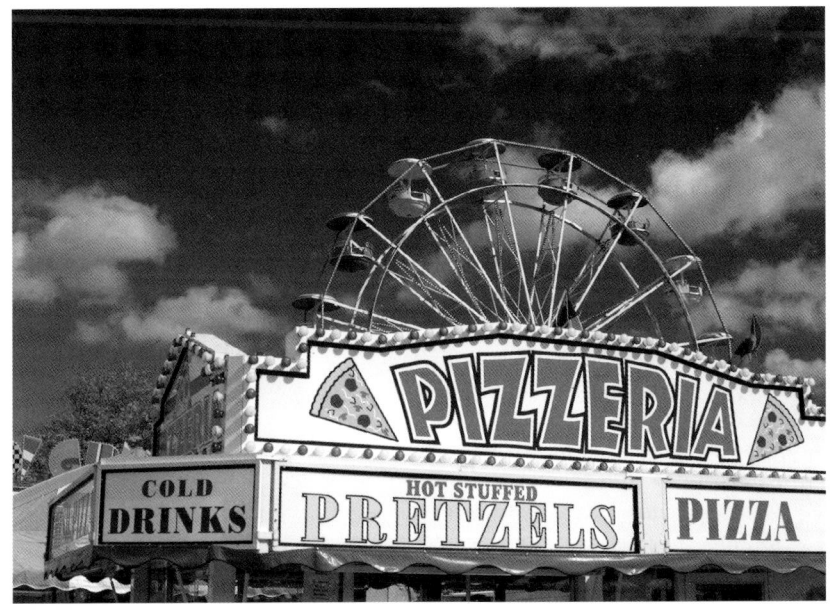

In average outdoor conditions, particularly on sunny days and under light cloud cover, the AWB system produces pleasing color balance. In more "difficult" conditions, such as open shade or under artificial lighting, switch to other white balance options for more accurate results.

Artificial light sources also produce light with certain color temperatures. Household tungsten lamps produce light with an orange cast (about 3200K). Most fluorescent tubes produce greenish light. Unusual lamps, such as sodium vapor and mercury vapor, produce light with a strange color that can be difficult to define.

In order to produce images with clean whites (when whites are clean, other colors are generally also accurate, although some artificial dyes have a strange color response), the 5D must be adjusted for the various color temperatures of light. It has a setting to automatically detect the type of lighting, called Auto White Balance (AWB). In addition, your 5D provides other options for controlling white balance in a broad variety of lighting conditions. Some of the advanced features are straightforward and intuitive. Others are complex, of the type you would expect in a camera designed for professional photographers. While you may not plan to use all of the diverse options, it's worth understanding how they work and why they might be useful.

Auto White Balance ▣

The Auto White Balance system is selected by setting the white balance dial (located on the top left shoulder of the camera) to AWB ▣. It is designed to analyze the color of light and set an appropriate temperature to render whites as white. That system works quite well outdoors on sunny or partly cloudy days, and indoors with flash. It's an especially useful choice when the light is changing rapidly (from sunny to cloudy to sunny again), or when shooting subjects that move from one type of lighting to another—sunlight to shadow, for example. But AWB does not always work so well under manufactured lighting such as sodium vapor.

Preset White Balance ▣

For more accurate white balance in mixed or artificial lighting, you may not want to trust AWB to correctly adjust the white balance. You can often get better results by selecting a specific white balance setting designed specifically for those conditions.

Rotate the white balance dial to the Preset icon ▣ and press the WB button in the center of the dial. A list of options will appear in the LCD monitor with more icons: Daylight ☀ , Shade ⌂ , Cloudy ☁ , Tungsten (household lamps) ✲ , Fluorescent, ▨ or Flash ◲ . Scroll to the desired option with the controller keys or the camera's control dial. Press the AF button in the center of the controller to confirm your selection.

Note: When using flash merely to fill shadows in a scene where sunlight (or another light source) is the primary source of illumination, do not select flash ◲ . Instead, make your white balance selection based on the type of lighting that is the main light source for the shot.

Preset WB Levels Adjustment: If desired, you can fine-tune the white balance level of the particular setting using the up/down keys of the controller. While the Preset white balance options are visible on the LCD monitor, select a plus (+) factor for a warmer (more yellow) effect, or a minus (-) factor for a cooler (more bluish) effect. You can make adjustments within a wide range.

You may find the WB levels option useful, however there is no way to determine the effect that any specific setting will produce before you take a photo. Hence, this feature calls for a lot of trial-and-error. You may decide to permanently leave the 5D set to a –1 factor for Cloudy WB if you find that the camera routinely makes images that are slightly too yellow on overcast days, for example. Or set a +1 factor for Flash WB if you find the camera routinely produces images that are slightly too blue when using flash. (If you decide on this technique, set the white balance level adjustment to the preferred amount and leave it there. Do not change it back after you finish taking a shot. Even after you turn the camera off, it will stay set for that specific WB option.)

Hint: The WB levels option is not very scientific because the exact color of light often varies within a broad range, as on a cloudy day, for example. In situations where the camera makes images with inaccurate white balance, I strongly recommend using the Custom WB feature 🖼 instead.

Creative Use of Preset White Balance: Using the "wrong" white balance setting can yield some interesting creative effects. For example, the Cloudy setting can be used when the sun is shining brightly to create a warmer appearance resembling the effect produced by a warming filter. The Flash WB setting produces a milder warming effect, while the Shade setting produces a very obvious yellow/orange color cast.

The Tungsten setting produces the opposite--a strong blue cast, useful with some winter scenes for a much "cooler" effect. Experiment with using the various Preset choices for creative purposes. You can always check the results in the camera's LCD.

Custom White Balance

This feature allows you to set the white balance value for any type of lighting. Though a sophisticated function, it is not overly complicated to set thanks to guidance that appears in the LCD monitor. It is well worth the bit of extra effort because this setting virtually guarantees good white balance under unusual lighting conditions.

Note: Custom WB applies only to photographs where flash is not the primary light source. If you routinely use flash, stick with the Preset option, perhaps using the white balance levels adjustment if necessary to produce a warmer or cooler rendition.

Be sure to carry a sheet of white paper or a gray card (to use as the target that you'll need in order to calibrate the camera). A sheet of paper is easier to carry, and is more readily available than a gray card. Photocopy the following steps for handy reference while you're out shooting.

Set the white balance dial to Custom WB 🖾 and follow these steps exactly as specified:

1. Press and release the WB button (on top of the camera) to open the white balance screen in the LCD monitor.

2. Be careful not to touch the shutter release button yet.

3. Look through the viewfinder and fill the central area of the frame (within the circle etched on the viewing screen) with your white or gray target. Be sure that the target is in the same light that will be used to make your images. (For example, do not cast a shadow over the target.) The target does not need to be in focus for this step.

4. Press the shutter release button all the way down. This calibrates the WB system. An image or your target will

now appear in the LCD monitor. If it looks neutral white or gray—depending on the target that you are using—the calibration process has been successful.

5. To confirm this Custom WB selection, press the AF button in the center of the controller. (If you're not satisfied—because the target exhibits a color cast—repeat the entire process. Press the AF button only when you are satisfied.)

On rare occasions, an error message will be displayed in the LCD monitor indicating that the system cannot calibrate the light. This is most likely to occur when a white target is illuminated by extremely bright light. In that case, try using a neutral gray card as a target because it reflects less light, the calibration process should be successful.

Note: The camera saves the last custom white balance setting even when the camera is turned off. If you repeatedly shoot in the same sports arena, for example, you can recall the setting simply by selecting Custom white balance. However, since the system only retains the last calibration, if you shoot in different light using Custom WB, be sure to recalibrate the system for the new conditions. Or, if you recall a previous setting, be sure you haven't changed it in the meantime.

Color Temperature

This option allows you to set a specific Kelvin temperature for white balance purposes. It is intended for photographers who use a color temperature meter, lighting with a known color temperature, or who follow the manufacturer's recommendations for certain types of lighting. If you aren't using these methods, other white balance options may be more useful.

Select Color Temperature **K** on the white balance dial and press the WB button. Two new displays will appear in the LCD monitor: numerals with K for Kelvin and the magenta/green compensation scale that runs from M9 to G9. Initially, ignore the scale and set a desired color temperature using the controller's keys.

The magenta/green compensation feature allows you to further adjust the white balance for magenta or green as if you were using filters over the lens, as in traditional film photography. (This feature is most helpful for fine tuning white balance for fluorescent bulbs, which tend to produce a green color cast.) Scroll over to the scale with the controller's right key and then select the level of compensation using the up/down keys. Again, this feature is intended only for those with expertise in assessing color temperature wishing to adjust the level (strength) of green or magenta "filtration." Frankly, most 5D owners will most likely use the Custom WB option when shooting without flash under artificial lighting.

White Balance Bracketing
When white balance bracketing is active, the camera generates three image files of a scene, each at a slightly different white balance setting. It's available with all of the WB options when shooting JPEGs. (It is not necessary with RAW since you can easily change the color temperature when processing your MRW files).

Access this feature via the drive mode selector button 🖐 on the top of the camera. Press the button and scroll down to the bracketing option for white balance on the LCD monitor. Two options are available: LoWB (for a slight variance) and HiWB (for a greater variance). After making your selection, press the AF button in the controller to confirm your choice.

When you take a single shot, the camera's processing system automatically generates the original image file plus two copies of the file, each with a slightly different white balance adjustment. One duplicate image will be slightly warmer while the other will be slightly cooler.

In my experience, this feature is most appropriate when using Auto White Balance or Preset white balance. It increases the odds of getting an image with color rendition that is most likely to please you. This feature has some disadvantages: it's available only with single frame advance; the extra files consume more space on a memory card; and though it takes less than a second, the extra processing time may cause you to miss a fleeting gesture in candid picture taking.

Color Modes

Digital cameras render color based on combinations of red, blue, and green and in terms of hue, saturation, and brightness. The various systems that define these colors are called color spaces. Color spaces were invented with different biases based largely on how images will be created or viewed. The 5D offers a broad variety of color space options. Select the one that is most suitable for the intended use of your images.

To access the 5D's color mode options (in M, S, A or P exposure modes only), press the Fn button (on the back of the camera to the right of the viewfinder) and scroll to the bottom item in the left column of icons that appears in the LCD monitor. Then use the left/right keys on the controller to scroll sequentially through the various color mode options. Press the AF button in the center of the controller to confirm your selection. The different selections are:

Natural Color
Typically called sRGB, this option produces rich, faithful colors. It's perfect for images intended for Internet use, or for enhancement with most of the image-processing programs. This is also the right choice if you plan to print directly from the camera or memory card using a photo printer that does not support the Adobe RGB color space (see below) in direct printing. (Check the printer's instruction manual for specifics.)

Most commercial volume printing firms also use sRGB images, so this option is fine for images that you take or send to a high-volume printing lab (photofinishers, on-line printing services, etc.). Be aware that most of these firms usually convert any Adobe RGB images you send to sRGB before making prints. On the other hand, labs offering professional quality custom printing often use the Adobe RGB color space, taking advantage of its wider color gamut.

Natural Plus
Similar to conventional sRGB, Natural Plus produces images with higher acutance—apparent sharpness around subject edges—and higher contrast. Select this option in flat lighting on a cloudy day, or for snappier images in atmospheric conditions such as haze, fog, or smog. However, on sunny days when contrast is naturally high, this setting could give ultra bright highlights and dark, murky shadows. Also think twice about using Natural Plus for portraits because the increased contrast and sharpness may not be flattering.

Other sRGB Color Modes
The 5D also offers a choice of specific color modes based on certain types of images, Scroll and highlight Color/DEC , then scroll to the desired sub-option. These six color modes are optimized for their specific types of shooting. (The camera automatically selects the pertinent option when it's used in one of the Digital Subject Programs, but these options can also be selected in other camera exposure modes.) They are listed below with Konica Minolta's description and my assessments of the characteristics of each.

Portrait: The first of the subject-specific sRGB color spaces, Portrait is "optimized for the reproduction of skin tones." The in-camera contrast level is automatically set to –1 while color saturation is set to +1. Images exhibit gentle contrast, a slightly warm balance, and moderately high color saturation.

Landscape: "Optimized for reproduction of outdoor scenery." Contrast, color saturation, and sharpness are automatically set to +1. As expected, this option produces images with higher than average contrast, color saturation, and sharpness for the most "punchy" effect overall.

Sunset: "Optimized for landscapes at dusk and dawn, the use of Auto White Balance is recommended"; Contrast and color saturation are automatically set to +1. This option pro-

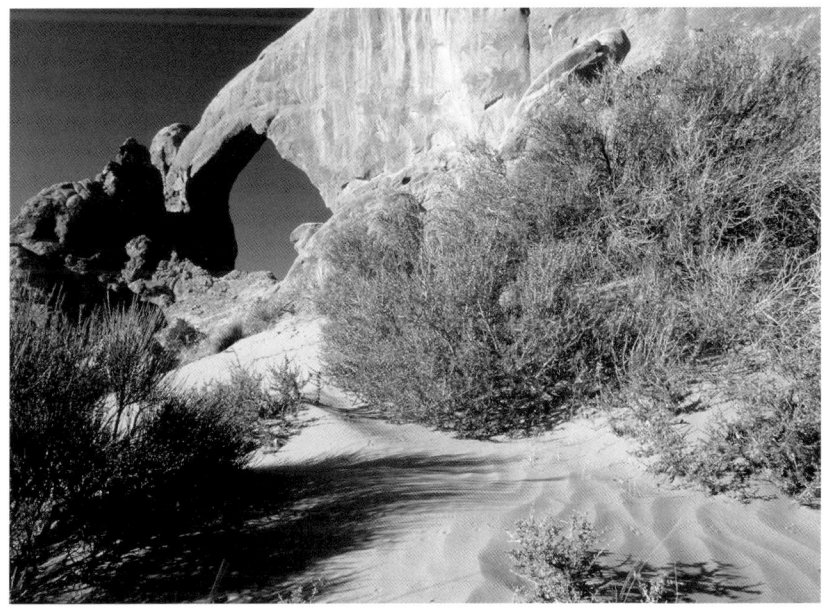

While you can achieve snappier contrast and richer color saturation with the options in the Function menu (Color/DEC), it's quicker and easier to use the Landscape Program mode.

duces images with a very warm (strong yellow) color balance as well as moderately high contrast and color richness.

Night View: "Optimized for night time scenery without flash." Contrast is automatically set to +1. In low light I found little difference in images made with this mode versus Natural sRGB, though the former exhibits slightly higher contrast and deeper color tones.

Night Portrait: "Optimized for night time portraits with flash." No automatic adjustments are made for contrast, color saturation, or sharpness. When compared to images made with Natural sRGB, the Night Portrait images exhibit slightly deeper color tones.

Black & White (B&W): This sRGB option causes the camera to generate images in monochrome. I found that the tones are neutral and the overall effect is pleasing, suitable for making prints without adjustments in Photoshop or other software. However, serious black & white photographers will want to adjust Levels and other controls in their imaging software, to produce the exact effect that's just right for any image.

Adobe RGB and Embedded Adobe RGB
The Adobe RGB color mode has a wider color gamut (recording range) than sRGB, so it can record more colors, which is useful for making prints. (However, when viewed on a computer monitor, sRGB images exhibit richer colors.) Two options are available here. The standard Adobe RGB item records the image in this color space but does not embed that data in the actual image file. When Embedded Adobe RGB is selected, the camera's processor embeds this color space into the actual image.

The term "embed" indicates that the color space is stored in the image data file and is immediately recognized by image processing software that is compatible with Adobe RGB color space, such as Adobe products. If the standard Adobe RGB option is selected in camera, the software will ask whether the image should be in sRGB or Adobe RGB color space.

Note: Not all image-processing software supports Adobe RGB. If you're using a program that does not, it should automatically change the color space to sRGB when opening an image. But if it produces an error message (such as incompatible color space) you should not use the Adobe RGB option in-camera. It's impossible to test the dozens of imaging programs on the market for their handling of files with Adobe RGB color space. You might want to experiment with test shots made using this color mode to determine what your own software will do with such images.

Except for Adobe RGB and Embedded Adobe RGB, all the color modes in the 5D are sRGB. If your software is compatible, there's a benefit to selecting Adobe RGB: the larger color gamut allows more colors to be recorded and reproduced when making prints. But the Adobe RGB color space is not the most appropriate for images intended for email, websites, or other Internet applications. Use the camera's other color modes for such images. You could also shoot in Adobe RGB mode if supported by your image-processing software, and convert the images to sRGB for Internet use.

Optimizing Images In-Camera

In-camera image optimization is particularly useful if you shoot JPEGs and print directly from the camera or memory card. If you fall into this category, you may wish to consider the Digital Effects Control (DEC) feature of the 5D. It allows you to alter the level of contrast, sharpness, and color saturation from very low to very high when using the camera's M, S, A, or P exposure modes. (There's no need for this feature if shooting in RAW format because the images can be adjusted in the converter software before conversion to another format.)

To adjust any of these three attributes, you must first select one of the color modes (use the Fn button as previously described). In the LCD display for your selected color mode, note three scales that appear, one for each attribute. The default for these is 0, and they can be adjusted within a range from –2 to +2 using the left/right controller keys. After you make any changes, press the AF button to confirm your selections.

Contrast ◖◗
Without internal adjustment, the 5D produces images with snappy contrast. To reduce contrast in harsh lighting conditions or to create flattering portraits that benefit from a soft look, you may want to adjust the contrast to –1 or to –2. In flat light, such as on an overcast day, you might want to try

a +1 level for more separation of light to dark elements, but think twice about selecting a higher contrast level for any other type of lighting. Low contrast is easy to fix in image-processing software, but excessive contrast can be difficult to moderate. In fact, you may want to permanently set a –1 level if you plan to enhance your photos in image-processing software.

Color Saturation 🄲🄾🄻

At its default setting, the 5D produces images with rich, vibrant color saturation, appropriate for most subjects. (When using a polarizing filter (over the lens), color saturation can be especially vivid.) However, if you find the colors to be excessive, set a minus factor when shooting in JPEG capture mode. Decreased saturation is often useful in portrait photography where muted color rendition is often more pleasing.

I find that a –1 saturation level produces color that is preferable for the majority of subjects, but this is a subjective judgment. If you plan to extensively manipulate your images, you'll probably want to start with a –1 or –2 level in-camera. Think twice about selecting a high saturation level; excessive color saturation can lead to loss of detail; that problem can be difficult to correct in image-processing software.

Sharpness 🄢

The camera produces quite sharp images at the default setting. You can increase to +1, but I suggest you do so only if you do not plan to use any sharpening filters in the computer. In my view, the +2 level produces excessive sharpening, which can be difficult or impossible to correct with image-processing software.

Some post-processing experts prefer to select the lowest in-camera sharpening level available (–2), using special sharpening techniques in image-processing software to enhance results. Frankly, I find that the default setting works well enough to produce sharp—but not artificially sharp—images. Before making a print, I apply light sharpening using Unsharp Mask in Photoshop or Elements.

Noise Reduction

Digital images made using long exposures (one second or longer) can exhibit noticeable digital noise even when low ISO settings are used. The effect is similar to the grain we see in prints made with high-speed films. These colored specks are most visible in shadow areas, particularly when they're brightened in image-processing software. Although the 5D controls digital noise quite effectively during standard processing, the camera includes a feature specifically designed for additional noise reduction. (Noise can also result from other causes, such as high ISO settings or under-exposure, but this particular feature is activated only if the shutter speed is one second or longer). When noise reduction is on, additional in-camera processing minimizes digital noise in these longer exposures.

To access this feature, press the MENU button and use the controller keys to select Recording Menu 1; scroll down to *Noise reductn*. Select *On* or *Off* and confirm it by pressing the AF button in the center of the controller.

Note: Be aware that noise reduction will not be active if the camera is set in Continuous Advance drive.

If you often make long exposures, as in night photography, you may appreciate this feature because it allows the camera to produce images with less visible noise. (Both the sharpness and the color of the specks are moderated.) However, there are two primary drawbacks.

First, the entire image becomes slightly softer than it would be without noise reduction. That can be corrected to a degree with the in-camera control for increasing sharpness or, preferably, in a computer using image-processing software.

Second, there is a delay after you take a shot of up to 30 seconds while the noise reduction is applied. During this time the camera is not operable, which can be quite frustrating.

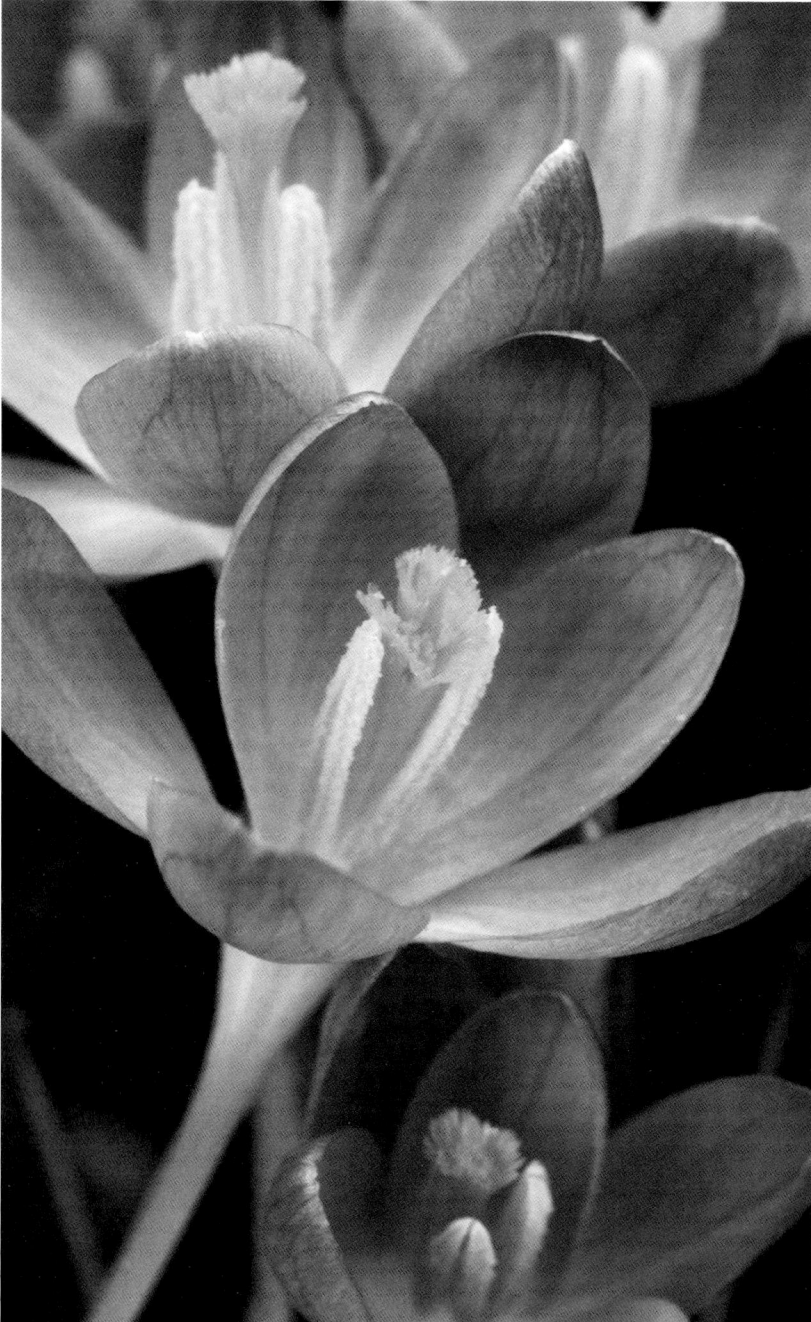

Using the LCD Monitor and Menus

The LCD Monitor

The 5D has a large 2.5-inch LCD monitor that is an extremely important tool for digital shooting. The monitor not only displays important recording data and camera settings, it lets you review pictures you have stored on your memory card as well as navigate within the vital menu system to control many of the camera's operations.

In order to save battery power, the LCD automatically darkens after a period of non-use. (The default is two seconds, but the time period can be adjusted in Setup Menu 3, see page 119.) Touching any button or turning any dial or knob quickly reactivates the monitor because the information is always live on the screen—only its backlight switches off to save power.

Image review occurs immediately after shooting via instant playback or by pressing the playback button ▶ , which allows you to look at any files on your memory card. You can set the length of time you want the instant-playback image displayed before the screen returns to data display.

↰ *You can make a vertical image display upright on your horizontal LCD monitor with a setting in Custom Menu 2.*

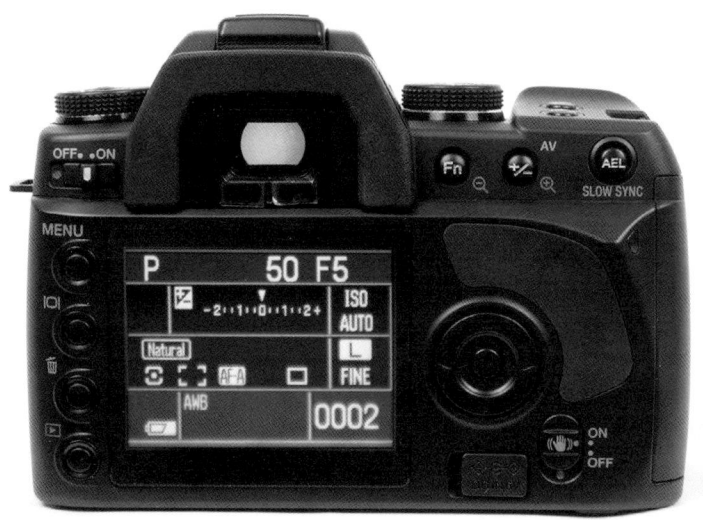

The LCD monitor not only plays back images you have recorded, it also displays a wealth of shooting information, providing instant information on the settings you are currently using.

Data Display

Data is displayed on the LCD monitor when images or menus are not being viewed. Since the screen is big, the letters and numerals are also large and easy to read (and you can even make them larger—simply press the display button |O| on the back of the camera two times). When the camera is placed in the vertical shooting position, the display automatically rotates for ease of viewing (see page 113).

The recording mode display presents a wide scope of useful information on settings and camera operations, ranging from readouts telling which exposure mode and f/stop are in use to battery status and the number of frames left on your memory card (see page 59 for detailed information). You can scroll between a full and partial display of recording information (or turn the monitor off) by repeatedly pressing the display button. You can also turn the LCD monitor off by programming it in Custom Menu 2 (see page 113) so it switches off automatically when you look through the viewfinder (there are two proximity sensors just below the viewfinder). This conserves power and eliminates the distraction of seeing the display while shooting. When you move the camera away from the shooting position, the data display switches back on automatically.

Note: When the LCD monitor is turned off, images are not displayed after they are taken.

Playback Options
Instant image review occurs automatically after each scene is shot. The default viewing period is two seconds, which can be changed in Recording Menu 1 **◘1** (see page 101).

   Although the feature for instant playback is useful for a quick look, the Playback mode offers you the ability to take your time and review all of the images stored on your memory card. Access this mode by pressing the playback button **▶** on the lower left back of the camera. Use either the control dial or the left/right controller keys to scroll forward or backward through the images. Use the down key to rotate images.

   To view a photo's histogram and Luminance Limit (highlight/shadow warning), which appear on a screen that also includes certain file and shooting information, press the up key on the controller (see pages 162-163 for details about these features).

   There are two other useful options in Playback mode. The first is a magnification feature. Use it to check sharpness in specific areas of an image, look for red-eye, gauge facial expressions in people pictures, and so on. In order to magnify an image in Playback mode, press the exposure compensation **⊠** button and scroll around the image using the keys on the controller to see different portions of the enlarged picture. To decrease magnification, press the Fn button. To return to full image viewing, press the display button.

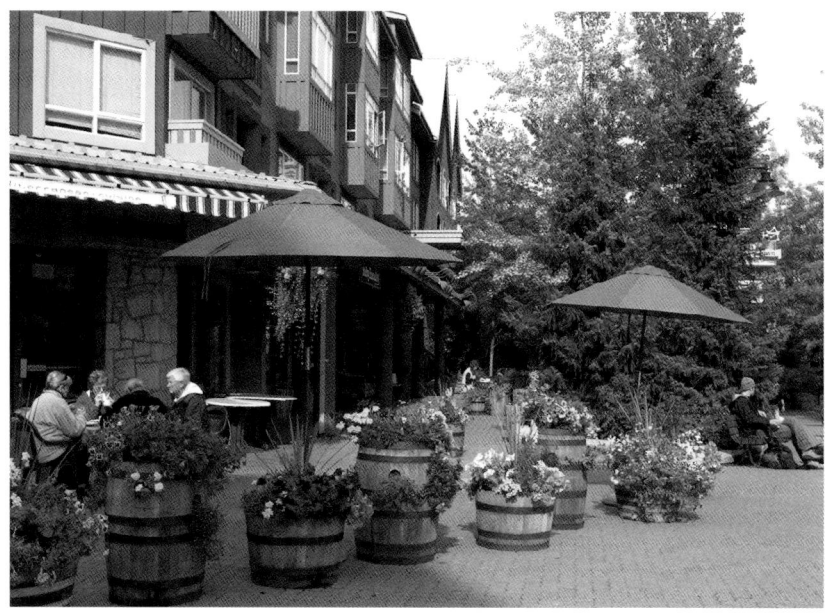

By pressing the exposure compensation button in Playback mode, I was able to magnify the image in the LCD monitor to confirm that all important areas of this picture were sharply focused.

Playback mode also includes an index display for reviewing thumbnails of multiple images. Simply press the display button ⅠⅠⅠ twice while in Playback mode. This feature is useful to search for a shot stored on your memory card since you can look at more than one picture at a time, but the images are small. The number of thumbnails displayed can be changed from 9 (default) to 4 or 16 using the Playback Menu 1 ▶1 , as discussed on page 106.

You can also use Playback mode to review images as a slide show on the LCD monitor (see Playback Menu 2 ▶2 , page 107 for setup information). Each picture stored on your memory card will display for five seconds before the next image automatically appears. Pause and restart the slide show by pressing the AF button. You can use the left/right controller keys to go back or forward within the slide show.

Cancel the slide show by pressing the MENU button or the down key on the controller.

Deleting Images

You can delete pictures one at a time in either instant review or in Playback mode. Simply press the delete button 🗑 (located on the lower left back of the camera) while an image is displayed. Scroll using the controller keys to highlight *YES* or *NO* in the confirmation screen, then press the AF button to complete.

   In addition to this feature, the 5D provides the ability to delete as many images as you specify, including the option to erase all images in a folder. Use the delete feature accessible through Playback Menu 1 (see pages 104-105).

Note: Although there is no in-camera method for recovering deleted images, several companies market software that's designed for this purpose. These programs do not provide a 100% success, but some are quite good at recovering deleted JPEGs and, sometimes, RAW files. Even some memory cards come with such software. Look for reviews on the Internet through a web search using keywords such as, "image recovery software programs."

Protect Images from Deletion

Before deleting any images, you may want to protect important ones from unintentional erasure using the lock feature. You can use the Playback Menu 1 to designate any number of images you choose to be locked, or protected, from deletion. You can always remove the lock from any image if you want at a later time. See page 106 for details.

Caution: All images, including those protected using the lock feature, will be erased when formatting the memory card.

The Menus

The Maxxum 5D/Dynax 5D offers an extensive list of menu options, including features for customizing camera operation to your own preferences. Some of the functions are simple, or at least intuitive, while others are more complex. This guide is intended to lead you step by step through the myriad features and provide practical recommendations on which functions to use, which ones to postpone for future consideration, and which may not be of use to you.

To access the 5D's electronic menus, press the MENU button (located on the left back of the camera). Scroll as instructed in this section using the left/right and up/down keys on the controller. Enter your selections using the AF button in the center of the controller.

There are four different menus, each with own set of tabs (or screens) as listed here:

- **Recording Menu 1   ◘1**
- **Recording Menu 2   ◘2**

- **Playback Menu 1   ▣1**
- **Playback Menu 2   ▣2**

- **Custom Menu 1   ☼1**
- **Custom Menu 2   ☼2**

- **Setup Menu 1   ⸕1**
- **Setup Menu 2   ⸕2**
- **Setup Menu 3   ⸕3**

The Recording Menus   ◘

The Recording menu lets you control several functions that determine how the photographs are captured and displayed, from how big the image file is, to the mode of flash used, to the order of images when bracketing for exposure. This

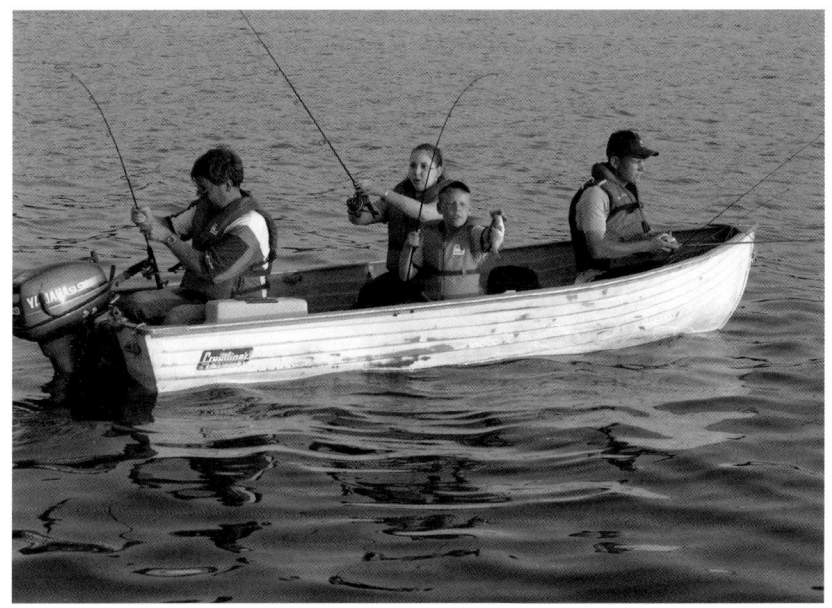

This scene posed a challenge because of high contrast and ultra bright highlight areas, making ideal exposure (in-camera) difficult to achieve. Making such assessments in advance can be useful when selecting Quality options including RAW because of its wide latitude.

menu consists of two distinct sections: Recording Menu 1 and Recording Menu 2.

Recording Menu 1 📷1

Press the MENU button and Recording Menu 1 will appear. Then use the controller down key to select one of the four functions listed below:

Quality: This selection allows you to select JPEG quality from *X.FIN* (extra fine—lowest compression), *FINE* (fine—slightly higher compression), or *STD.* (standard—the highest level of compression). See pages 72-77 for description of how to use these settings.

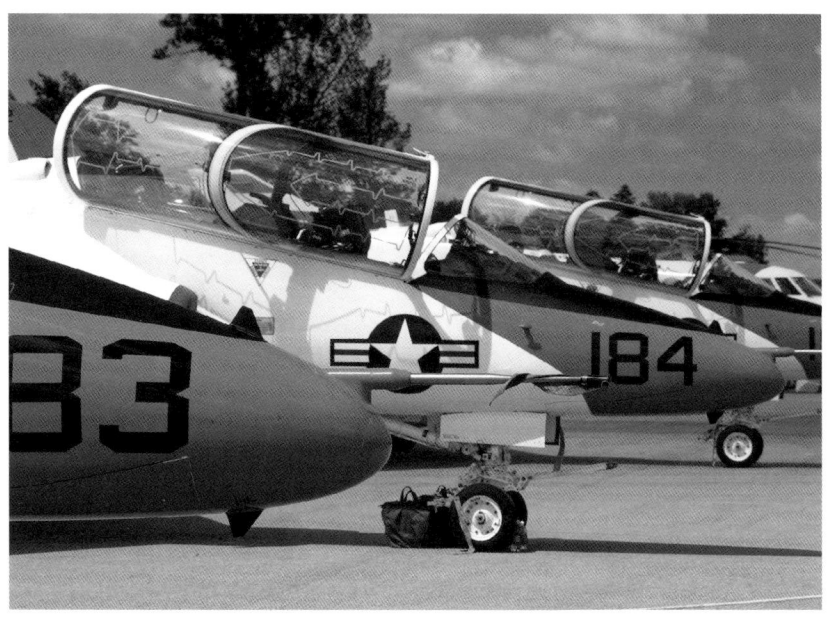

A 5-second time limit in instant playback is adequate for quickly confirming that exposure and composition are acceptable. For a longer and closer scrutiny of sharpness and other factors, set instant playback to 10 seconds or switch to the full Playback mode.

First scroll right using the controller key, then up/down to choose the level of compression you require. Press the AF button in the middle of the controller to confirm your selection and return to the menu screen.

You can also scroll right and then up/down to select *RAW* or *RAW+* (which captures both a RAW and a JPEG file simultaneously). Register your choice by pressing the AF button.

There are no added compression options because RAW (MRW) files are not compressed. I often use RAW format because of the image enhancing options available in conversion software (see page 219).

The JPEG portion of the RAW+ option can be used as an email attachment to friends or clients when you don't want to spend a lot of time processing your image files. It is also useful because some browser programs do not recognize the MRW but will allow you to view the JPEGs.

Image size: For JPEGs, select *L* (Large resolution of 3008 x 2000 pixels), *M* (Medium resolution of 2256 x 1496 pixels), or *S* (Small resolution of 1504 x 1000 pixels) as discussed in detail on pages 72-77.

When shooting RAW, no image-size options are provided because the camera always uses 6-megapixel capture.

From the Image size menu selection, again scroll right when shooting JPEG by using the controller key, then up/down to choose the specific resolution (L, M, or S) you wish to set. Press the AF button to confirm your selection and return to the menu screen.

Instant Playback: This item sets the length of time an image is displayed on the LCD monitor immediately after a shot is taken. Select either 2, 5, or 10 seconds. Use *2 sec.* if you conserve battery power or just want to glance at the shot to make sure you recorded it. Select *10 sec.* if you want to analyze your pictures before deciding whether to keep or delete. Use *5 sec.* as middle ground. Remember, you can examine any image for longer periods of time by using the camera's Playback mode.

To set the time period for viewing instant playback, scroll down from Recording Menu 1 to *Inst. Playback.* Then scroll right using the controller key to enter then up/down to select from the three different options described above. Enter your selection by pressing the AF button.

Noise Reductn: This setting activates the digital noise reduction feature for exposures longer than 1 second, as discussed in detail on page 91.

From *Noise reductn.,* use the controller keys to first scroll right and then up/down to select *On* or *Off.* Enter by pressing the AF button.

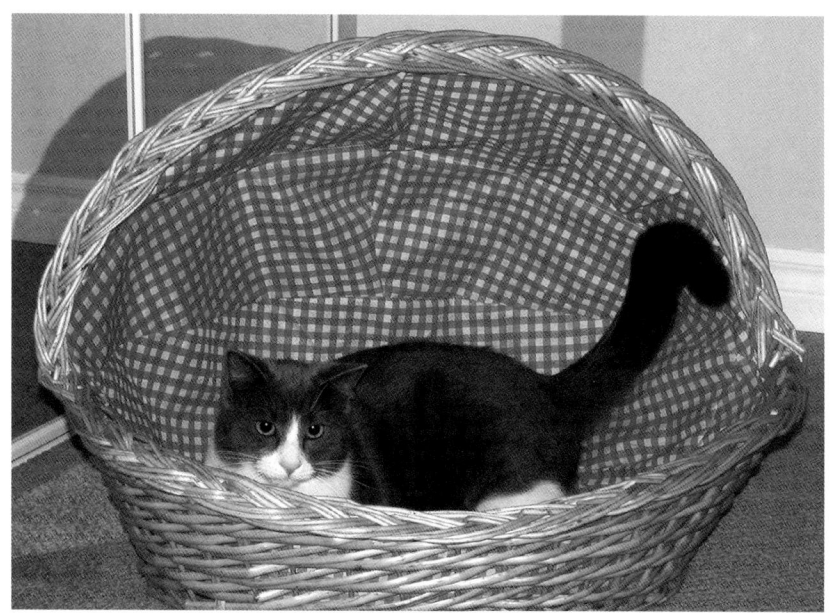

When taking photos of pets indoors, red-eye (or green-eye) is common. To minimize this problem and save processing time in the computer, select Red-eye reduction Flash mode.

Recording Menu 2 📷2
Press the MENU button and scroll with the right controller key to highlight Recording Menu 2. Then use the controller down key to select one of the four functions listed below:

Flash mode: The options include *Fill-flash*, used as the primary lighting when conditions are dark; used to soften and fill shadows in bright or backlit conditions; *Red-eye reduction*, used to prevent or reduce red-eye by firing a set of pre-flashes; *Rear flash sync* fires flash at the end of a long exposure so that light trails follow a moving subject; and *Wireless/Remote flash*, for off-camera wireless flash photography using a compatible Program Flash unit and the built-in flash. (Refer to pages 171-189 for more details about flash photography.)

From *Flash mode*, use the controller keys to first scroll right and then up/down to select one of the four options described above. Enter by pressing the AF button.

Flash control: The default setting is *ADI flash* (ADI stands for Advanced Distance Integration)—the more sophisticated option. It is only available when D-series Konica Minolta lenses are used and only with the built-in flash or a D-series accessory Program Flash. If you are using other lenses or an older Konica Minolta flash unit, the camera will automatically switch to Pre-flash TTL metering without considering subject distance. That should still produce excellent flash exposures except with very light or dark-toned subjects. You can also select the *Pre-flash TTL* option, described in more detail in the chapter on flash, page 182.

From *Flash control*, use the controller keys to first scroll right and then up/down to select one of the two options described above. Enter by pressing the AF button.

Bracket order: This sets the order of the exposure compensation sequence in exposure bracketing. The first option is *0, –, +*. Your alternative choice is *–, 0,+*. Your selection will be dictated by personal preference.

From *Bracket order*, first scroll right using the controller key then up/down to select one of the two options and enter by pressing the AF button.

Reset: This control returns many of the camera's recording functions to the factory-set defaults. It's useful after you have been experimenting with some of the camera's many features. To get the 5D back to "normal," use this feature to restore the following:

Exposure Compensation to 0, *Flash Compensation* to 0, *AF Area* to wide, *AF mode* to AF-A (automatic switching between Single-shot and Continuous AF), *Focus area selection* to spot AF (using the central AF area point), *Metering mode* to multi-segment (evaluative honeycomb pattern),

Drive mode to Single-frame advance, *Preset White Balance* to Daylight with 0 compensation; *Color Temperature* to 5500K with 0 Green/Magenta adjustment, *Color mode* to Natural sRGB, *Digital Effects Control* to 0, *Flash mode* to Fill flash or red-eye reduction (depending on which of the two was most recently used), and *Flash control* to ADI.

From *Reset*, scroll right using the controller key; a confirmation screen will display. Use the controller keys to select *Yes* for reset or *No* to cancel reset. Use the AF button to confirm.

The Playback Menus ▶

There are two Playback menus that offer several useful options for reviewing and managing images you have recorded to the memory card.

To access the Playback menus, press the MENU button. Then, using the controller keys, scroll to the Playback icon ▶ and press the AF button to activate the menu. Scroll to Playback Menu 1 or Playback Menu 2.

Playback Menu 1 ▶1

This section includes several choices for image review, along with their respective sub-choices. It also includes the option to format your memory card. Use the controller key to scroll down to one of the selections:

Delete: This setting will permanently erase images from your card, either singly or in batches that you select. Caution is urged when you use this option because images deleted from your memory card cannot normally be recovered.

From the *Delete* item, scroll right for more options to refine your choice. Select from the options below using the up/down controller key and press the AF button to complete any of these operations:

- *Marked frames* lets you select images to erase. This option displays a frame selection screen showing a set of thumbnail images. Scroll through the thumbnails using the left/right controller keys and select frames for deletion with the controller's up key; deselect any frame with the down key. Press the AF button to display a confirmation screen, then select *YES* or *NO*. Confirm by using the AF button to complete the operation. (Cancel this process at any time before completion by pressing the MENU button.)

- *All in folder* deletes all unprotected frames in a folder previously selected in the *View folder* menu option (see page below).

- *All on card* deletes all unprotected images that have been written to the memory card.

Format: This item formats the memory card, permanently erasing all data. Even protected images are deleted.

When *Format* is highlighted, press the AF button and choose *YES* or *NO* from the confirmation screen. Verify your choice by again pressing the AF button, and a final screen will confirm the formatting activity.

Never remove a memory card when formatting is underway; it could damage to your card. I recommend reformatting the card every time after you download images to your computer's hard drive or other backup system.

View folder: This item provides an option to view images only in a single folder or in all folders on your memory card by scrolling to *Single folder* or *All folders*, respectively. I strongly suggest selecting the *All folders* option. This will allow the camera to display all images in Playback mode, not merely the images in a specifically selected folder.

From *View folder*, use the controller keys to first scroll right and then up/down to select one of the two options described above. Enter your choice by pressing the AF button.

Lock: There are five options to protect or unprotect images on the memory card from deletion. Once a file is locked, an icon appears on the image's playback display ⊶ , and that image cannot be deleted by using the delete button or any of the menu delete options (except by using the *Format* option in Playback Menu 1).

From *Lock*, use the controller keys to first scroll right and then up/down to select from the choices described below. Press the AF button to enter your selection:

- *Marked frames* functions similarly to *Marked frames* selection in the *Delete* menu. Instead of deleting one or more frames, you protect one or more frames.

Scroll through the thumbnails using the left/right keys and select a frame for protection with the up key; deselect any frame with the down key. Press the AF button to display a confirmation screen, then select *YES* or *NO*. Confirm by using the AF button. (Cancel this process at any time before completion by pressing the MENU button.)

- *All in folder* locks all frames in a folder previously selected in the *View folder* menu option.

- *All on card* locks all images recorded to the memory card.

- *Unlock folder* will unlock all the protected frames in a specific folder that has been designated in the *View folder* option described above.

- *Unlock card* unlocks all protected images on memory card.

Index format: Choose the number of thumbnails (*4, 9,* or *16* frames) you can view at one time on the LCD when you press the display button.

From *Index format*, scroll right to select from the three choices listed above. Confirm by pressing the AF button.

Playback Menu 2 ▶2
This menu includes the less frequently used options listed below.

Scroll down to highlight one of these selections:

Slide show: When you select *Enter* and press the AF button, the camera will play back all the images on the card at a rate of one image every five seconds. To pause and restart the slide show, press the AF button. To move ahead or go back, press the left/right controller keys. To cancel the slide show, press the down key on the controller.

DPOF set: This option designates files on your memory card for direct printing using a DPOF (Digital Print Order Format) compatible printer (downloading into a computer is not necessary). The three options are selected in a similar way as the same options in the *Delete* and *Lock* menus:

From *DPOF set*, use the controller keys to first scroll right and then up/down to select one of the three sub menus described below. Enter your choice by pressing the AF button.

• *Marked frames* lets you choose one or more files for DPOF. After you scroll to this option, the frame-selection screen appears.

Scroll through the frames and enter those for DPOF by using the up key. A small printer icon with the number of prints next to it indicates these frames. Increase or decrease the quantity of prints between one and nine (zero deselects the frame) by using the up/down controller keys. Press the AF button to create a folder (misc.) that will store your selections.

• *All in folder* selects images in a specified folder for DPOF.

• *All on card selects* all the images on your memory card for DPOF.

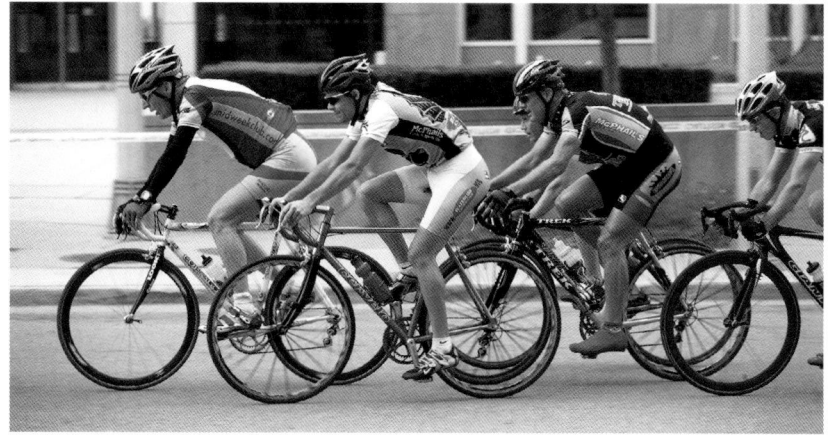

The Release option in the Custom menu's Priority setup allows you to shoot even if focus has not been confirmed. This is likely to increase the number of unsharp photos that you record, but may be necessary when shooting action photos.

Date imprint: When *On*, the date is printed with the photo when DPOF printing is used.

Index print: This option creates an index of thumbnail prints for all the images selected for DPOF. Highlight *Off* to cancel the index print. The number of images printed per sheet varies from printer to printer.

Cancel print: Use this option to delete the misc. folder of DPOF image files. If you do not manually delete the folder, the DPOF information will remain on the memory card until reformatted.

From *Cancel print*, use the controller keys to first scroll right and then up/down to select from the two options described below. Enter your choice by pressing the AF button.

• *All frames C* will cancel all DPOF data on the memory card.

• *All frames F* will cancel DPOF data in a specific folder.

The Custom Menus ✿

Like many other digital SLR cameras, the 5D includes two Custom menu screens so that you can tailor camera settings to your own preferences. Most camera owners do not take full advantage of the Custom menus. But many of these features can be handy, and they exist because there is no way to predict which custom functions each owner will find to be most valuable; consequently many are provided.

To access these functions, press the MENU button. Then use the controller keys to scroll to the Custom icon ✿ and press the AF button to activate the menu. Scroll again to choose the specific Custom Menu you want.

Custom Menu 1 ✿1

The options in this menu are preferences more than necessities, and your 5D will work if these functions are left in their default settings. It is a good idea to use your camera for a couple of months and really get to know the basics before plunging into most of these. Nonetheless, here is a brief explanation of each item.

Use the controller key to scroll down to your selection from the following six choices:

Priority setup: The first item, *AF*, is the default setting. It ensures that the camera will not take a photo unless focus has been confirmed in Single-shot AF—a suitable precaution. You can also select *Release*, which allows the camera to fire in the AF modes whether focus is confirmed or not. Sports photographers may want to use this option with erratic subjects in low light, preferring to get a slightly out-of-focus image to no image at all. An icon for RP (Release Priority) displays in the data monitor when this is selected. Remember to reset this item to *AF* afterwards, though.

From *Priority setup*, use the controller keys to first scroll right and then up/down to select one of the two options described above. Enter your choice by pressing the AF button.

FocusHoldButt: A select number of Konica Minolta lenses have a button used to recall a preset focus point when pressed. If using such a lens, select *Focus hold* for the button to lock focus. Press *D.O.F. preview* for the button to preview depth of field.

From *FocusHoldButt,* use the controller keys to first scroll right and then up/down to select one of the two options described above. Enter your choice by pressing the AF button.

AEL button: This controls the function of the camera's AE lock button. The default setting is *AE hold,* in which the AE Lock (AEL) button is active only while you depress it. You can also select *AE toggle,* which activates AEL continuously once the AEL button is pressed (no need to hold it in). Press the AEL button again to deactivate. *AE toggle* might be useful in landscape photography to lock in the exposure values while you slowly recompose the shot. However, it can also lead to serious exposure errors if you forget that *AE toggle* has been set and do not turn AE lock off when switching to a different subject, or when the light level changes.

Two other AEL options are also available. In *Spot AE hold,* the camera automatically switches to spot metering when the AEL button is pressed and held down. And *Spot AE toggle* provides the same function but without holding the AEL button; AEL remains active until the button is pressed again. I don't recommend this because these options can create metering confusion and exposure errors. If you want to use spot metering, simply select that option using the metering mode dial.

From *AEL button,* use the controller keys to first scroll right and then up/down to select one of the four options described above. Enter your choice by pressing the AF button.

Ctrl dial set: This changes the function of the control dial. The default setting is *Shutter speed,* where the control dial manages shutter speed in Program Shift or Manual mode. To set a specific aperture (f/stop) in M mode, you must press and hold the exposure compensation button while rotating the control dial.

The option for *Aperture* changes the role of the control dial in Ps and M mode to controlling the f/stop. Consequently, you must press and hold the exposure compensation button while rotating the control to set the shutter speed in M mode

From *Ctrl dial set*, use the controller keys to first scroll right and then up/down to select one of the two options described above. Enter by pressing the AF button.

Exp. comp. set: When using flash, the camera's exposure compensation button will adjust both the ambient light and flash exposure with the *Ambient & flash* selection. With the *Ambient only* option, only the ambient light exposure will be compensated. (A Flash Exposure Compensation feature is available with the Fn button.)

From *Exp. comp. set,* use the controller keys to first scroll right and then up/down to select one of the two options described above. Enter your choice by pressing the AF button.

AF illuminator: The default setting for this is *On*. When the built-in flash is up, it will fire several short bursts in low light to assist the AF system in acquiring focus. You can turn this feature *Off* if it becomes inconvenient. Except in very dark conditions, the AF system should still be reliable.

From *AF illuminator*, use the controller keys to first scroll right and then up/down to select *On* or *Off*. Enter by pressing the AF button.

Custom Menu 2 ✿2
Six additional items are available here for further customizing the camera.

Scroll down with the controller key to highlight your selection.

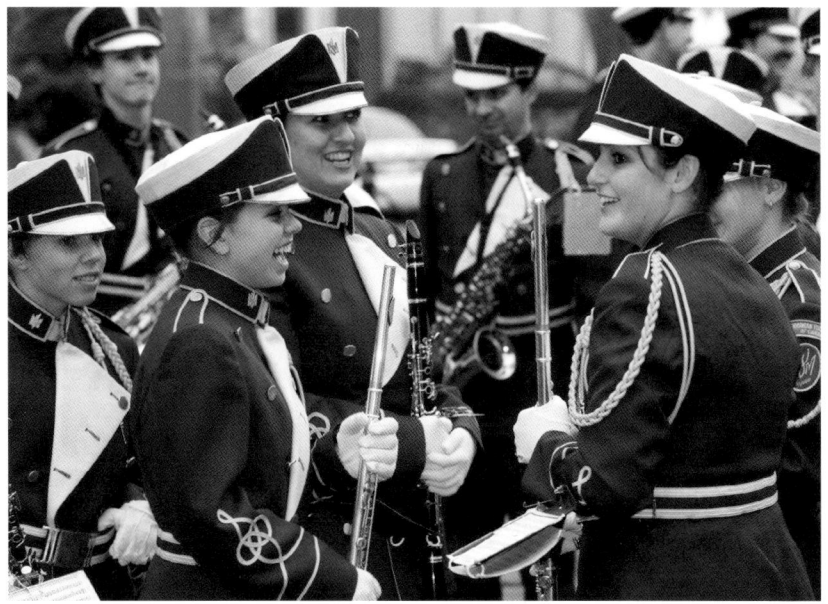

When using exposure compensation with flash in outdoor photography, you may want to choose Ambient & flash in the Custom menu to adjust both the ambient light and flash exposures by using the exposure.

Shutter lock (card): There are two shutter lock options in Custom Menu 2. This is the first, or top, listing. *On* prevents the camera from firing unless a memory card has been loaded (this is the default). This way you can't shoot without a card. Off enables the camera to shoot when a card is not loaded (not recommended).

From *Shutter lock* (for card), use the controller keys to first scroll right and then up/down to select *On* or *Off*. Enter by pressing the AF button.

Shutter lock (lens): This is the second listing. Again the default is On. The camera cannot be fired unless a lens is mounted. Because the shutter won't open, the CCD sensor is better protected from dust and other elements when no lens is on the camera. However, you can also select *Off* to trip the shutter when no lens is mounted. This is necessary only when the 5D is attached to a telescope or microscope using a special adapter.

From *Shutter lock* (for lens), use the controller keys to first scroll right and then up/down to select On or Off. Enter by pressing the AF button.

AF area setup: This item allows you to change the time that the autofocus points are illuminated on the viewing screen for focus confirmation. Select *0.3s.* for a brief indication. You can also select *0.6s.* or *Off* (the focus point is never illuminated

From *AF area setup*, use the controller keys to first scroll right and then up/down to select one of the three options described above. Enter your choice by pressing the AF button.

Monitor disp.: The *Automatic* setting (default) turns the LCD monitor off automatically when the viewfinder is being used. (Sensors detect your eye at the viewfinder.) The default setting is both logical and useful for conserving battery power. You can also select *Manual*, causing the LCD monitor to be on (with data display or image playback) even when you're looking through the viewfinder to take another shot. In that case, you would need to use the display button |O| to turn off the LCD monitor.

From *Monitor disp.*, use the controller keys to first scroll right and then up/down to select one of the two options described above. Enter your choice by pressing the AF button.

Rec. display: Sets format for recording data display. When set to *Auto rotate* (default), the recording data in the LCD will shift between horizontal display and vertical display as the shooting orientation of the camera is shifted respectively. Select *Horizontal* to keep the recording data display fixed in horizontal format.

From *Rec. display*, first scroll right using the controller key then up/down to select one of the two options described above. Enter your choice by pressing the AF button.

Play display: For playback display setup. *Auto rotate* displays a vertical image upright on the horizontal LCD monitor (which makes the image smaller) as well as on a computer monitor when using DiMAGE MasterLite software. If you prefer to view vertical images using the entire LCD monitor, select *Man. rotate* instead.

From *Play. display*, use the controller keys to first scroll right and then up/down to select one of the two options described above. Enter your choice by pressing the AF button.

The Setup Menus ✦

The final menu, consisting of three distinct screens, controls the operation of the camera.

To access these functions, press the MENU button. Then use the controller keys to scroll to the Setup icon ✦ and press the AF button to activate the menu.

Setup Menu 1 ✦1
It's a good idea to become familiar with the six items in this menu because they are ones that you will definitely want to set initially and perhaps adjust from time to time.

Scroll down from Setup Menu 1 to highlight your selection.

If you often shoot vertical images, consider setting the Man. Rotate ⇨ *option in Play display so your vertical photos will fill the LCD monitor in Playback mode. Although I prefer the default setting, most 5D owners will use the Man. Rotate feature.*

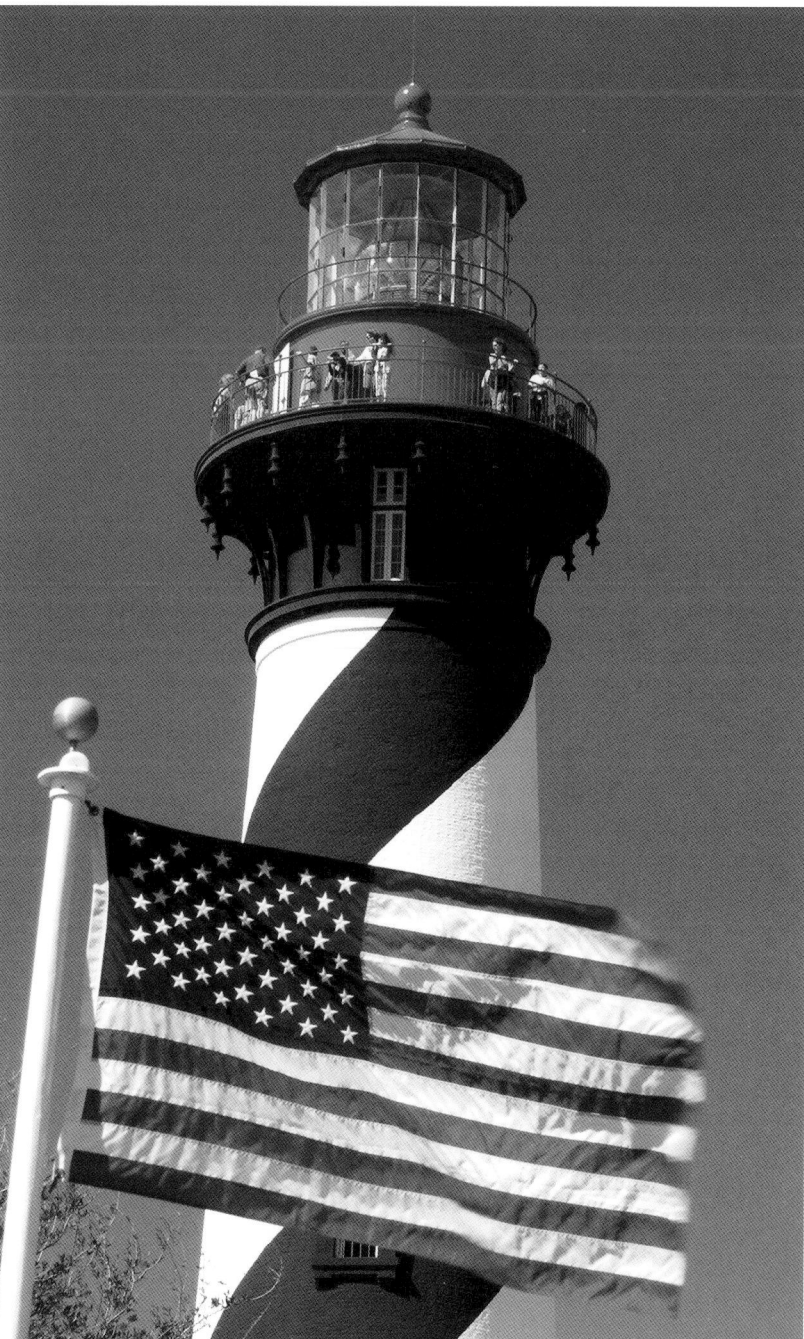

LCD brightness: Scroll right to select Enter to use a slider that makes the LCD monitor darker (Low–) or brighter (+High). The higher you set monitor brightness, the easier it is to see data or images on the LCD monitor in bright conditions.

In the slider screen, use the right/left controller keys to adjust brightness from Low– to +High. Enter by pressing the AF button.

Transfer mode: The default setting is *Data storage*, which is used to download images from the camera to a computer connected with a USB cable. Select *PTP* for making prints directly from the camera using a PictBridge compatible printer.

From *Transfer mode*, use the controller keys to first scroll right and then up/down to select one of the two options described above. Enter your choice by pressing the AF button.

Video output: Allows you to choose the appropriate connection standard for viewing images on a television. Two options are available for video system compatibility: *NTSC* (North American standard) and *PAL* (most other countries). Check which standard to use in your geographic area.

From *Video output*, use the controller keys to first scroll right and then up/down to select one of the two options described above. Enter your choice by pressing the AF button.

Audio signals: *On* (default) causes the camera to beep when focus is confirmed in Autofocus mode. Select *Off* to disable this audio feature.

From *Audio signals*, use the controller keys to first scroll right and then up/down to select *On* or *Off*. Enter by pressing the AF button.

Language: Determine the operating language you prefer from the list of eight options, including *English*, the default setting.

From *Language*, use the controller keys to first scroll right and then up/down to select one of the available language options. Enter by pressing the AF button.

Date/Time set: Use to set the date and time for the first time or to change them when needed. Such data will not be printed on your images. However, it will be recorded by the camera for every image that you make and the information can later be accessed with image editing software.

From *Date/Time set*, first scroll right using the controller key. A screen with *YYYY/MM/DD* display will appear. Use the up/down controller keys to adjust the date and time while scrolling from field to field with the left/right keys. Enter the complete setting by pressing the AF button.

Setup Menu 2 ⊬2

This section provides several items for creating and naming new image file folders. If you find all of this to be confusing, just leave all of the file folder options at their default settings.

Scroll down using the controller key to highlight your selection.

File # memory: Files are placed within folders on the memory card. This menu function manages how the camera labels files in different folders. The default setting is *Off*. A new file will be labeled with a number that is one greater than the last image saved in that particular folder. When *On* is selected, a new file will have a number that is one greater than the previously saved file, even if it is saved to a different folder.

From *File # memory*, use the controller keys to first scroll right and then up/down to select On or Off. Enter by pressing the AF button.

Folder name: Use to determine which of two formats are assigned to name folders on the memory card. Each consists of eight characters. *Std. form* (default) creates a label such as 100KM028, where the first three digits represent a folder number, KM refers to Konica Minolta, and 028 designates the 5D camera model. You may prefer to select *Date form*. The folder format follows a sequence of 100YMMDD, so 10070608 is a folder created on June 8, 2007. If you select the *Date form* option, a new folder will be created on each day when you make an image with the camera. All images made that day will be saved in that folder.

From *Folder name*, first scroll right using the controller key then up/down to select one of the two options described above. Enter by pressing the AF button.

Select folder: This item allows you to specify the folder to which images should be saved. When you select this item, you'll see a list of current file folders that have been created. Specify the one that you want to use to store the next set of images that you will shoot.

From *Select folder*, use the controller keys to first scroll right and then up/down to select from a list of existing folders. Enter by pressing the AF button.

New folder: Use this item to create new folders. From *Select folder*, scroll down to highlight *New folder*, then right to highlight *Enter*. Press the AF button to create a new folder that will use the *Folder name* format currently in use. Every time you create a new folder, the folder number increases automatically by one greater than the previous folder on the memory card.

Setup Menu 3 ⚙️

The following items are available. Scroll down from this menu heading using the controller key to select the item you want to set.

LCD backlight: This determines a time period to keep the LCD monitor lit before the backlight goes off, thereby conserving battery power. Press any camera button to restore the backlight. The default is *5 sec.*, but you can also choose *10 sec., 30 sec.,* or *60 sec.* I suggest 10 seconds.

From *LCD backlight*, use the controller keys to first scroll right and then up/down to select one of the four different time periods. Enter by pressing the AF button.

Power save: In order to conserve battery power, the camera automatically switches into "sleep mode" after a period of non-use. The default for this feature is *3 min.* You can also select *1 min., 5 min., 10 min.,* or *30 min.* Select one of the longer times if you want the camera always ready to shoot, but carry an extra battery because power consumption will be higher. The camera can be quickly revived (in about one second) from sleep mode by pressing any camera button or by touching the shutter release button.

From *Power save*, use the controller keys to first scroll right and then up/down to select one of the five different time periods. Enter by pressing the AF button.

MenuSec.Memory: This item manages how the menu display will appear when you press the MENU button. Select *On* and the display will recall the last open menu. When set to *Off* (the default), pressing the MENU button will call up Recording Menu 1.

Delete conf.: For delete confirmation. Before considering the options in this item, it's important to understand the concept. Whenever you are viewing an image (whether in instant review or in Playback mode), you can choose to delete that shot by pressing the delete button 🗑 . When you do so, the camera asks (in a note on the LCD monitor) "*Delete this frame?*" The default answer is *No*. To delete, you must scroll to *Yes* and then press the AF button to start the deletion process. However, when the *Delete conf.* menu item is set to *Yes*, the highlighted answer to the delete question becomes *Yes*, saving a scrolling step and therefore making the deletion process quicker. (However, the *No* default decreases the odds of inadvertent deletion.)

From *Delete conf.*, use the controller keys to first scroll right and then up/down to select *Yes* or *No*. Enter by pressing the AF button.

Clean CCD: Use this to gain access to the CCD sensor if you notice dust specks in your photos. A fully charged battery or the optional AC adapter is required.

Improper cleaning may damage the CCD sensor. If you choose to use this process, follow these steps:

• After selecting the *Clean CCD* item, scroll right and highlight *Enter* by pressing the AF button.
• A note will then appear in the LCD monitor informing you to shut the camera off after the cleaning is finished.
• It will then ask whether you want to continue; select *Yes* if you are ready.
• Remove the lens or body cap.
• The reflex mirror will flip up, revealing the CCD sensor.
• Hold the camera facing downward and pump a blast of air from a large blower bulb toward the sensor; repeat this a couple of times to dislodge any dust particles. Use extreme care not to touch anything inside the lens mount.
• After cleaning is finished, turn the camera OFF and replace the lens or body cap. The reflex mirror will return to its normal position.

Caution: *Use extreme caution. After exposing the CCD, use a large blower brush (sold by photo retailers) to blow away specks. Do not use compressed air because the propellant may damage the CCD. Konica Minolta does not recommend the use of sensor cleaning kits (swabs or brushes and liquids) that are marketed by third-party manufacturers.*

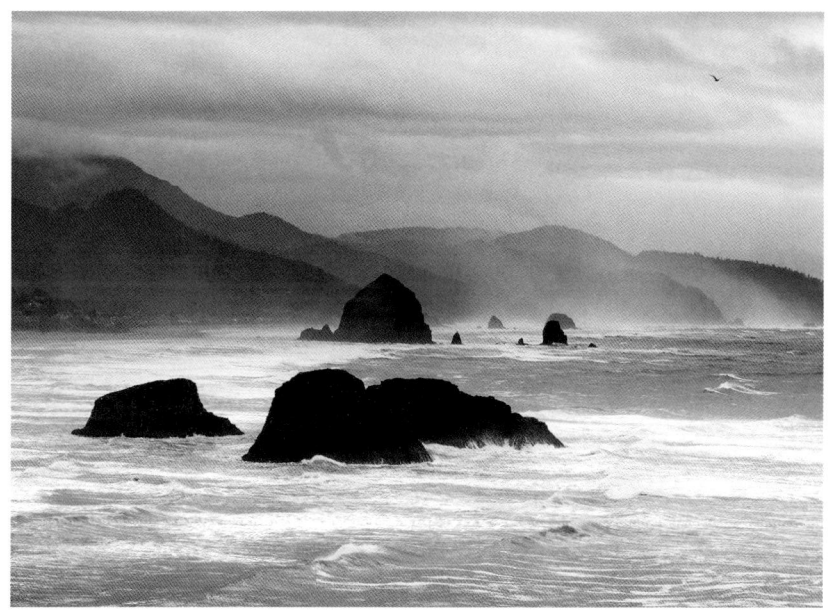

Use care when changing lenses. Salt spray, sand, or dust can settle on the sensor and show up in photos. These blemishes are most visible in large mid-tone areas such as the sky (although visible speck in this photo is actually a seagull in flight).

Damage to the CCD may require an expensive repair or replacement of the sensor module. If you cannot remove dust using a blower brush, contact a Konica Minolta authorized service center to arrange for professional CCD cleaning service.

Reset default: This feature allows you to reset the camera to all of the default settings in each of the different menus sections simply by pressing *Yes*. Of course, if you are satisfied with the setting adjustments you have made, simply ignore this option.

From *Reset default*, first scroll right using the controller key to display a confirmation screen. Scroll again to select *Yes* or *No*. Enter by pressing the AF button.

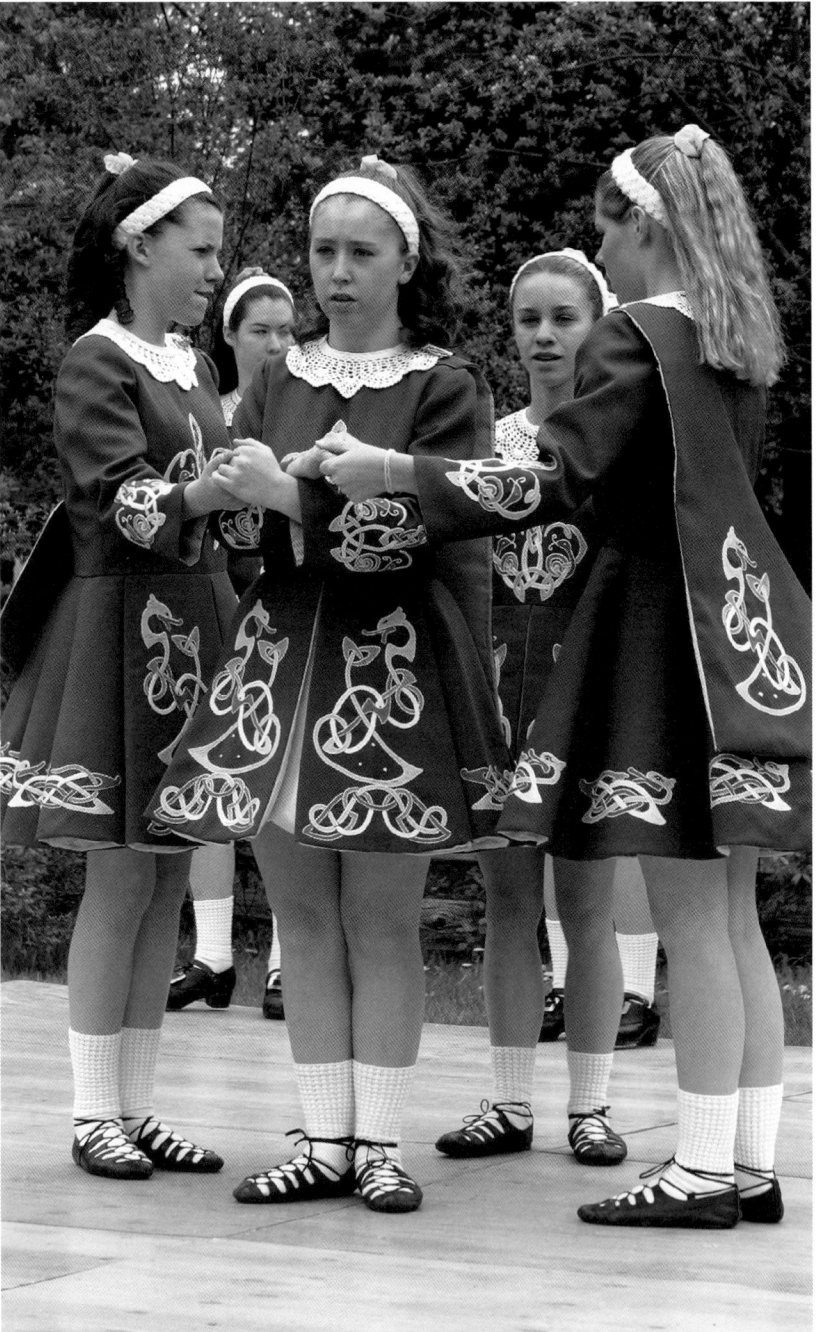

Camera and Shooting Operations

Image Sharpness

Various factors contribute to the sharpness of an image. While focus, depth-of-field, and even use of flash play a role, proper handholding technique is also essential. If you don't use proper technique, camera movement may degrade image sharpness and your pictures will be disappointing. A good way to evaluate your technique is to review your photos. If the focused subject is not crisp, but another element in the scene is sharp, the problem is usually caused by an improperly focused image. However, if nothing in the photo is tack sharp, the cause is probably camera movement.

To reduce camera shake, make sure that your shutter speed approximates the reciprocal of the effective focal length of the lens in use. For example, a 100mm equivalent lens would require a hand-held shutter speed of about 1/125 second. (When considering this, remember that due to the size of its sensor, the 35mm equivalent focal length of a lens on the 5D is the actual focal length multiplied by 1.5x.) If you cannot achieve a high enough shutter speed at your desired aperture setting, you can increase your ISO (but beware of noise). You can also use a tripod or other camera support. If the shutter speed is adequate, make sure that you use proper handholding technique to maximize image sharpness.

When it's impractical to use a tripod, use the Anti-Shake system to produce sharp images, especially if you're shooting in low light like on this heavily overcast day.

Handholding tips

Hold the camera's grip in your right hand with your index finger on the shutter release. For horizontal (landscape format) pictures, cradle the lens and body in your left hand, so that your fingers can comfortably operate the lens. For vertical (portrait format) shots, turn the camera so your right hand is on top and the opposite end of the camera is cradled in your left hand. With either format, keep your elbows in, pressed gently against your body for additional support. Spread you legs apart in a firm, but comfortable, stance.

When you are ready to take a picture, exhale and roll your finger across the shutter releaseæmaking sure to hold the camera level. Practice in front of a mirror, until you feel comfortable holding the camera and tripping the shutter.

Konica Minolta's innovative image stabilization technology actually moves the sensor to compensate for camera shake. Called the A/S or Anti-Shake system, it functions with almost all Konica-Minolta autofocus lenses.

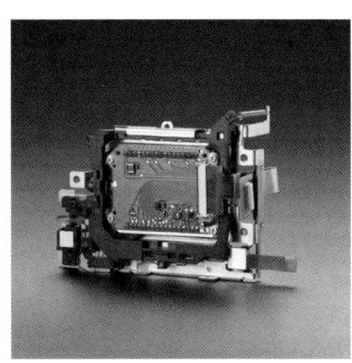

The Anti Shake System (A/S)

Konica Minolta has incorporated an innovative in-camera Anti-Shake (A/S) image stabilization technology into the Maxxum 5D/Dynax 5D. Since the entire system is located within the camera body, it works with nearly all Konica Minolta Maxxum/Dynax lenses and some aftermarket lenses. Unlike other manufacturer's image stabilization systems, which work by shifting elements within the lens, Minolta's in-camera system shifts the sensor. Because it works inside the camera body, the A/S system allows photographers to use image stabilization with virtually any lens at any time.

How to use A/S

Turn the feature on with the Anti-Shake switch located on the lower right back of the camera. The system consists of both a sensor that detects camera/lens motion and a mechanical device that helps produce sharper photos. When the A/S sensor detects camera motion, a microcomputer analyzes data on focal length, aperture setting, and focusing distance and sends a signal to a Smooth Impact Drive Mechanism (SIDM), which mechanically shifts the entire CCD sensor unit to compensate. The incoming light rays are refracted and the projected image is returned to the center of the frame, which produces a sharper image.

The A/S feature is designed primarily for hand-held use at shutter speeds shorter than 1/4 second. When the A/S system is active, the Anti-Shake scale (a five step, stair-like icon at the right side of the viewfinder data panel) is displayed. In bright light, with the system on, the scale may not appear because shutter speeds are high enough that no image stabilization is necessary.

You should practice using A/S in low light. Point the camera and frame your subject. The more steps displayed in the scale, the greater the need for image stabilization. When all five steps in the A/S scale are displayed, maximum CCD shift is underway. In this case, the system may not be able to produce the sharpest image so consider using a faster shutter speed to make the shot.

Note: If the A/S scale blinks, an Anti-Shake function error has occurred. Turn the camera off and allow it to cool. If it still blinks when you turn the camera on again, remove the battery for 30 seconds and reload it. If the problem persists, contact a Konica Minolta service facility.

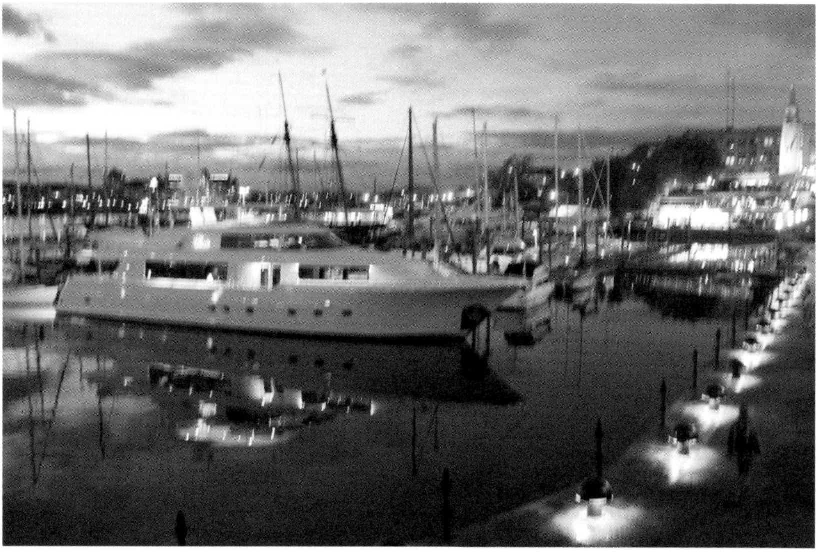

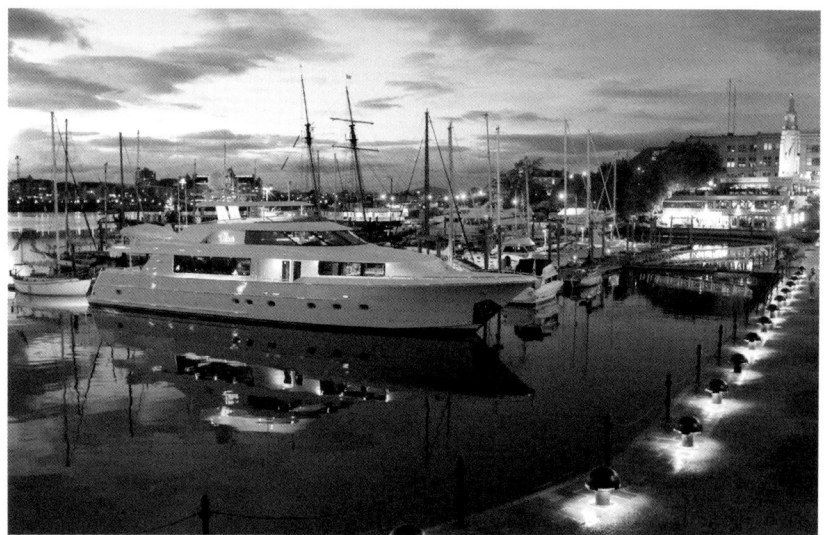

Even when using ISO 1600 for this low light boat scene, a shutter speed of 1/10 second produced blur from camera shake (top photo). Activating the A/S system provided a significant improvement (bottom photo), confirming the value of this feature when a tripod is cannot be used.

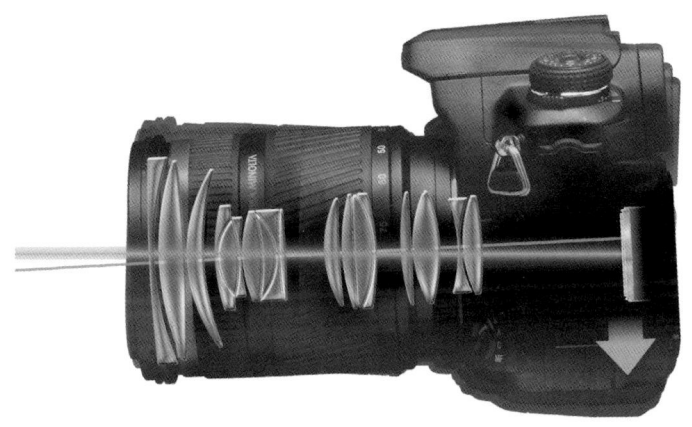

When camera shake is detected, the entire CCD sensor module shifts to compensate, producing a sharper photo with little or no blurring.

Practical Application

The A/S system works best if you stay within two steps of your normal minimum handholdable shutter speed. Use even faster shutter speeds if practical, especially if maximum A/S activity is denoted on the scale in the viewfinder. This recommendation may be conservative, especially if you're particularly steady when handholding any lens, but it will pay off in extra sharpness. The system will also allow you to use smaller apertures with less risk of unsharp images at longer shutter speeds, thus expanding the image's depth of field.

With large, heavy telephoto lenses, use a tripod and disengage the A/S system. When shooting from an unstable platform, such as a boat, activate the A/S system and use fast shutter speeds: at least 1/60 second with a 28mm focal length and at least 1/500 second at the 300mm end of a 100-300mm zoom lens. When using flash with the AS system activated, the fastest possible sync speed is reduced to 1/125 second. Finally, be aware that A/S system use increases power drain by roughly 30%, so take extra batteries if you plan on using it a lot during a day of shooting.

The Focusing System

The 5D has a sophisticated TTL phase-detection autofocus (AF) system that utilizes CCD-line AF sensors (9 points: 8 lines and a center cross-hair sensor) to assure quick, accurate focusing in almost all picture-taking situations. The location of these sensors is denoted on the viewfinder screen. The center cross sensor is the most sensitive because if works for both vertical and horizontal patterns.

The AF system functions in light that is the ISO 100 equivalent of –1 EV–18 EV. There is also a built-in AF illuminator on the built-in flash and accessory flash units, which helps the camera to focus in low light. All A-mount (Maxxum/Dynax mount) lenses are compatible with the 5D. (The older, manual focus MD and MC series cannot be used.)

Three options define how the AF areas (or focus points) are used by the system: Wide AF area, Spot AF area, or Focus area selection. The camera also offers four AF modes: Single-shot AF (AF-S), Automatic AF (AF-A), Continuous AF (AF-C), and Direct Manual Focus (DMF), which uses the autofocus system but allows you to fine-tune focus manually. You can also operate the 5D using full manual focus.

AF Modes

Use the AF/MF switch located on the lower left front of the camera to activate autofocus. Set the switch to the AF position. Then press the Fn button and use the controller down key to scroll down the left column of the LCD display to highlight the AF mode display. Use the left/right controller keys to select the mode you wish to use, then press the AF button to confirm.

Single-Shot (AF-S): This option is intended for static subjects. Activate AF-S by holding the shutter release button partway down. When focus is acquired, the effective AF area point lights red in the viewfinder and the focus signal lights steadily in the viewfinder data panel (at the bottom of the viewfinder screen). As long as slight pressure is maintained on the shutter release button, focus remains locked—useful for recomposing without changing focus.

If the camera cannot find focus, the focus signal will blink in the viewfinder data panel; you cannot take a picture until focus is confirmed unless you have selected *Release priority* in Custom Menu 1 (see page 109). If you are not using the center cross sensor, it may help to shift to it. Should the subject move (toward or away from your position) before you take a shot, start the process over to set focus for the new camera-to-subject distance.

Automatic AF (AF-A): The AF system switches automatically from Single-shot AF to Continuous AF mode if motion is detected in the subject. This default mode is recommended for multi-purpose use. If focus acquisition is not possible, the focus signal will blink in the viewfinder data panel; you cannot take a picture until focus is confirmed (indicated by the focus confirmation icon displayed in the viewfinder data panel) unless you have selected *Release priority* in Custom Menu 1.

This mode is useful for subjects that may begin to move soon. Response to motion may take a second or two as the camera adjusts for the changing camera-to-subject distance. Hence, the first shot or two in a series may not be perfectly focused.

Continuous AF (AF-C): This mode tracks a moving subject. Focus is never locked automatically, but shifts continuously as the camera-to-subject distance changes. Focus lock is not available, and if you recompose, focus will change. (Some Konica Minolta telephoto lenses incorporate a focus hold button; with such lenses, you can lock focus in AF-C mode.) The active AF area point (whichever one finds focus) will be illuminated in the viewfinder. If focus cannot be acquired, the camera will not allow you to take a photo; the focus lock indicator will blink in the viewfinder data panel.

Note: When AF-C is selected, the flash unit's focus-assist feature will not operate.

AF-C is ideal for action photography because tracking focus starts instantly without the delay that occurs in AF-A mode when the camera must switch between AF-S and AF-C. The system is most reliable (virtually foolproof) in brightly lit outdoor photography. It's not as reliable in low light.

Direct Manual Focus (DMF): This option allows you to fine-tune focus in AF-S mode without switching to manual focus. To use it, let the camera autofocus on a stationary subject. When focus is confirmed, use the manual focus ring on the lens to make slight focus adjustments—for a person's eyes instead of the nose, for example.

Note: Do not attempt to adjust focus before you receive the camera's focus confirmation signal.

Focus Area

Setting the focus area determines which AF areas will be used in finding and maintaining focus. Press the Fn button and scroll through the icons to select from three choices:

Wide Focus Area ▱ **:** This is the 5D's default mode. All of the system's focus areas are active and the camera uses automated AF area selection. Focusing is completed when one or more of the areas, or points, find focus. The active focus point (or points, when the scene includes several objects at the same distance from the camera) will light red on the viewing screen.

The automated system cannot read your mind, so it will not always select the focus area that covers your primary subject. In a scene with several objects, the system will select the closest subject or the object with the greatest contrast or most distinct texture. With "difficult" subjects (those with unusual patterns, for example), the central focus area will often set focus so that the object in the center of the frame will be sharpest. This is because the central focus area is crosshatched—it includes both horizontal and vertical sensors and is capable of acquiring focus even with subjects that may frustrate the other single sensor focus areas.

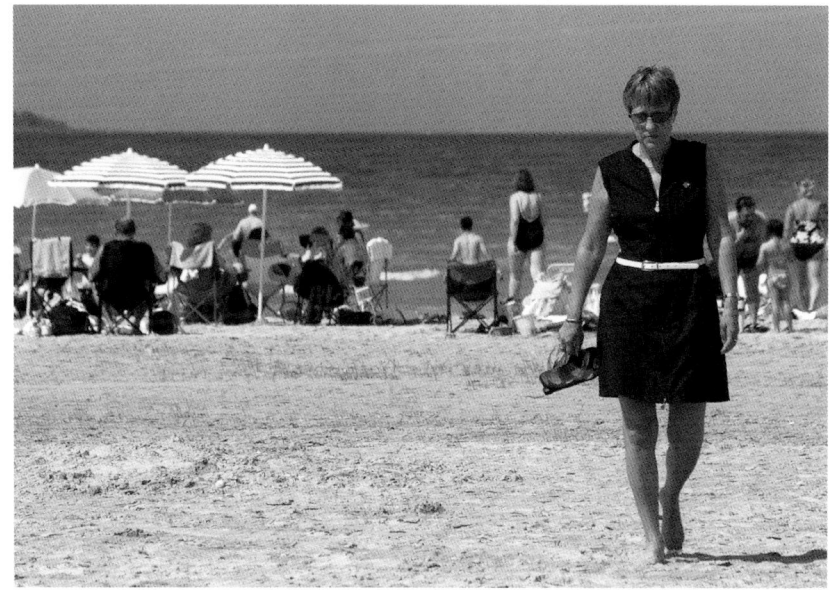

The Wide Focus Area option is useful for quick shooting when more time-consuming focusing techniques are impractical. As long as one of the sensor-points covers the intended subject, even when not in the middle of your composition, accurate focus can be achieved instantly.

The wide focus option, with its automated focus point selection, is ideal for action photography because it can focus on off-center subjects. It also works well for snapshots and point-and-shoot style photography. Naturally, the system will not always produce the intended effect, possibly focusing on a secondary element that's a closer or a more reliable target than your preferred subject.

Spot AF Area 🔳 **:** The camera uses only the central area to set focus. In addition to using the Fn button and controller keys, you can access Spot AF at anytime by pressing the AF button. This is useful in a situation described above, where the AF system is having trouble focusing on the intended subject. Using Spot AF, aim at your subject and lock focus by keeping the shutter release button half pressed while recomposing. It is also a useful focusing selection when subjects are approaching the camera at high speed, such as an animal or a racecar. Spot AF also provides more reliable focus acquisition in low-light photography.

Focus Area Selection ⊞ *:* In this mode, any of the focus areas points can be user selected, and the active point of focus can be changed manually at any time. Use the controller keys to select one of the outside focus areas while looking at the subject through the viewfinder. To quickly select the central focus area, press the AF button. When a focus area is selected, it will be briefly illuminated in red on the viewing screen when it finds focus.

As long as you press and hold the appropriate controller key to designate a specific focus area point, focus will remain locked; focus will not change if you recompose. When you use this technique, exposure is also locked. You cannot use this feature to set focus for one part of a scene while optimizing exposure for an entirely different area. When you're ready to switch to a different focus area point, use the controller arrows to make your selection. Press the shutter release button when you're ready to take the picture.

The ability to manually select any of the several focus area points is common to many brands of SLR cameras. This feature certainly sounds useful and logical. However, unless I'm shooting an action subject, I generally use only the central focus area, often with focus lock. But, in spite of my experience, you may find circumstances where you'll want to select one of the other eight "local" focus area points, and that option is certainly available to you.

Manual Focus

To use full manual focus set the AF/MF switch located on the lower left front of the camera to the MF position. This disengages the autofocus system so you can focus manually using the focus ring on your lens. If you are having trouble focusing, or you want to set focus in anticipation of an event, you can estimate the subject distance and set the focus accordingly. The focus signal in the data panel confirms focus by lighting steadily, and the active focus area lights up on the viewfinder screen. However, in this focus mode, you can take a picture anytime, even if focus is not confirmed.

I recommend switching to MF occasionally, especially in macro, landscape, and architectural photography when you may want to set the point of focus in the scene to control depth of field (see pages 144-146). The Manual Focus mode is also ideal for critical focus on a small, specific subject element: the eyes in a portrait or the stamen in the heart of a blossom, for example. Finally, it's a convenient method for focusing on one segment of a scene while setting exposure for an entirely different area.

Drive Modes

The function of the drive modes is similar to that performed by the motor drive in a film camera. These modes control the firing and recocking of the camera's shutter mechanism.

Set the drive mode by using the drive mode button on the top right of the camera ☜ . After pressing the drive mode button, use the controller's up/down keys to highlight your selection:

- Single-frame/Continuous Advance ☐ / ☐
- Self-timer ☼₂ / ☼₁₀

Use the left/right controller key to select a specific frame advance or self-timer option as described below.

Single-Frame Advance ☐
The 5D's default drive, Single-frame Advance will shoot one frame each time you press the shutter release button until the memory buffer is full. Select this any time you simply want to shoot one image at a time rather than in a bracket or a burst.

Continuous Advance 🖵

In Continuous Advance the camera will continue to record images while the shutter release button is held down until the memory buffer is full. This is useful when you want to shoot a series of images, whether of friends being silly in front of the camera or of action at a sports event. It will shoot up to 3 frames per second (fps) as long as the shutter speed is 1/250 second or faster. If longer shutter speeds are used, the framing rate will be slower.

Note: The framing rate can be quite slow when flash is used because the flash must recycle after each image in order to fire again. The recycle time depends on the amount of flash output used when making an image. There's a long recycle time when high output is required (great flash-to-subject distances), and a quick recycle time when lower output is required (with close subjects or in bright light).

The number of JPEG frames you can shoot in a single burst depends on the image size and quality. Larger, less compressed files fill the camera's memory buffer faster and take longer to be written to the memory card. Also, some memory cards are manufactured with greater write speed than others. Faster cards allow more images per burst. Using a card with moderately fast write speed, you should be able to shoot about ten Large/Extra Fine JPEGs in a series. With a card made for extremely fast recording, I was able to shoot up to 20 frames in a sequence. However, the framing rate slowed after the seventh shot to about 2fps.

2-Second Self-Timer ⟳2

This option allows a 2-second delay between the time when the shutter release is pressed and when the shutter actually fires. Because it raises the mirror at the beginning of the countdown, this feature is useful for triggering the camera without creating movement or vibrations—serving a function similar to a true mirror lock-up. It is often used for long exposures or when telephoto or macro lenses are utilized and the camera is on a tripod or other support. Focus and exposure are set when you first press the shutter release button, so it is best used with fairly static subjects.

134

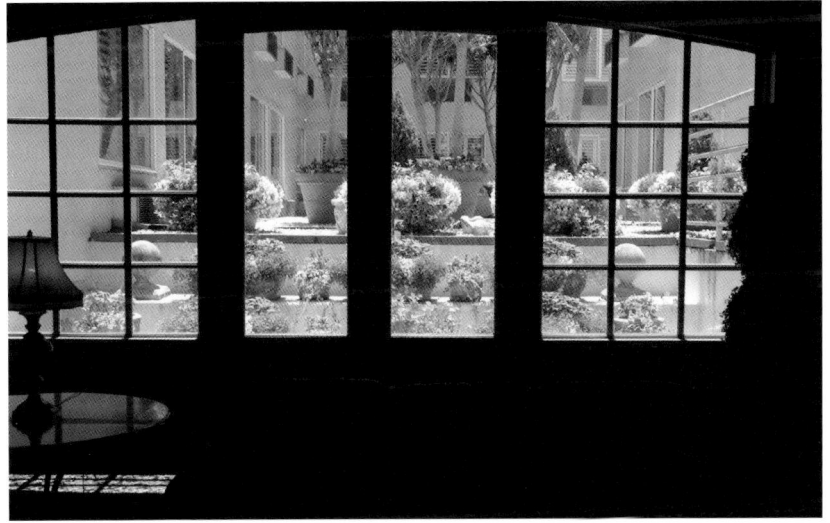

When using a tripod for maximum sharpness at long shutter speeds, it's worth taking advantage of the self-timer or a remote control accessory. Either can eliminate vibration that usually occurs when you trigger the camera in the conventional manner.

10-Second Self-Timer ⏱₁₀

When the 10-second option is selected, the camera will delay 10 seconds after the shutter button is pressed before it fires. This can be useful when the photographer wants to be in the picture and when the camera is mounted on a tripod. During the 10-second delay, you should have time to get into the picture. Focus and exposure are set when you first press the shutter release button. If the lighting changes during the 10-second delay, the exposure may not be correct.

Hint: If you photograph birds or animals, it's best to use one of the optional remote control accessories, RC-1000S or RC-1000L instead of using the Self-timer. This will allow you to trip the shutter at exactly the right instant without jarring the camera. (The mirror lock up feature is available only when using Self-timer and is not often practical with moving subjects; during the delay interval the subject may have disappeared.)

135

Exposure

After first using your camera to take a few shots using the AUTO mode, you'll want to advance to the next step, taking advantage of the camera's exposure control features for more serious photography.

Before proceeding to specifics about features, it's worth reviewing some technical concepts. The term exposure, in digital photography, can be defined as the amount of light that will strike the camera's light-sensitive CCD. Ideally, the exposure should be "correct." In other words, the image should depict the scene as we expect, with clean whites, rich, dark blacks, and midtones that are not excessively light or dark. Important detail should be visible in both highlight and shadow areas.

Every camera's light metering (measuring) system is calibrated to provide ideal exposure with midtone subjects such as grass, rocks, trees, or a Kodak gray card. Using such midtone based metering, if the subject is white (or another very light tone), or if the scene includes a vast expanse of bright snow, sand, sky, or water, the image may be too dark: underexposed. Conversely, a black lava field (or other very dark-toned subject) may be overexposed: too bright, rendered as gray.

Two factors control the amount of light that produces the image: the length of time that the camera's shutter mechanism is open and the size of the aperture (opening) in the lens. The selection of shutter speed and aperture can be left entirely to the camera or can be managed by the photographer using the camera's various exposure modes. The user can also bias exposure, using overrides or the Manual mode. All of these functions are discussed later in this chapter.

The Role of Shutter Speed and Aperture

In order to create an image with the desired amount of light, the correct combination of shutter speed and aperture must be selected. This ensures that the image is not excessively bright or excessively dark. The longer the shutter speed—

one full second versus 1/1000 second, for example—the greater the amount of light that will strike the image sensor. The larger the aperture selected, the more light that will enter during any given exposure time.

Shutter speeds are denoted in seconds, or fractions of a second. Aperture size is denoted with f/numbers, also called f/stops. The smaller the f/number, the larger the aperture size. A wide aperture such as f/4 will allow far more light to enter the camera than a small aperture such as f/16 during any given time period. The camera's autoexposure system considers scene brightness and sets an f/stop and shutter speed that should produce a well-exposed image.

Note: Even the most sophisticated light meter—such as the segmented honeycomb pattern system—will not always produce a perfect exposure. Extremely light or dark-toned subjects may cause exposure errors. Also, an accurate exposure may not be the most pleasing or most appropriate for creative expression. That's why the 5D includes options for adjusting the exposure.

Equivalent Exposure

Many combinations of shutter speeds and apertures will produce the same, or equivalent, exposure. A long shutter speed and a small aperture can allow the same amount of light to strike the sensor as a fast shutter speed and a large aperture. You do not need to calculate which combination of shutter speed and aperture is suitable, because the camera's light metering computer completes this task.

Measuring Brightness

There once was a time when cameras did not contain any built-in system for measuring subject brightness. In those days you needed to use an accessory light meter or rely on estimates, experience, or expertise to make appropriate settings.

Today virtually all cameras include at least a basic, low-tech metering system. Since the 1990's, many SLR cameras have included three light metering options; as you might expect, the 5D includes all three. These include 14-segment honeycomb pattern (evaluative, using artificial intelligence), the old-style center weighted averaging system, and spot metering. You'll find more specifics about each later in this chapter.

ISO

The amount of light required for an accurate exposure depends on the ISO setting you have selected on the camera. ISO is an international standard for quantifying a film's sensitivity to light. While digital cameras don't use film, ISO numbers are still used to set the sensor's sensitivity. A low ISO number such as 100 denotes low sensitivity to light. A high ISO number such as 800 or 1600 denotes high sensitivity to light. This factor is automatically taken into account by the camera's light meter when making calculations about aperture size and shutter speed that should produce a good exposure.

Note: ISO numbers are mathematically proportional, as are shutter speeds and f/stops. As you double or halve the ISO number, you double or halve the sensor's sensitivity (i.e., at ISO 800, the sensor circuits are twice as sensitive to light as at ISO 400, and at ISO 800, the sensor circuits are half as sensitive to light as at ISO 1600).

The 5D allows you to choose an ISO from 100 to 3200, although you'll rarely need to use the highest option. Select ISO 100 for the best image quality and higher ISO levels as needed.

Start by pressing the ISO button on the top of the camera. While the button is depressed rotate the control dial (or use the controller's keys) to change the ISO while keeping an eye on the change in the LCD monitor. Stop when you reach the desired ISO setting. Your selection will be effective as soon as you touch the shutter release button.

While scrolling the ISO options, you'll note that the 5D also offers an Auto ISO setting. With Auto ISO selected, the

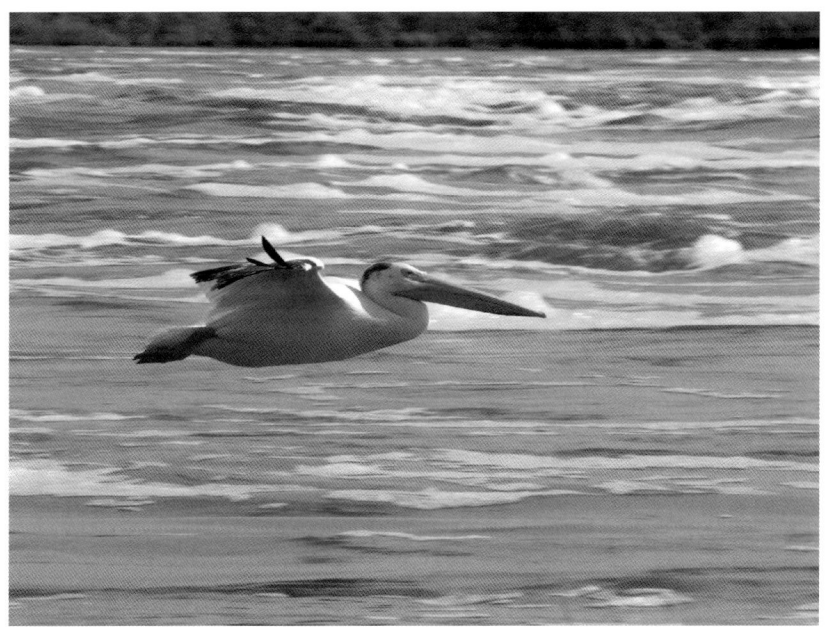

The range of ISO options offers flexibility for different shooting situations. A high ISO setting, such as ISO 800 used in this case, can be valuable when you need fast shutter speeds to capture a moving subject without blurring, especially when using a telephoto lens.

camera will set a low ISO in bright light and a higher ISO in darker conditions for fast shutter speeds to minimize the risk of blur from camera shake. (The Anti-Shake function is useful for this purpose too, but it cannot compensate for subject movement or for camera shake at extremely long shutter speeds.)

Hint: In very low light, the Auto ISO feature may select a very high ISO setting in order to provide fast shutter speeds to minimize the risk of blur from camera shake. In that case, expect to see more digital noise in your images. Noise is primarily colored specks that are most visible in shadow areas. If you want full control over ISO, do not select the Auto ISO option.

When scrolling through the ISO options, you'll note two additional settings that can be selected: Lo 80 (for low key) and Hi 200 (for high key). These are part of the Zone Matching concept that's somewhat complex. In practical terms, here's the purpose of these options.

Select Lo 80 for a low key scene: primarily composed of dark toned and dark colored subjects such as a man in a dark tuxedo against a black limousine parked next to an indigo blue building. Select Hi 200 for scenes made up of predominantly light tones, such as blonde ladies in white swimsuits on a beach with white sand and surf. In either case, the camera adjusts exposure and contrast for a technically optimal rendition of a low key (primarily dark toned) or high key (primarily light toned) scene.

Exposure Modes

The Maxxum 5D/Dynax 5D provides a wide range of exposure modes, which allow for a variety of operational settings. These are selected by using the exposure mode dial on top right of the camera.

Auto Mode (AUTO)

The fully automatic mode was designed for maximum operating simplicity with the camera in total control of the aperture/shutter speed combination. In AUTO, the camera uses its default settings, although you can set some overrides, including ISO, exposure compensation, metering pattern, and white balance, and so on. Frankly, for anyone who wants to use a point-and-shoot approach, I suggest leaving all features at their factory-set default levels. However, if an image is obviously too bright, or too dark, you might want to set some exposure compensation with the ☒ button (located on the back upper right of camera) before re-shooting for better results.

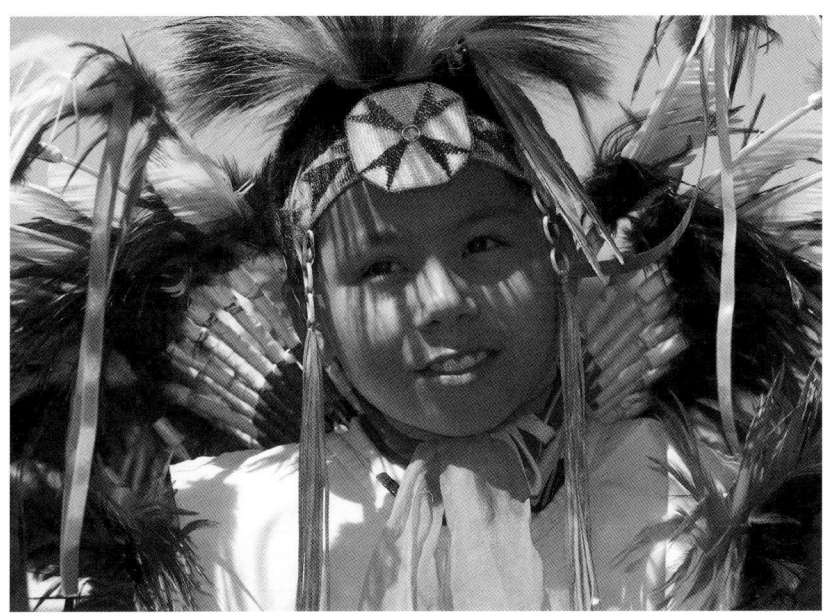

When using flash outdoors with the Portrait Subject Program, try setting a minus level for Flash Exposure Compensation to achieve a subtle effect. A setting of -0.7 was used for this image in order to maintain some shadows for the most natural flash effect.

Digital Subject Programs

The 5D provides five fully automatic modes, or programs, that use "intelligent" automation to make suitable settings for common situations and subjects (see the program list on pages 141-142).

After selecting one of the Digital Subject Programs by choosing its icon on the exposure mode dial, located on the top of the 5D to the right of the viewfinder housing, you can set certain camera functions, while others cannot be adjusted.

Portrait 🄽 : Selects a moderately wide aperture to soften the background; a telephoto lens is recommended for an even softer or a less distinct background. Color rendition and contrast are optimized to produce "warm, soft skin tones." Flash can be used when desired or needed for proper exposure.

Sports Action 🄽 : Favors fast shutter speeds to "freeze" a moving subject. Continuous AF and Continuous Advance are activated automatically. Flash can be used if desired, but its range is limited, so it's inappropriate for distant subjects.

Landscape 🄽 : Sets a moderately small aperture for great depth of field (zone of acceptably sharp focus) while boosting color saturation (richness), sharpness, and contrast for a snappy, vivid effect. Flash can be used, but with this mode's bias for small apertures, the use of the built-in flash is probably not practical.

Sunset 🄽 : Optimized to produce rich, warm tones with relatively high contrast and color saturation for pleasing results when shooting a sunrise or sunset.

Caution: Avoid viewing the sun directly or through the lens because doing so can hurt your eyes.

Night Portrait 🄽 : Designed for flash photography in low light or night when a slow shutter speed is needed to record the low-light background not exposed by the flash. It sets a long shutter speed—also called Slow Sync mode—as required with dark scenes. It's useful when you intend to use flash to illuminate a nearby subject, such as a person against a city skyline at night. At the start of the long exposure—several seconds or more—the flash will fire to illuminate the nearby subject. Use a tripod to avoid blurring from camera shake.

Hint: Slow Sync mode can also be selected in any camera exposure mode (except Manual) by pressing the AEL button when flash is active.

Program (P)

In Program (P) mode the camera sets the shutter speed and aperture, but unlike AUTO, this mode allows you to change the aperture/shutter speed combination. All other camera functions can be set by the photographer, unlike AUTO mode.

The camera sets an aperture (f/stop) and shutter speed to provide a correct exposure. You need not accept this combination of settings. You can activate a selection called Program shift (Ps) by pressing the shutter release button halfway until the aperture and shutter speed are displayed in the viewfinder. Turn the control dial (in front of the shutter release button) to select a different aperture/shutter speed combination.

Note: The Program shift feature does not change exposure. It allows you to select from its various shutter speed/aperture combinations that let the camera maintain an equivalent exposure. When using flash in P mode, the Program shift feature is disengaged. However, you can force the camera to select Slow Sync mode (at very long shutter speeds) by pressing the AEL button.

Although P mode allows you to shift the aperture/shutter speed combination, I recommend using Aperture Priority (A) or Shutter Priority (S), discussed in the next sections. When you select an aperture (f/stop) in A mode or a shutter speed in S mode, the camera retains that setting and will not discard it when it switches to "sleep" mode (as it does in Program mode) to conserve battery power. So if you have set f/22 or 1/15 second, the camera will maintain either of those settings until you intentionally make a change.

Aperture Priority (A)

Selected by choosing the A on the exposure mode dial, this automatic exposure mode allows you to set any desired aperture using the control dial. Your selected f/stop is confirmed in the data panel in the viewfinder and on the LCD monitor. The camera automatically responds by setting a shutter speed that should yield a good exposure, according to its light meter's calculations. (In some cases, exposure compensation will be required for a perfect exposure.) All of the 5D's features and overrides are available for your selection.

When using flash with the 5D set to A mode, the camera will set a shutter speed no longer than 1/60 second unless you press the AEL button to enter Slow Sync mode, a feature discussed on page 178. The shutter speed will be no faster than the highest possible flash synchronization speed: 1/160 second, or 1/125 second when the Anti-Shake function is on.

Keep an eye on the shutter speed in Aperture Priority mode. The exposure time may be too long to hold the camera. Review the hints about the shutter speeds necessary for sharp pictures on pages 123). To reduce the risk of blur from camera shake, turn the A/S system (⬛) on, using the ON/OFF switch on the lower right of the camera back.

The A mode is often used to control depth of field, which is the range of apparent sharpness in front of the focused subject, and behind it. See the following "Short Course" to learn more.

Depth of Field—A Short Course
While the elements in your photos are usually three-dimensional, they are recorded on the sensor in two dimensions with a single plane of sharp focus. However, when an image is viewed, there is an area in front of and behind the plane of sharp focus that is perceived to be in focus. This range of apparent sharpness is referred to as depth of field. The factors that influence the amount of depth of field are:

• The focused distance
• The focal length in use
• The shooting aperture

If the focal length and subject distance are constant, depth of field will be shallower with large apertures (lower f/numbers) and deeper with small apertures (higher f/numbers). If the aperture and focused distance are constant,

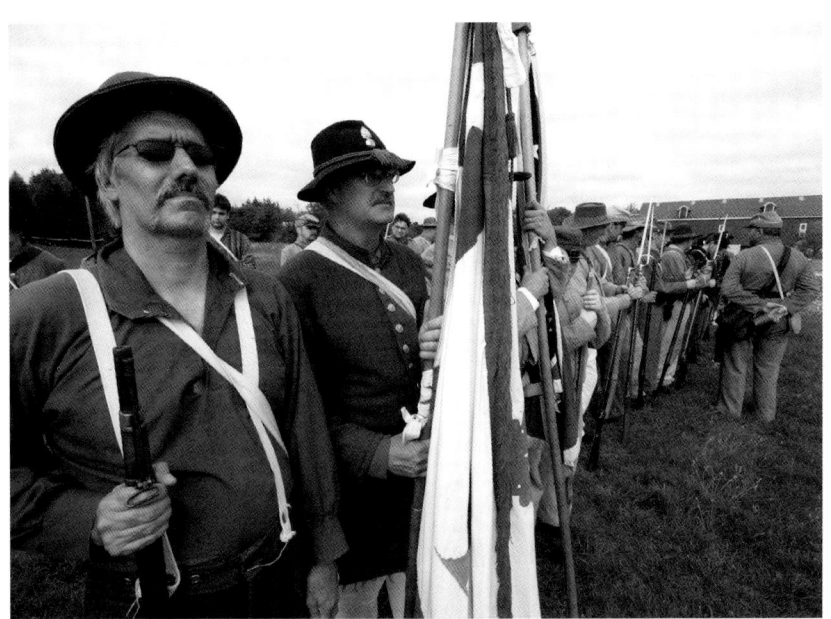

The effect of depth of field changes what the camera "sees" in the scene. This photo, shot with a wide angle focal length and a small aperture, exhibits a great range of acceptable sharpness from foreground to background.

depth of field will be shallower with longer lenses (telephoto range) and deeper with shorter lenses (wide-angle range). If the focal length and aperture are constant, depth of field will be greater at longer focused distances and shallower with closer focused distances.

These things should be considered when planning your composition and the look of the finished photograph. Aperture Priority (A) mode is particularly useful because it allows you to select a desired aperture that will be maintained until you change it. The camera sets an appropriate shutter speed for a "good" exposure, although you can use overrides for a brighter or darker effect.

Depth-of-Field Preview: Today's lenses, including those manufactured for the Maxxum/Dynax cameras, use open-aperture metering. This means that they don't close down to the shooting aperture until a split second before the shutter opens to record an image. Until then, the aperture stays wide open, allowing the viewfinder to be as bright as possible for composing, focusing, and metering. This bright viewfinder is an advantage of modern camera technology, but having the lens at its maximum aperture doesn't allow you to judge depth of field at the shooting aperture. (Remember, as a lens closes down, depth of field increases.)

The 5D has a feature that closes the lens down to the selected aperture so that you can preview the depth of field as it will appear in the finished photograph. By pressing the depth-of-field preview button (located on the lower right front of the lens mount platform), you will see the effect of the lens aperture closing down. The viewfinder will become darker and, depending on the lighting conditions and the selected shooting aperture, you should be able to see the elements in the scene well enough to judge sharpness. While this button is pressed you can also change the aperture to experiment with how depth of field changes with various f/stop settings.

This invaluable feature allows you to fine-tune image sharpness. Sometimes you will want to assure that all elements of a composition—from foreground to background—will be rendered sharply in focus. Other times you will want some elements—usually a cluttered background—to be soft or de-focused, so they don't compete with the subject. Either way, the depth-of-field preview is the easiest and most precise method of judging the degree of sharpness of various parts of a composition.

Depth of Field Shooting Tips: In close-up photography, depth of field is limited. So to maximize it, choose the smallest aperture possible, such as f/22. You may also wish to control the point of focus to further maximize depth of field. (Remember that focused distance is part of the formula even at close ranges.) Take advantage of the camera's depth-of-field preview button. This will allow you to preview the depth of field in your composition. If depth of field is not adequate, you can use a smaller aperture, or readjust the point of focus. For example, when photographing a flower, you may find that overall sharpness will be improved by focusing on a different part of the flower. Also, for best results in close-up photography, use a tripod or other camera support whenever possible.

For portrait photography a soft, out-of-focus background is preferred because it will not draw the viewer's eye away from the subject. To accomplish this, choose a large aperture (small f/number.) Because telephoto lenses have less inherent depth of field than shorter focal lengths, they are ideal for isolating the subject against a softly blurred background. You can always check the effect using the camera's depth-of-field preview.

For landscape photography, maximizing depth of field will render much of the scene in focus. Besides using a small aperture (higher f/number), controlling the point of focus will make the most of the depth of field. As a rule of thumb, depth of field will extend about 1/3 in front of the point of focus and 2/3 behind it. Thus, focusing somewhere in the front-to-middle portion of the scene will yield the greatest amount of sharpness. You can check the depth-of-field information provided with your lens, or use the camera's depth-of-field preview button to make sure that elements of the scene are as sharp as possible. Take advantage of the lens or focal length to create a pleasing scenic view. Not only does a wide-angle lens allow you to capture sweeping vistas, but it also maximizes the depth of field in the photograph.

Hint: If you want to be sure your photo contains a definite amount of depth of field, take the same shot at several apertures: f/11, f/16 and f/22, perhaps. There's no expense involved, because you're not paying for film or processing, and one of the images should exhibit the desired range of acceptably sharp focus.

Shutter Priority (S)

When shutter speed is more important than the depth of field, switch to the camera's S mode. This mode allows you to select a desired shutter speed, and the camera will then set the appropriate f/stop for a suitable exposure. (In some cases, exposure compensation will be required for a perfect exposure.)

When using flash in S mode, the camera will allow you to select a shutter speed as long as 30 seconds. However, you cannot set a shutter speed faster than the flash sync speed of 1/160 second, or 1/125 second when the Anti-Shake function is on.

The following chart may be useful as a tool for learning the meaning of many common shutter speed abbreviations that you are likely to encounter in any camera exposure mode. It does not include every available option, but once you understand the concept, you'll have no difficulty in determining the exact shutter speed.

1000:	1/1000 second
60:	1/60 second
15:	1/15 second
1″:	one second
1″5:	one and a half seconds
15″:	fifteen seconds

Shutter Speed Considerations: Aside from using a shutter speed that will produce a sharp photo—without blur from camera shake—there's another important reason for selecting a slow or fast shutter speed, which is the ability to render or control subject motion. To appreciate the concept, take several shots of moving cars at a fast shutter speed such as 1/500 second. Do the same at a slow shutter speed such as 1/15 second. Analyze the resulting images and you should find that the first set is quite sharp while the second depicts the subject with motion blur.

This knowledge can be useful for creative purposes, allowing you to control the way that a moving subject will appear in your images. Think of a waterfall for example. If you shoot at 1/500 second, the droplets of water will appear to be frozen in mid-air; that may not provide the flowing effect that you want. Put the camera on a tripod and switch to a shutter speed of 1/4 of a second and the water will be blurred, producing a convincing effect of the motion of the flowing water.

Note: When you select a faster shutter speed in S mode, such as 1/500 second, the camera will set a wider aperture to assure correct exposure, so depth of field will therefore be reduced. When you select long shutter speeds, the camera will set a small aperture, so the image will then exhibit greater depth of field. This is more noticeable when you shoot at a low ISO setting, such as ISO 100. If you want to use fast shutter speeds, plus smaller apertures for more depth of field, switch to ISO 400 in bright light and ISO 800 on overcast days.

In action photography, we often think of using fast shutter speeds to freeze the subject: render it without motion blur. But sometimes it may be preferable to convey the feeling of motion by using a relatively slow shutter speed, such as 1/30 second. In this case the subject will be blurred instead of "frozen" or static. This option works best with subjects moving across the frame from the left or right, thus traveling across your line of vision. Pan (move the camera) at the same speed as your subject is moving. It helps to use a tripod with a pan head and to begin to a little before tripping the shutter release. In the resulting image, the subject should be quite sharp, though with some motion blur, while the background will exhibit obvious blur. If the action is occurring close to the camera, try also using flash in Rear curtain sync mode during a long exposure for some of your shots, as discussed in the chapter on flash photography.

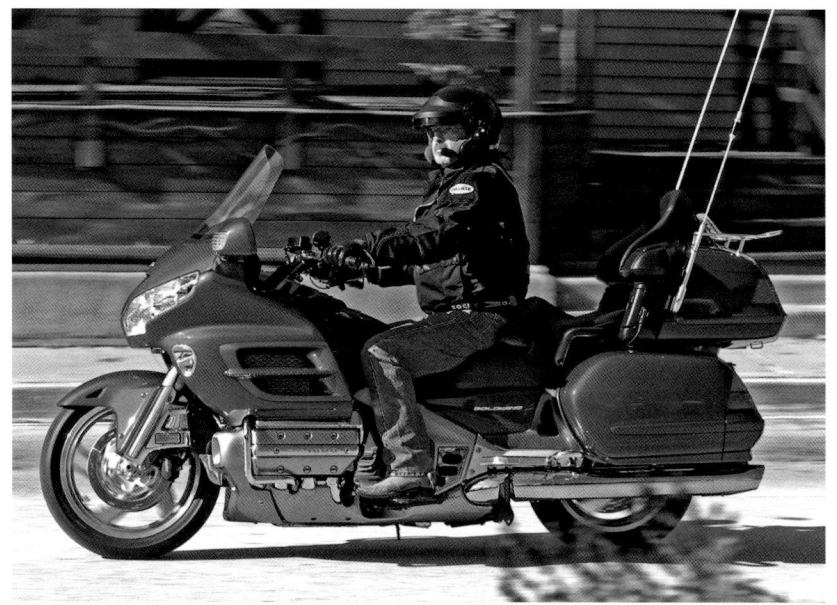

As this example illustrates, the pan/blur technique can be useful for simulating motion in a still photo made at a shutter speed of 1/15 second. Longer exposures produce more impressive effects but make it more difficult to achieve optimal results.

The pan/blur technique takes practice because it requires you to move the camera at exactly the right speed. You may need to shoot quite a few frames to get one that's nearly perfect, technically and aesthetically. Through persistent trial and error, you'll become more skilful with effective panning. And in the meantime, you won't need to spend a lot of money on film and processing, one of the significant advantages of digital versus 35mm photography.

Exposure Control Range Warnings

Despite the best efforts of the autoexposure system to produce correct exposure, there are times when subject conditions are beyond the system's range. In such cases the camera provides various warnings so you can take corrective action.

When using the AUTO, P, or Digital Subject Program modes, both the aperture and the shutter speed displays in the LCD monitor will blink if the exposure is beyond the limits of the autoexposure system. If the scene is too bright, the fastest shutter speed and the smallest aperture will blink. You can address the warning by lowering the ISO or by placing a neutral density filter on your lens.

If on the other hand the scene is too dark, the camera's slowest shutter speed (30 seconds) and the largest possible aperture for the lens will blink. In this case, try increasing the ISO and use flash.

In A mode, the display for shutter speed will flash to indicate exposure outside its range. For example, if you select a large aperture (low f/number) in bright light when using a high ISO setting, the camera's highest shutter speed (1/4000 second) may not be fast enough to provide a correct exposure. When this happens, lower the ISO, add a neutral density filter, or adjust the f/stop until the shutter speed stops flashing. In dark conditions, the camera's longest shutter speed will blink. If so, change the f/stop until the blinking stops, set a higher ISO, or use flash.

If you are shooting in S mode, depending on the shutter speed, ISO setting, and brightness of the scene, the camera may not be able to set an aperture that produces a correct exposure. In that case, the aperture will go to its largest or smallest limit, and then blink. With a bright scene, lower ISO or increase shutter speed until the aperture display stops blinking. In dark conditions, raise the ISO, decrease the shutter speed, and/or use flash.

Manual (M)
Manual mode allows you to select any aperture/shutter speed combination even if that will produce exposures that are different from the camera's recommendation. That's because Manual mode was intended to provide the ability to intentionally overexpose or underexpose an image for creative purposes. A scale in the viewfinder data panel, and in

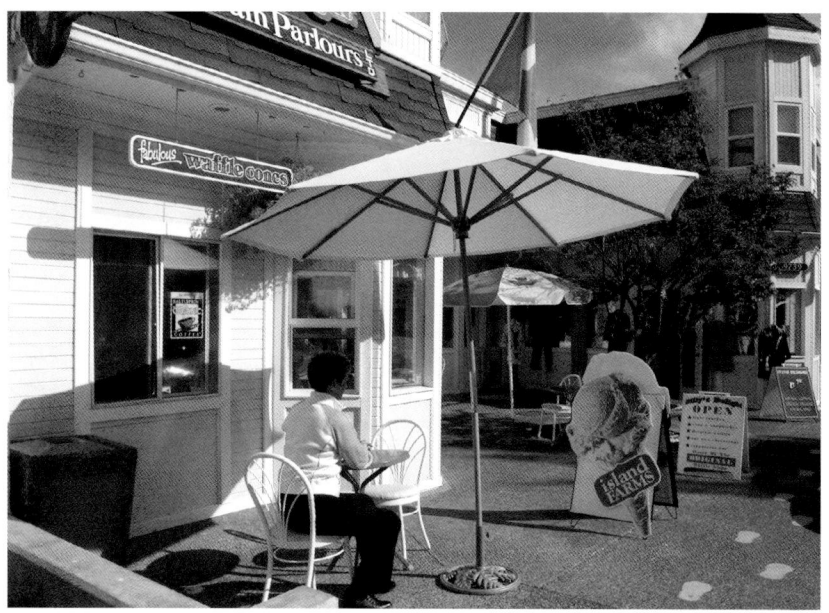

When you select M exposure mode, the 5D provides information to help you produce a correct exposure. With a very dark-toned or very light-toned subject, you may decide to deviate from the camera's recommendations. You may also wish to set different exposures for creative effects.

the LCD monitor, shows the amount of deviation from the meter-recommended exposure at the aperture and shutter speed you have set.

Experiment with M mode by selecting a shutter speed with the control dial. In order to change the aperture, press and hold the exposure compensation button 🔲 on the back of the camera while rotating the control dial. (This selection process can be reversed, using a function available in Custom Menu 1, see page 110.)

Depending on your aperture/shutter speed selections, an image may be correctly exposed, according to the light meter (0 on the scale), or overexposed (+) or underexposed (-). The scale also shows the extent that your exposure will vary from the recommended "correct" exposure. A reading of +1 for example, indicates that the image will be overexposed by one Exposure Value (EV), while -1 indicates underexposure by one EV. The scale is marked in increments of one-third (0.33) EV.

One EV is equivalent to one aperture stop or one shutter-speed step. It's quite a large increment in digital photography; over or underexposure by one EV is generally obvious in an image. An EV factor of 0.33 is less noticeable in an image.

The entire manual operating technique is somewhat complex and recommended only for experienced SLR camera users. There are quicker, more intuitive and more convenient methods for adjusting exposure. In fact, most photographers (including many professionals) prefer to use Aperture Priority (A) and Shutter Priority (S) modes, applying overrides to achieve a desired exposure effect. Unless you're ready for extensive exposure experimentation, or if you are already proficient in manual exposure control, you may want to experiment before relying on M mode.

Note: The 5D includes a feature called Manual Shift that allows you to change the f/stop and/or shutter speed without affecting the exposure. To use this, set the aperture and shutter speed. Now, you can lock in that exposure level by pressing and holding the AEL button. Any subsequent changes—to f/stop for depth of field control, or shutter speed for control of the rendition of motion—will not change the image brightness. If you do enjoy shooting in fully manual mode, this feature may be helpful to you.

Bulb Exposure

The longest shutter speed that you can select is 30 seconds, but there is another option for making even longer exposures: BULB. The term relates to a historically early photo accessory that used a blower bulb attached to a hose to trip the camera's shutter.

Set the exposure mode dial to M, and then decrease the shutter speed until the LCD display says BULB. The camera's shutter will remain open as long as the shutter release button is held all the way down. (An optional remote-control cord accessory can be used to lock the shutter release for greater convenience and less risk of camera shake.) A tripod must be used for sharp images during long exposures, and it is best to put the eyepiece cap in place to prevent light from entering through the viewfinder and affecting the exposure.

The camera's light meter is disengaged, so you will need to use a handheld meter to calculate exposure. This option is most useful for night photography to record the moon and stars, a dark cityscape, or fireworks, for example. The Anti-Shake system is also disabled.

Hint: Some articles in photography magazines and on the Internet provide recommended exposure times and apertures for various types of night photography. Some even call for exposure times as long as several hours in order to record the movement of stars during an entire night (but be aware that long exposures can create sensor noise. See page 91 for details on noise reduction). Because the camera requires a steady source of power to keep the electronic shutter open, start with a fresh battery, or use the optional AC adapter accessory if you want to try this type of photography. (Battery life will vary with the temperature: short in cold conditions and much longer in warm locations.)

Select a Metering Method

It's important to understand the camera's light metering strategies in each of the three options available by pressing the Fn button on the back of the camera.

14-Segment Honeycomb Pattern (Evaluative) Metering ◉

Also known as multi-segment metering, this system uses artificial intelligence to analyze brightness in 14 segments of a scene, and also considers subject distance and position data provided by the autofocus system in its analysis of subject conditions. Because the system compares exposure data with pre-programmed exposure models, it is quite successful at metering subjects with unusual reflectances.

For example, in strong backlighting—a friend posing against a setting sun, for example—the system increases exposure automatically to reduce the risk of a dark image. It uses the same strategy for any scene possessing high reflectance, whether a sunny, snow-covered landscape or a close-up of a bride in white. The metering system should also compensate for a dark-toned subject, such as a lava field, reducing exposure to render it as black, instead of gray.

While this is a very sophisticated metering method, the system's recommendations still may not always be ideal. For example, an image of a snowy scene may be slightly underexposed, while the black lava may be overexposed. Surprisingly often, however, the exposure will be close to optimal, perhaps slightly over a perfect level. During extensive testing, the Maxxum 5D/Dynax 5D that I used tended to produce overexposure more often than underexposure in honeycomb pattern metering.

Slight exposure errors may or may not be a problem, depending on whether you can correct the errors with image processing software. But even when shooting with RAW, which generally offers more capacity than JPEG for post-shooting exposure correction without degrading image quality, it is worth taking the time to get a well-exposed image in-camera, using exposure compensation as required.

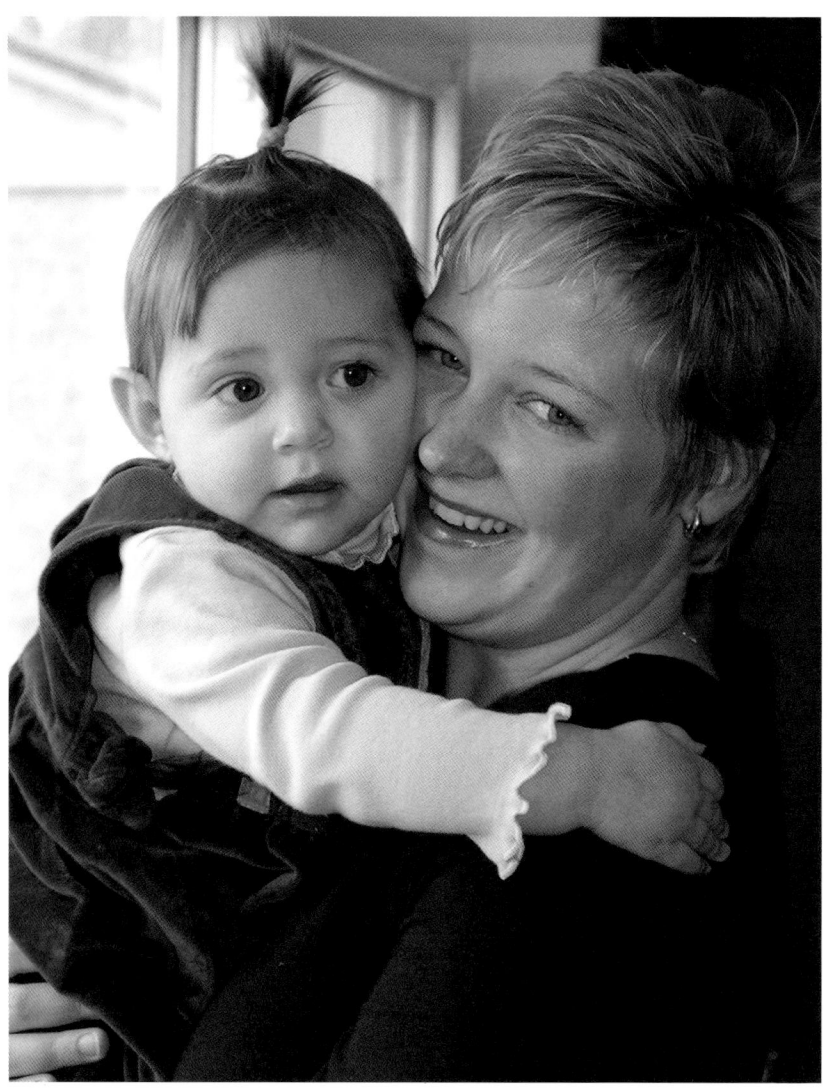

Take a spot meter reading from a midtone portion of your subject—such as the shadowed side of the mother's face in this case—and your photo should exhibit pleasing exposure.

Spot Metering ◘

Spot metering measures only the portion of the scene within the small circular area in the center of the viewfinder. To use it, point the lens so that the central circle etched on the viewing screen covers the target you intend to meter.

One of the most valuable uses of spot metering is to measure light values in different parts of a scene for comparison or to determine the exposure gradient in the scene. Another common scenario is a spot lit performer (small in the frame) against a dark background. Or you might be faced with shooting a small, midtone subject located in very bright surroundings, such as a cabin in the snow on a sunny day. These types of shots often produce exposure that is not optimal with other metering patterns.

In the above cases, meter your primary subject, then press and hold the AEL button to make sure that the locked-in exposure does not change while you recompose. When you take the shot, the exposure will be optimized for the primary subject.

With experience, this is a useful type of metering. But it can also be tricky because the exposure is significantly affected by the brightness of the selected area. If the target is a midtone (a tanned face, for example), the exposure will be accurate. But if you take a spot meter reading of a light-toned area, underexposure will occur. And if you spot meter a dark area, the image may easily be overexposed. Consequently, spot metering can produce images that vary within a wide range of exposure. It is recommended for photographers who are confident in judging the relative reflectance of different subjects.

Note: If you take a spot meter reading off a white or a black subject, serious exposure errors will result unless you also use one of the camera's compensation features. For example, if spot metering a brightly lit area of snow, you might need to set a +1.5 EV exposure compensation factor for a correct overall exposure.

Center Weighted Metering ◯

An old-style (conventional) light-metering system, center weighted measures brightness over most of the scene and averages it, but it applies extra weight to a large central area. The system does not employ any "intelligent" evaluation.

Photographers who have a lot of experience with early SLRs that used this system often use center weighted metering, selecting an approximate amount of exposure compensation (based on extensive experience or rules of thumb) to achieve a desired effect. When applied with some expertise, this technique can produce excellent exposures. However, in general you will get better results with the camera's honeycomb-segment metering system. You are also better off using spot rather than center weighted metering with difficult subjects or when precisely metering a small area is advantageous.

Exposure Compensation

After taking a shot, check it on the LCD monitor. If you think it's too bright or too dark, set some exposure compensation and re-shoot. When shooting in the camera's various automatic exposure modes, this feature is accessed with the ▤ button on the upper right back of the camera. While pressing and holding the ▤ button, rotate the control dial to select a + (plus) or − (minus) setting. Watch the scale in the LCD monitor change to reflect your settings and stop when you reach a desired level of compensation.

The camera can make changes toward the plus side or the minus side in 1/3 EV increments. EV denotes exposure value, and one full EV change equals one full aperture stop or one full shutter speed step.

When shooting with multi-segment metering, few scenes will require more than a + 0.7 or - 0.7 EV of exposure compensation. Take a shot without compensation and review it in the Playback mode—preferably using the histogram (discussed on pages 163-169)—for an exposure analysis. If you're not satisfied, set a plus compensation factor for a brighter image or a minus factor for a darker image, and re-shoot.

Hint: Avoid making JPEG images that are overexposed, with excessively bright highlight areas. If the light-toned subject elements are too bright, they contain no detail. While you may be able to darken them later in a computer, you cannot replace detail that was not recorded by the sensor. The opposite applies to scenes that include important detail in shadow areas; avoid underexposure because that may cause a loss of shadow detail.

Exposure Bracketing

This function allows you to shoot three successive frames while the camera automatically sets a different exposure for each. This increases your chances of getting the most optimal exposure with any given subject in any given lighting condition.

Exposure bracketing is selected in the Drive mode with the drive mode button 🖐 on top of the camera. Scroll down using the keys on the controller to the choice for exposure bracket. Now scroll right to select one of the four options.

• Three frames in a continuous burst (press and hold the shutter release) with a 0.3 EV compensation difference.

• Three frames in a continuous burst (press and hold the shutter release) with a 0.7 EV compensation difference.

• Three frames in single advance (press the shutter release separately three consecutive times) with a 0.3 EV compensation difference.

• Three frames in single advance (press the shutter release separately three consecutive times) with a 0.7 EV compensation difference.

In continuous bracketing, only the last image of the series will be displayed in the LCD monitor.

The sequence for bracketing is 0 for the first frame, minus (-) exposure compensation for the next frame, and plus (+) exposure compensation for the last frame of the series. This sequence can be changed in section 2 of the Recording menu as described in the menus chapter (see page 103).

Note: When flash is active, the bracketing function varies the flash exposure only. Only single frame bracketing is available, so you'll need to take three distinct shots each time the flash has recycled and is ready.

Autoexposure Lock (AEL)

In any of the autoexposure modes, the AEL option lets you meter a portion of a scene and lock the exposure value so that you can recompose your shot. This is useful in spot metering under difficult lighting conditions, such as strong backlighting where the autoexposure system may read too much light in the scene and underexpose your subject.

To activate this function, point the lens at a midtone area that you wish to meter and press the AEL button on the back of the camera in the upper right corner. Hold the button as you recompose and set autofocus with a light touch on the shutter release button. When you're ready to take the shot, fully depress the shutter release.

If you plan to use the AEL technique with spot metering, set some exposure compensation if your target is light-toned or dark-toned. This should help to assure correct exposure. For example, set perhaps +1.3 if you plan to take the light meter reading from a white egret. Or maybe set -1 if taking the meter reading from a black cat. Then activate the AEL, recompose for the desired framing, and take the shot.

Note: When flash is active, the AEL button cannot be used to lock exposure. In this case it is used to set a long shutter speed for slow sync flash photography with all exposure modes except Manual.

Exposure Evaluation

So far we have primarily discussed the simplest method for assessing exposure: checking the image on the LCD monitor during instant playback or during review in the full Playback mode. In fact, there are two additional methods for a more scientific evaluation of exposure and detail in highlight and shadow areas. Available in instant playback or in the camera's full Playback mode, the histogram and Luminance Limit display are valuable tools.

Both features provide feedback on exposure and contrast, serving as instruments to help you evaluate your image. Once you review the information they provide, you can choose to re-shoot the image with a different exposure and/or contrast setting if you desire. Though some people count on "fixing" exposure problems with software after downloading their image files into the computer, you can't process detail that was never captured in the first place. Whether shooting in JPEG or RAW, image processing is faster and much more reliable if you've used the camera to shoot the exposure and contrast properly in the first place.

To activate these features, press the top (up) key on the controller while viewing an image in instant image review or in the camera's Playback mode. The image displayed will now be smaller in the LCD monitor. A "hilly" type of graph—called a histogram—will appear below the image. Any excessively bright or excessively dark areas will blink within the displayed image, thanks to the Luminance Limit display.

Let's look at these two features in more detail, starting with the Luminance Limit display.

Luminance Limit Display

This feature functions as a highlight/shadow warning because it indicates areas in the photo that are over or underexposed. You will see a thumbnail of your image. When bright areas of the image flash, the system is warning that the highlights are "blown out," or too bright to hold much (if any) detail. When shadow areas flash, they are "blocked up," or too dark to show much (if any) detail.

Each type of warning (highlight or shadow) flashes alternately; the display uses a different type of pattern for each in order to avoid confusion. This Luminance Limit is not as informative as the histogram display, but it's logical, intuitive and easier to interpret. It can certainly help you avoid the most serious exposure problems.

Consider a situation where highlight detail or texture is important, as in a bride's dress or the texture of a flower petal. After taking a shot, check the image, looking closely for a highlight warning in the pertinent area. If it flashes, you'll probably want to re-shoot. Set a –0.3 exposure compensation; review the image in Playback mode and check for a warning again. If necessary, re-shoot again, using a –0.7 exposure compensation factor, and check the image again for a highlight warning. Keep an eye on shadow warnings at the same time, if there is also important detail in shadow areas.

Hint: Although highlight detail is often the most important, be careful when shooting a dark-toned subject, such as men in black tuxedos or a Hawaiian lava field. Underexposure—particularly images made at ISO 400 or higher settings—will tend to overemphasize any digital noise that might be present. When possible, re-shoot the image a few times, increasing the amount of plus exposure compensation for each shot. You can always darken the image in the computer, which will not affect digital noise. However, lightening the shadow areas in post processing will usually cause any pre-existing noise to be more noticeable.

Sometimes shadow detail or texture is important—as in the fur of your black cat. In that case, pay attention to the shadow warning. If an important shadow area blinks, you may well choose to re-shoot. Set a bit of plus compensation to increase the exposure, allowing the camera to record more detail. But beware of overexposing any important highlights you may want to include in the image; setting too much plus exposure compensation can produce flashing in the highlight areas.

Setting a lower contrast level in Digital Effects Control (DEC) in the Function sub-menu (see page 89) can also be useful for scenes that include dark shadows as well as bright highlight areas, as on a bright, sunny day. When you reduce image contrast, there's less risk of blown-out highlights and blocked-up shadows. You can always boost contrast later, in a computer, but it's more difficult (and sometimes impossible) to fully correct excessive contrast or to recover highlight and shadow detail. Even with software that includes the appropriate tools to do so, the manipulated image may not look natural.

The Histogram
More complicated than the Luminance Limit feature, the histogram is a more scientific method for making a technical evaluation of your images. It consists of a graph that appears on the LCD monitor indicating brightness distribution from black (on the left side of the graph) to white (on the right side) along the horizontal axis. A dark image will be weighted to the left, a bright image will be weighted to the right. Midtone brightness distribution is represented in the central area of the graph. The vertical axis indicates the pixel quantity existing for the different levels of brightness.

If the graph rises as a typical bell-shaped curve, from the bottom left corner of the histogram to a peak in the middle, then descends to the bottom right corner, all the tones of the scene are captured. If the graph starts or ends too far up on either the left or right vertical axis of the histogram, so that the "slope" looks like it is cut off, then the camera is cutting off data from those areas. Some loss of detail is inevitable when the contrast range is beyond the capabilities of the camera—a dark-toned subject surrounded by extremely bright sky or water, for example.

When the histogram is heavily weighted towards either the dark or bright side of the graph, detail may be lost in the sparser of the two areas—dark sections of your photo may fade to black, and brighter sections may appear completely washed out.

However, some scenes are naturally dark or light in tone. Think of a dance troupe in white against a whitewashed adobe wall. Then think of a black panther lurking within a stand of brown trees. In these cases, most of the graph can be on one side of the scale. The luminance distribution will be heavily weighted to the right side for the dance troupe and toward the left side for the panther.

Yet if detail in highlight area is important, try to control your exposure so that the slope on the right reaches the bottom of the graph before it hits the right vertical axis and "drops off" that side (though the real world is not perfect and you can't always accomplish this exactly).

If a scene includes important detail elements in shadow areas, try to manage so that the slope on the left reaches the bottom of the histogram before it hits the left vertical axis. Check the histogram after taking a shot and, if necessary, reshoot using a plus exposure compensation setting. Then check the histogram again for the new image. Also check the right side of the graph to see whether the new exposure has produced blown out highlights. Of course, when shadow detail is most important, you may need to tolerate some loss of detail in the brightest areas.

The histogram display is valuable when shooting in tricky lighting conditions with both dark and bright areas. With a bit of experience in evaluating histograms, you'll know if you are getting the desired effect in high contrast situations such as this.

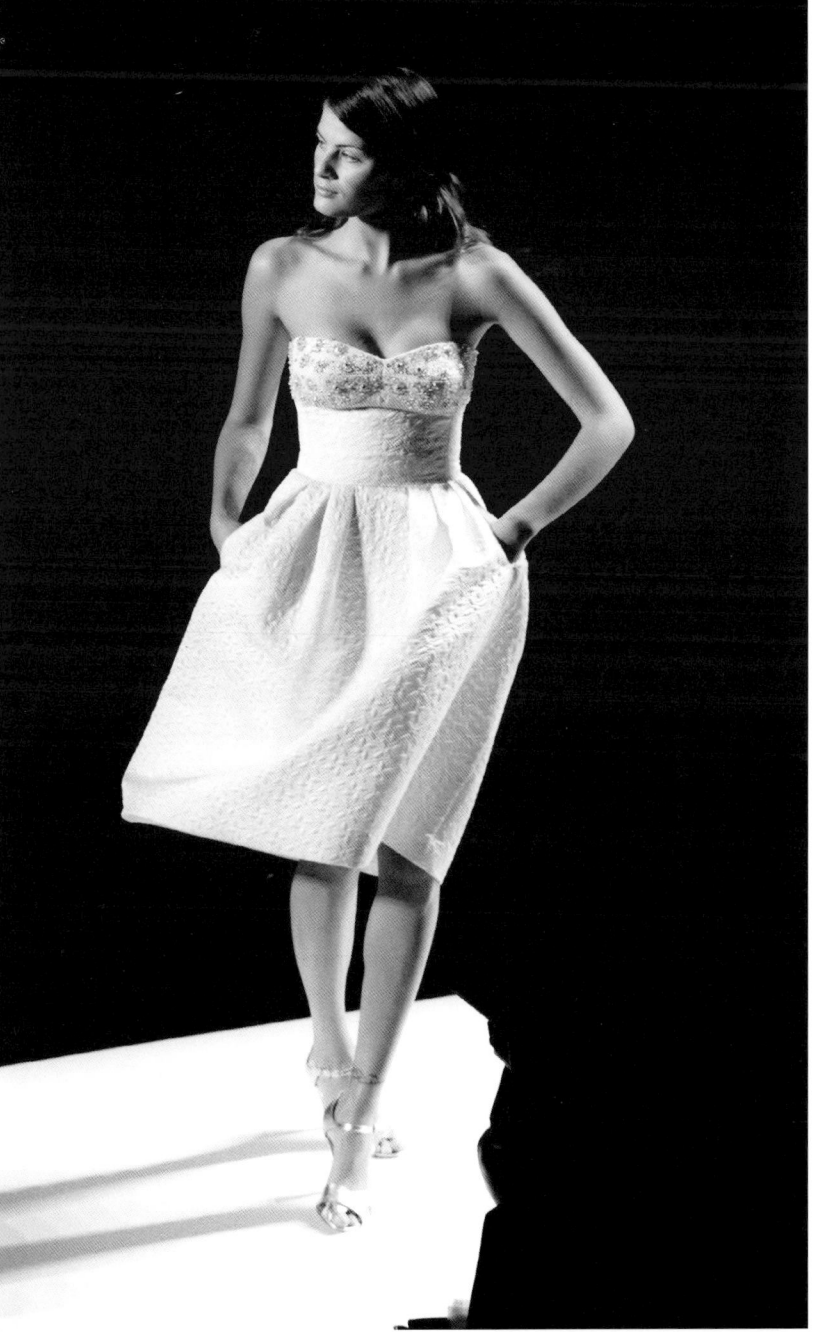

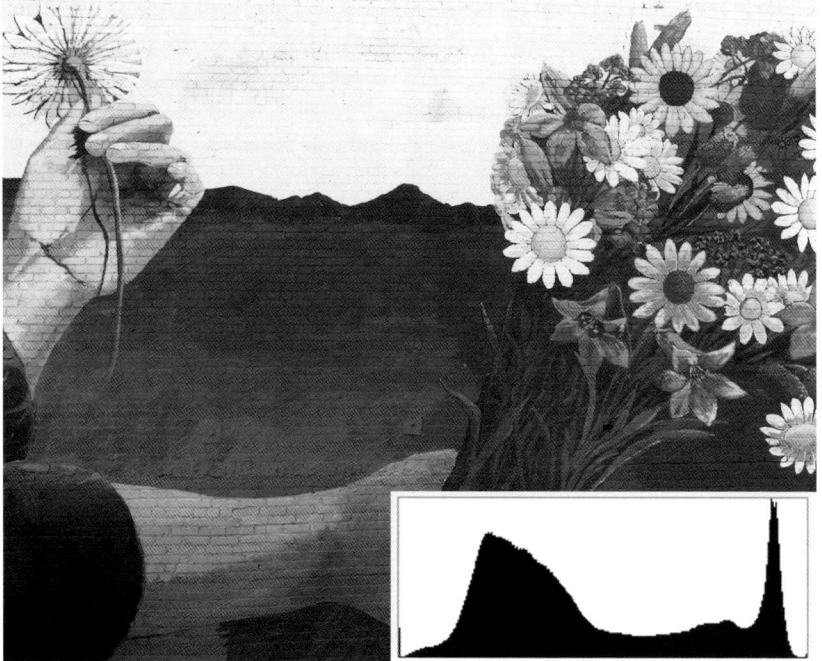

Image A   *(photo © Kevin Kopp.)*

Image A: If the graph rises from the bottom left corner of the histogram, then descends towards the bottom right corner, all the tones of the scene are captured. (There may be a few peaks and valleys involved, but the graph still rises from the left and ends very close to the right axis).The image will include pure black, pure white, and a good distribution of midtone, for an exposure that's correct overall:

Image B: With some images, the slope will drop before it reaches either the left or right side of the scale. In other words, the graph starts too far in from one or both sides of the histogram. This indicates that the image does not contain rich dark blacks or bright pure white tones. (Remember, black is represented on the left of the graph and white on the right.)

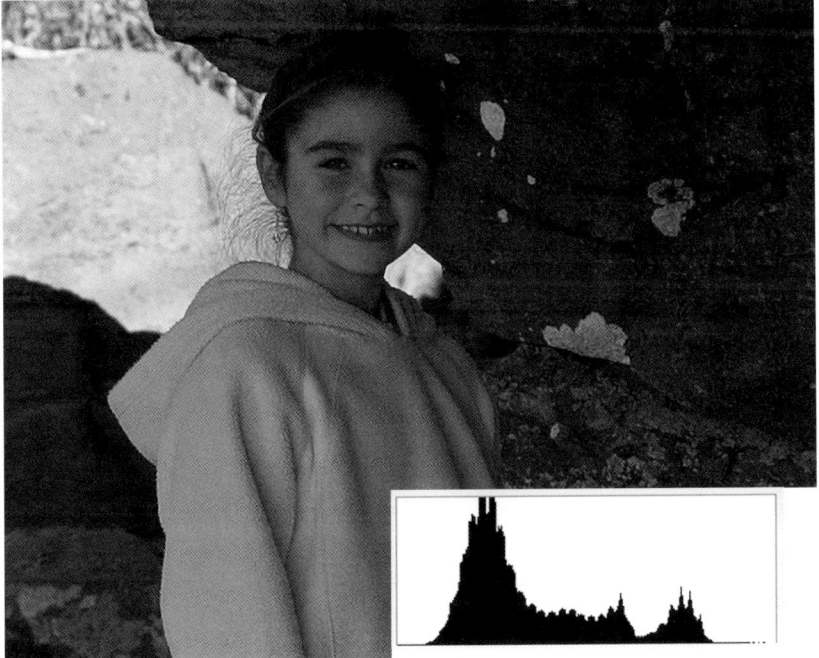

Image B   *(photo © Kevin Kopp.)*

The image consists primarily of midtones and grayish blacks and grayish whites. This does not necessarily mean poor exposure; in fact, it signifies low contrast. That's easy to correct in the computer, or by setting a slightly higher contrast level in-camera (accessed with the Fn button as described on page 89.) Of course, you may decide to set some plus or minus exposure compensation as well, before taking the shot again. That will produce brighter whites or darker black tones.

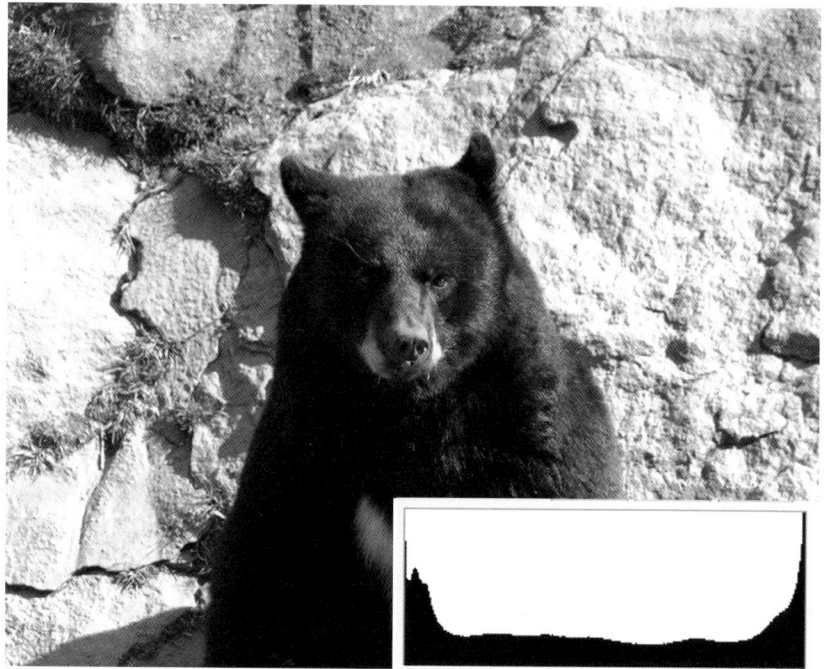

Image C   *(photo © Kevin Kopp.)*

Image C: In images made in extremely high contrast (including very dark shadow areas plus very bright highlights) the histogram may show a slope that is cut off at both ends. In other words, the slope does not gently reach the bottom of the horizontal axis near either end of the histogram. This indicates that detail will be lost in both highlight and shadow areas. Dark sections of your photo may fade to black, and brighter sections may appear completely washed out.

Try re-shooting an image of this type, using a low contrast setting in-camera. For nearby subjects, try using flash to even out the lighting for gentler overall contrast. If the light is changing, wait until a cloud covers the sun, moderating excessive contrast.

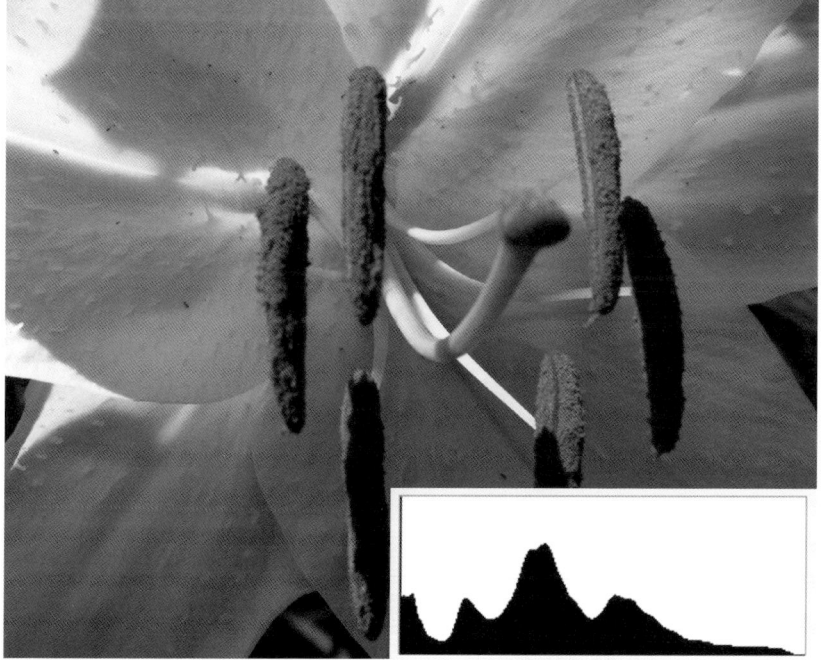

Image D   *(photo © Kevin Kopp.)*

Image D: In some images, as in a portrait of a bride in white or a sunlit flower for examples, highlight details are important. In those cases, be sure the slope on the right reaches the bottom of the graph before it hits the right side. Otherwise, the image will not hold detail in bright areas of the subject: they will be blown-out. Re-shoot, using a minus exposure compensation setting.

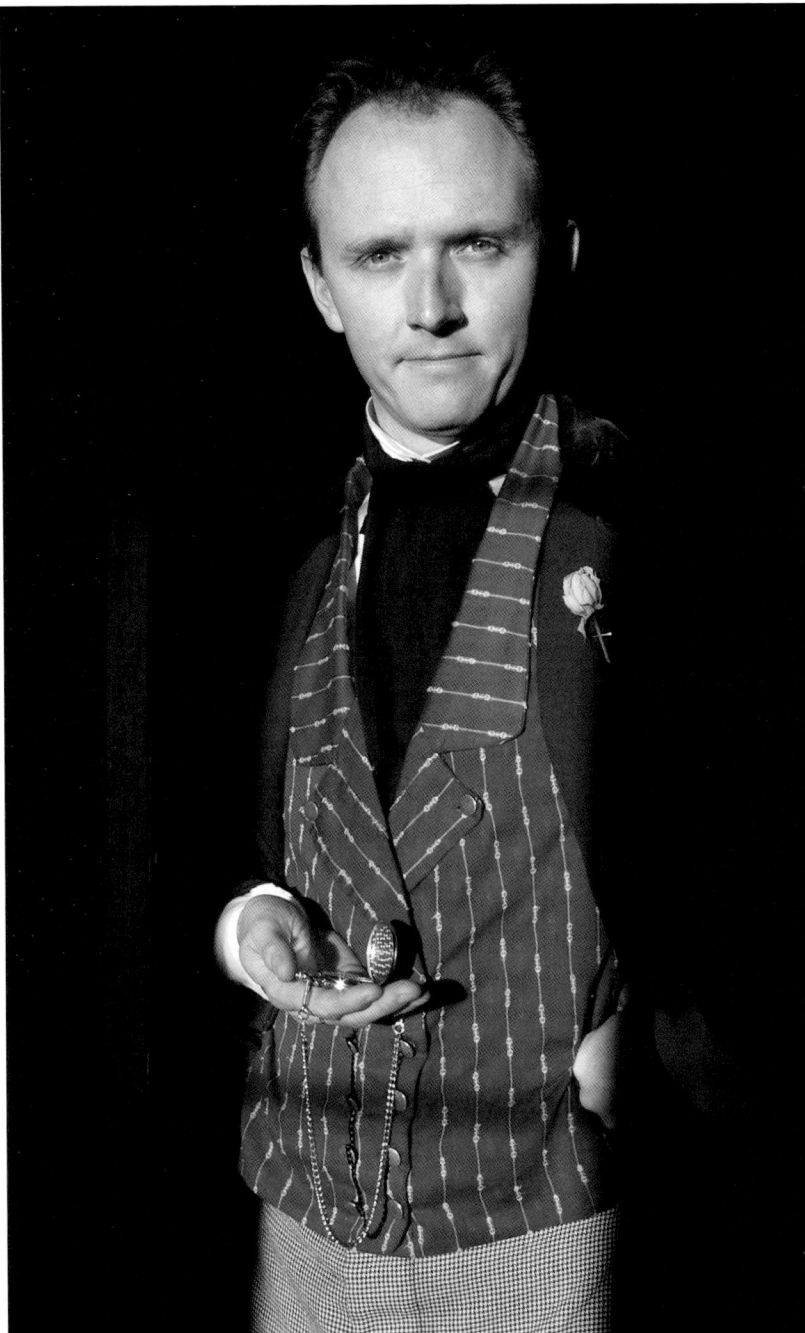

Flash Photography

Electronic flash is not just a supplement for insufficient lighting but can also be a great tool for creative photography. Flash is highly controllable, its color is precise, and the results are repeatable. However, the challenge is getting the right look and many photographers shy away from using flash because they aren't happy with the results. This is because on-camera flash can be harsh and unflattering and taking the flash off the camera used to be a complicated procedure with less than sure results. The sophisticated flash options available with the Maxxum 5D/Dynax 5D—especially with a compatible accessory flash unit—eliminate many of these concerns.

Achieving just the right effect is also easier with a digital camera than it was with a 35mm camera. This is because the LCD Monitor provides instantaneous feedback that alleviates the guesswork. With digital, you take a picture and you know immediately whether the flash exposure was right or not. You can then set exposure compensation, change the angle of bounce flash, move an off-camera flash unit to a better location, and more.

The Built-in Flash

Even when using the built-in flash unit, very good photos are possible, particularly in outdoor locations when flash is not the primary light source. Flash photography can be totally uncomplicated. Simply set the camera to the Program exposure mode and manually raise the flash head. By the time

A little bit of light from the flash often goes a long way in creative photography. Here the flash was used to add a bit of sparkle to a subject almost perfectly exposed by existing light.

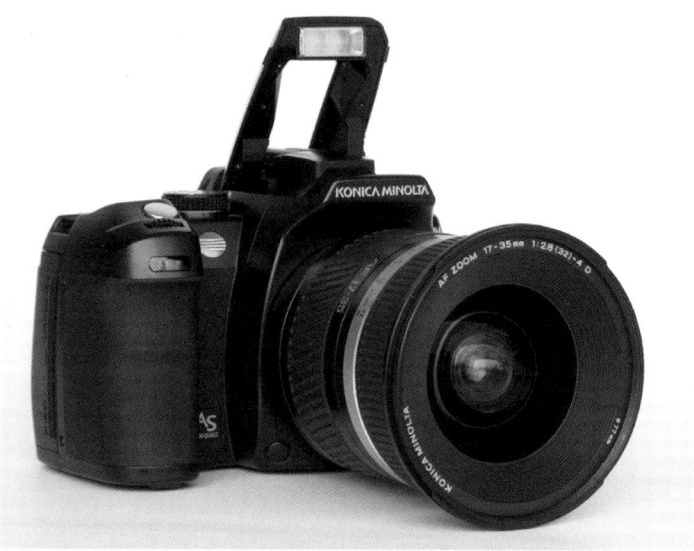

While small and not very powerful, the camera's built-in flash unit can come in handy as long as you are aware of its limitations. You can extend its range by increasing your ISO a little or opening up the lens aperture. If you have the time, check your first flash picture in the camera's LCD and try moving closer to your subject if the exposure is not adequate.

you have composed and focused, the flash should be charged and ready to fire as confirmed by a lightning bolt symbol in the viewfinder data panel. The camera will set a suitable aperture (f/stop) and shutter speed, called sync speed in flash photography. It will also set the right flash power output or intensity. As long as your subject is within the flash range, the image should be well exposed.

While the lighting bolt symbol is blinking, which indicates that the flash unit is recycling or charging, you cannot take another shot. When the blinking stops, the flash is ready and you can make another image. Remember, however, that the built-in flash draws power from the camera's battery. Frequent flash use will reduce battery life so if you plan to use flash a lot, it is a good idea to carry at least one spare battery.

Flash Range

The small built-in unit is not particularly powerful but it has adequate range for most snapshots and people pictures. The effective range varies with the aperture (f/stop) that's used: it's greater at f/4 than at smaller apertures such as f/8, for example. Effective range also varies depending on the ISO selected: it's greater at higher ISO settings because the CCD sensor is more sensitive to light. The following chart provides effective flash range at f/4, a common maximum aperture at the short end of many variable aperture zoom lenses, and at f/5.6, a maximum aperture that's common with these lenses at the medium to longer focal lengths.

Hint: Photocopy this chart—or summarize the most useful information—and carry it in your camera bag for future reference. Although I have emphasized the maximum flash range, don't ignore the minimum range. Moving close to a subject for a frame-filling close-up—especially when using high ISO settings—can produce excessively bright flash photos.

ISO Setting	f/4	f/5.6
Lo80	1 - 2.7m 3.3 - 8.8 ft.	1 - 1.9m 3.3 - 6.2 ft.
100	1 - 3m 3.3 - 9.8 ft.	1 - 2.1m 3.3 - 6.7 ft.
200 or Hi200	1 - 4.3m 3.3 - 14 ft.	1 - 3m 3.3 - 9.8 ft.
400	1- 6m 3.3 - 20 ft.	1 - 4.3m 3.3 - 14 ft.
800	1.4 - 8.6m 4.6 - 28 ft.	1 - 6m 3.3 - 20 ft.
1600	2 - 12m 6.6 - 39 ft.	1.4 - 8.6m 4.6 - 28 ft.
3200	2.8 - 17m 9.2 - 56 ft.	2 - 12m 6.6 - 39 ft.

Although the flash range is impressive at ISO 800, 1600, and particularly at ISO 3200, remember that image quality will be lower due to more prominent digital noise at high ISO settings. Consequently, you might consider buying one of the powerful accessory Program flash units (with at least double the range) if you often use flash for distant subjects. Aside from the other benefits of an accessory flash, greater power output will allow you to shoot at lower ISO settings more frequently, for superior image quality.

Accessory Flash Units

In addition to greater power output, accessory flash units include extra features for improved flash control.

D-Series Flash Units

The (D) designation indicates that a unit supports the camera's sophisticated ADI (Advanced Distance Integration) flash metering, available when D-series lenses are used. ADI uses distance information from a D-series lens to control the flash output and is less affected by very bright, or very dark, subjects than Pre-Flash TTL metering. The HS abbreviation—appended to the two most recent flash units—indicates that they support high-speed flash sync. These flash units are fully compatible with the 5D.

Program Flash 2500(D): This is a simple, lightweight, affordable model with moderate power as denoted by its ISO 100 GN, or Guide Number, of 82/25 in feet/meters. The flash head can be tilted upward in a range from 0° to 90°, useful for bouncing flash from a ceiling or a portable reflector panel accessory. A focus-assist AF illuminator (near infrared beam projector) is built-in. The 2500(D) can also be used in Manual mode at full power, or 1/2, 1/4, 1/8, 1/16, and 1/32 power.

Program Flash 3600HS(D): This is a larger model with greater power output (its ISO 100 GN is 118/36 feet/meters at the 85mm zoom head setting). It's also full-featured with illuminated LCD data panel, wide angle diffusion panel (for

The Maxxum/Dynax Program Flash 5600HS(D). Photo © Konica Minolta.

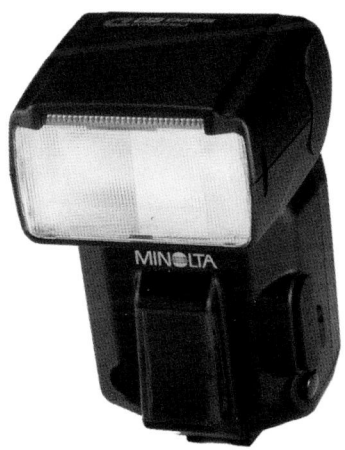

use with lenses as short as 17mm), power zoom flash head to match lenses of 24mm to 85mm (and longer), tilting head, focus-assist illuminator, plus custom functions for additional creative options.

Program Flash 5600HS(D): The premium flash unit, this one is suitable for serious photographers and professionals. It is compact but has a GN ISO 100 of 184/57 feet/meters at the 85mm zoom head setting. This model includes all the features of the 3600HS(D), plus others. The focus-assist illuminator is optimized for the nine-point AF sensor used in the 5D. The power zoom head offers positions from 24mm to 85mm. For lenses as short as 17mm, use the built-in adapter. In addition to conventional upward tilt capability, this unit allows for tilting the head 10° downward for close-up photography, and allows for rotation to the side for bouncing flash from a wall.

Macro Flash Units

Macro Flash units consist of two parts: the flash head(s) that attach to a bracket or a macro lens, plus a controller that's attached to the camera's hot shoe; the two are connected with a cable. The optional Macro Controller MFC-1000 accessory must be used with these flash units.

Macro Ring Flash 1200: For use in extreme close-up photography with Konica Minolta macro lenses, each of the four flash tubes in the circular head can be individually selected if desired. Four focus-assist lamps are also included as aids in low light focusing.

Macro Twin Flash 2400: This model is similar in many respects to the 1200, and is also intended specifically for extreme close-up (macro) photography. However, instead of a single, circular flash head, the 2400 consists of two separate flash heads on adjustable arms, which are useful for adjusting the position of the lighting.

Other Maxxum/Dynax Flash Units

Some older Program flash units can also be used with the 5D, but they're certainly not "fully compatible." The 3200i, 2000i, 3500xi, 2000xi, SF-1 and X-series units can also be used with the 5D but provide fill flash only. The 5400HS, 5200i, 5400xi and the 4000AF can be used, with the optional Flash Adapter FS-1100, but only with fully manual flash control. These units may be acceptable for photographers who use an accessory flash meter device (for determining suitable settings in manual flash control), but they're not recommended for others.

Flash Photography and Camera Exposure Modes

Whether you're using the built-in flash or an accessory flash unit that's attached to the camera's hot shoe, you can shoot with any of the exposure modes available with the 5D.

Full-Auto Program (AUTO)

In Full AUTO the camera sets the shutter speed and aperture used for each shot as required for a good exposure. Settings such as: ISO, white balance, exposure and flash exposure compensation are set at the camera's default settings. This mode is a good choice if you want to let the camera do all the work, or if family members what the 5D to act as a "point-and-shoot" camera. This mode will give you the greatest simplicity reliability in flash photography.

Program (P)

Program Exposure controls the shutter speed and aperture used for each shot. (With flash photography, you cannot use the Program shift feature to select a different f/stop or shutter speed combination.) The camera also sets the proper flash power output or intensity.

Aperture Priority (A)

Just as with ambient light photography, you can select a desired f/stop in a mode. The camera will set a flash sync speed from 1/60 second to 1/160 second or up to 1/125 second when the Anti-Shake system is on.

After taking a shot, make sure that the Flash Signal (in the viewfinder data panel) is blinking to confirm adequate flash exposure. If it does not blink, select a wider aperture (lower f/number) or move closer to the subject, and re-shoot. You can also choose a higher ISO setting on the camera, but do this with care as it can increase digital noise. You may also want to try setting a + flash exposure compensation factor at least with a nearby subject. That technique is rarely useful with a distant subject because the flash unit may have already been generating maximum output, and simply cannot produce greater intensity. You can also increase the ISO, but again be aware that this increases noise.

The Flash Signal is useful but you should also review photos on the LCD monitor to confirm that the flash effect was pleasing and appropriate for the subject. If not, try again, using some of the techniques discussed in this chapter.

If you want to make a long exposure with flash, to be sure of recording the darker surroundings lit only by ambient light, try this. Before taking the photo press and hold the AEL button, which will activate slow sync. This causes the camera to choose a longer shutter speed, which will produce an exposure with better ambient light recording and hence, a brighter background. A tripod is recommended for this technique.

Shutter Priority (S)

In S mode, you select a shutter speed and the camera will set the corresponding aperture. You can set shutter speeds as long as 30 seconds and as short as 1/160 second, or 1/125 second when the Anti-Shake system is on. The shutter speed cannot exceed the flash sync speed so make sure you don't select a shutter speed higher than the ones listed.

Changing the shutter speed will not affect the flash exposure. However, it does allow you to control how ambient light areas, not lit by the flash, will be rendered. This is especially useful when you have a flash lit subject in front of somewhat dark background that you want to be rendered naturally in the photo. An example of this would be a subject with a city scene at dusk or a beautiful sunset behind them. If you don't intentionally use a longer shutter speed, the picture will probably have a flash lit subject against a very dark or black background.

In these situations make sure you use a tripod when shooting at long shutter speeds to prevent blur from camera shake. Shutter priority mode is also useful when you want to render ambient light motion blurs and a sharp flash-exposed subject. You should set the camera for Rear flash sync (see page 102) and use a slower shutter speed to capture the ambient exposure of the moving subject. The camera should then produce an image with a sharp subject (illuminated by the brief burst of light) with light trails that follow the moving subject instead of preceding it.

If you do not get a good flash exposure on the first try here are some suggestions: If the flash exposure of a close subject is too dark, set a + exposure compensation factor. If the flash exposure of a subject that is further away is too dark, move closer to the subject or set a higher ISO level for greater sensitivity to light (always keep in mind that increasing the ISO may increase noise). You can also fine-tune the ambient portion of the exposure—i.e. the background that is not lit by flash—by using the exposure compensation dial on the top right of the camera.

See page 173 for specifics on the range of the built-in flash. If you're using an accessory flash unit with a data panel, it will provide information as to the flash range at any ISO and aperture/shutter speed setting; that reduces the need for trial and error shooting with subjects that are very close to the camera or very far away.

Manual (M)

Just as in ambient light photography, you can select any aperture in M mode. However, you must set a shutter speed that syncs with the flash; your choices are the same as in S mode. As long as your subject is within the maximum range of the flash unit with the aperture you have set, the camera should produce a good flash exposure. When using one of the accessory Program flash units with a data panel, you'll find useful information as to flash range; that varies depending on the ISO, the f/stop that you selected and the position of the flash unit's zooming head.

During flash photography in the camera's Manual mode, the exposure scale in the viewfinder operates, but it is not providing data on flash exposure. Instead, the scale provides an indication as to the brightness level of the background that will not illuminated by flash.

If the marker on the scale indicates -2 for example, the background will be about 2 EV (or stops) darker than the primary subject. (In other words, the scale denotes the difference between the background lit by ambient light and the nearby subject illuminated by flash.) The scale provides data in a +2 to -2 EV range. If the background brightness will be substantially different than subject brightness—common in very dark locations or in extremely bright backlighting—an arrow at the end of the scale blinks.

This feature is most useful in outdoor photography in backlighting with a subject against an ultra bright background: sky, sand, snow, water, etc. By selecting an appropriate shutter speed, you may be able control background brightness in such cases. By filling in the front with flash you will create and exposure that falls more within the dynamic range of the CCD sensor.

In many typical conditions, the brightness of the background is not substantially higher or lower than the subject brightness, so the +2 to -2 scale should be adequate. If you wish to make an image with a brighter or darker background, simply adjust the shutter speed. A longer shutter speed should provide a brighter background while a faster shutter speed should provide a darker background. (Naturally, the fastest shutter speed selectable when flash is active is 1/160 second, or 1/125 second when the Anti-Shake system is on.) Watch the scale in the viewfinder and stop making adjustments when the marker indicates a desired level of difference between subject brightness and background brightness.

Flash Metering Options

The camera allows you to select either of two options for flash metering control. The following information clarifies some of the concepts relating to those options.

ADI Flash (Advanced Distance Integration)
This is the most sophisticated TTL (through the lens) option. It's available only when using D-series Konica Minolta lenses and either the built-in flash or an accessory D or HS(D)-series flash unit. The camera's microcomputer considers distance data provided by the lens. This increases the odds of a good exposure because it is less influenced by high or low subject reflectance, therefore more likely to produce a good exposure with white or black subjects that

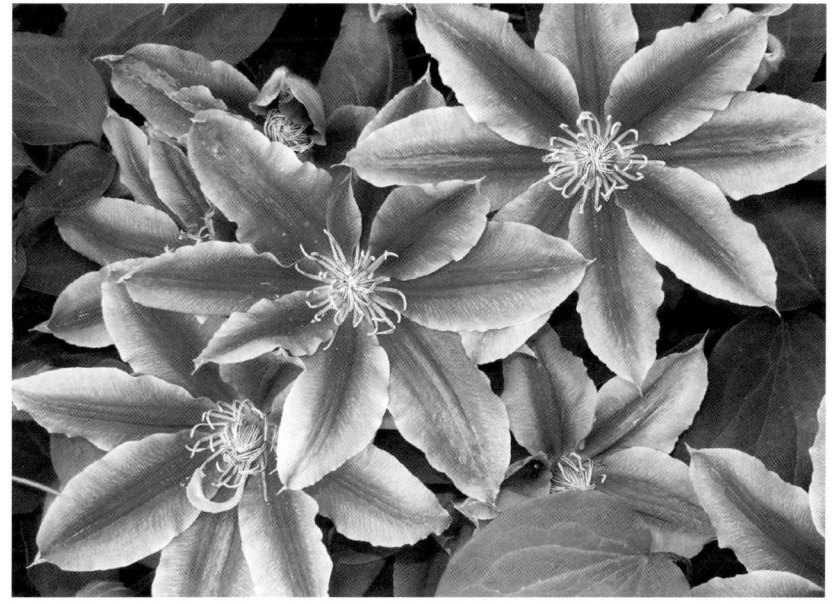

When using lenses designated with a D (including the DT series), the 5D uses sophisticated ADI flash metering that provides excellent exposures. For tight close-ups such as this, use an optional Program Flash unit to prevent uneven lighting due to the lens blocking some of the illumination produced by the built-in flash.

might otherwise lead to under or over exposure, respectively. I recommend this option for those who use a D-series lens and a compatible flash unit.

Note: If the AF system is unable to find focus or if you're using manual focus, the camera will automatically switch to Pre-Flash control. The same will occur in wireless off-camera flash photography, or if you use the (non D-series) Macro Twin Flash 2400, Macro Ring Flash 1200. When using the Maxxum/Dynax Program Flash 2500(D) unit, be sure to select ADI flash on both the camera and the flash unit. Finally, note that Konica Minolta recommends selecting Pre-Flash control when using filters that reduce light transmission (such as a polarizer) or when you use an accessory flash unit's wide angle adapter (diffuser) or the built-in flash.

181

Pre-Flash
This is the standard TTL (through-the-lens) flash metering mode for use with non D-series lenses or with certain flash units, as explained previously. With this technology, a brief burst of flash is fired before an exposure is made but no distance data from the lens is considered. The camera's microcomputer analyzes data from the pre-flash and makes the appropriate output setting. Most of your flash exposures will be fine, unless the subject is unusually light or dark, or is located against a very bright or dark-toned background.

Hint: Light tones and back lighting can lead to under exposure while very dark tones can lead to over exposure. Check your images on the LCD Monitor. If an image would benefit from different flash intensity, set some plus or minus flash exposure compensation, as discussed later in this chapter.

Flash Modes

In addition to flash control (metering) options, the 5D includes a menu option for selecting a desired flash mode. The following applies to the built-in flash and to accessory flash units that support the pertinent features.

Fill-Flash
This is the default flash mode that's suitable anytime. It works well in low light or in bright light, whether flash is used as a primary light source, to supplement the ambient light, or to fill-in shadows. In dark locations the flash will put out the necessary power required in its role as the main light. Outdoors, in strong sunlight, flash output will be automatically reduced, so it should not overpower the ambient light.

Red-Eye Reduction
This mode is recommended for use in dark locations for pictures of people or animals. When selected, the flash unit fires several bright bursts of light intended to reduce the size of the subject's pupils and hence, to minimize

the red-eye syndrome (with pets this is often a blue of green effect, but the cause is the same). After the pre-flashes, the actual flash burst is fired. This feature is occasionally successful in reducing red-eye when used with the built-in flash, but people tend to be annoyed by the bright pre-flashes.

Hint: I do not recommend using Red-eye Reduction mode unless you find that the camera/flash produces terrible red-eye in certain circumstances. There are two drawbacks. The bright pre-flashes may cause your subjects to blink or appear unnatural. And there's quite a long delay from the instant that you press the shutter release until the actual exposure is made; during that time, your subjects' expression or position may change completely.

Effective Ways to Reduce Red-eye
Here are simple steps that you can take to reduce the occurrence of red-eye.
• Ask the subject not to look directly at the lens
• Turn up the room lights to cause the iris in the eye to close down reducing the risk of red-eye
• Use an accessory flash unit that sits higher above the camera, and hence, further from the lens; a greater flash to lens axis distance minimizes red-eye
• Using an accessory flash unit, bounce the light from a ceiling or wall if your flash unit includes a tilt or swivel head feature
• Use wireless off camera flash (described later); hold the remote flash unit above and to one side of your subject
• If your image-processing program includes a red-eye correction tool, use it as per the instructions available with the software

Rear Flash Sync

In conventional flash photography, flash fires at the start of the exposure. When you select Rear flash sync however, the flash will fire at the end of an exposure. This feature is useful when shooting moving subjects at long shutter speeds (preferably 1/15 sec. and longer) to produce natural looking motion streaks, which follow the subject instead of preceding it. Some photographers also use rear sync for long exposures of static objects or people, moving the camera to produce interesting flash blur effects.

Motion Blur—how it works

In order to create realistic motion trails that follow the object, the flash must be fired in reverse of the action. If the flash is fired at the beginning of the action using standard front curtain sync, the 5D will record the "frozen" object at the beginning of its travel and then record the motion trail as time progresses. This captures the action but the motion trail will appear to be in front of the moving object. However, if the operation takes place in reverse, the camera will record the ambient light motion blur and then freeze the object at its most forward point of travel. Thus, the photo will appear natural, with the motion trail following the object. This technique can produce dramatic action shots so take the time to experiment with your camera and flash until the effects you want become second nature.

Wireless/Remote Flash

When you use one or more 5600HS(D) and/or 3600HS(D) flash units, you can take the accessory flash off-camera. There is no need to use a TTL connecting cable (wire) between the camera's hot shoe and the remote flash unit(s). The off-camera flash is triggered by a brief burst of light from the camera's built-in flash. Metering control is TTL, making it quite easy to get good exposures without any calculations.

This is a valuable technique that deserves detailed consideration, so it's discussed in a separate section later in this chapter (see page 189).

Modifying Flash Intensity

Regardless of the flash options or shooting techniques that you use, not all of your flash exposures will be perfect, technically or aesthetically. Some will exhibit more or less flash than you want for a certain subject or a specific situation. After taking any flash photo, review the image on the camera's LCD Monitor. If you would prefer more or less flash intensity, simply set flash exposure compensation or try using the camera's flash exposure bracketing feature.

Flash Exposure Compensation
Particularly in outdoor photography, you may find that you prefer a more subtle fill-flash effect than the system produces. If so, try setting a -1 flash exposure compensation factor in the Function sub-menu accessed with the Fn button. Then, re-shoot and you should be pleased with the more subtle flash effect. For more intense flash, sometimes necessary to correct for underexposure caused by a white subject or an extremely bright background, try a +1 flash exposure setting. The amount of compensation will vary based on the subject and your personal preferences.

Flash vs. Ambient Light Exposure Compensation

In some situations, you may want to use both flash exposure compensation (to adjust flash output) as well as ambient light exposure compensation. That technique might seem complicated but it's really quite straight forward if you understand the following concepts. Imagine two different types of scenes: a portrait setup in a dark basement and a portrait setup outdoors at the beach with a bright background of sand and surf.

Flash Photography in Low Light
The following concepts apply in dark locations when flash is the primary light source for a nearby subject but it does not illuminate a dark, more distant background.

The flash metering system will control the brightness of the nearby subject. The ambient light metering system will attempt to control the brightness of the background, but there are limits to what can be done with deep, dark backgrounds. For a brighter or darker rendition of the nearby subject, use flash exposure compensation; that feature will have no effect on the brightness of the more distant background.

For a brighter or darker rendition of the background (not illuminated by flash) set a plus or minus ambient light exposure compensation, but again, the camera can only do so much. That should have no effect on the subject if it is illuminated only by light from the electronic flash.

Flash Photography in Bright Light
The concept is similar in a bright outdoor location, but with a twist. In the beach scene, the portrait subject is not only illuminated by electronic flash, but also the sun is producing some of the light.

In this case when you use ambient light exposure compensation, it will have some effect on the brightness of the subject too. That's because flash is not the only light source. Flash exposure compensation will have no effect on the brightness of the distant background.

These concepts are important in serious flash photography when you want to adjust exposure for the subject or for the background, or for both. Experiment with simultaneous use of the camera's ambient light and flash exposure compensation features. Try different levels for each and check the resulting images on the camera's LCD Monitor. With some experience, you'll soon become adept at estimating what settings will produce the most accurate, or creatively pleasing, exposure for the subject and the background in flash photography.

High Speed Flash Sync

A feature that's available only with HS(D) series flash units, high-speed sync (HSS) allows the flash to sync at shutter speeds faster than the normal 1/160 second sync speed available in conventional flash photography.

When set on the flash unit, HSS will allow you to make flash photos at a shutter speed as fast as 1/4000 second. This can be useful when you want to photograph a nearby subject, in extremely bright light, at a very wide aperture, such as f/1.7 or f/2.8 available with some lenses. If you used conventional flash, at the conventional 1/160 second sync speed, the image might be over exposed. By making the photo with a faster sync speed, such as 1/500 second, correct exposure is assured.

To utilize this feature, attach a 5600HS(D) or 3600HS(D) flash unit to the camera's hot shoe and set the flash unit to the HSS mode. Note that HSS cannot be used when Rear flash sync is set on the camera.

Select the camera's Shutter Priority (S) mode and set a desired shutter speed, such as 1/500 second. Check the information on the flash unit's data panel as to flash range. If the range is not suitable for the camera-to-subject distance, select a different shutter speed and check the data panel again. Changing the camera's ISO setting also changes the flash range at any shutter speed.

Although you can select shutter speeds (sync speeds) as fast as 1/4000 second, you'll rarely need to use anything faster than about 1/500 second. That's because flash range reduces dramatically as you select faster shutter speeds. Unless you're using a very high ISO setting for extreme close-ups in very bright sunshine, a sync speed of 1/250 second to 1/500 second will often be perfect when shooting at very wide apertures.

Bounce Flash

Direct flash can often be harsh and unflattering, causing heavy shadows or a "deer in the headlights" appearance in your subject. Bouncing the flash changes the lighting angle, softens the light, and creates a more natural-looking effect.

Most compatible accessory flash units feature heads that are designed to swivel and tilt, allowing a shoe-mounted flash to be adjusted so it is not aimed directly at the subject. You can point the flash toward the ceiling or a wall to produce soft, shadowless lighting. However, the ceiling and walls must be white or neutral gray, or they may cause an undesirable color cast. Just make sure the flash range is sufficient to be reflected off the flat surface and still reach the subject.

Wireless/Remote Flash

Wireless/Remote Flash can produce flash photos with professional lighting effects. You can take advantage of this feature if you own an accessory 5600HS(D) or 3600HS(D) flash unit.

Remove the hot shoe cap and mount an accessory flash unit in the camera's hot shoe. Turn on the 5D and the flash unit. Select *Wireless* from the *Flash mode* option in the camera's Recording Menu 2 ✿2.

Remove the flash unit. Raise the camera's built-in flash to activate it and position the camera and the accessory flash as desired around the subject. To use more than one accessory flash in wireless/remote operation, simply repeat the process above with each unit.

Flash Range

It's important to position the remote flash unit so it's not too close to, or too far from, the subject. When using a standard—not high-speed—flash sync speed, the following range applies: At ISO 100 and f/5.6, the range will be 1 to 5 meters or 3.3 to 16.4 feet. There is no value in using higher ISO settings for greater flash range because the camera and flash must be within 5 meters or 16.4 feet of the subject.

Wireless/Remote Flash Techniques

When the accessory flash unit is charged and ready, its AF illuminator lamp blinks twice, indicating that you can take the photo. The built-in flash will fire a low intensity burst, just enough to trigger the remote flash but not enough to light the subject. You can use high-speed flash sync, if desired, as long as the remote flash unit is quite close to the subject. (Flash range is low when a high sync speed, such as 1/500 sec., is used.)

Initially, practice with a single remote flash unit. If you own two HS(D) flash units, try more advanced setups with one illuminating the subject and the other illuminating the background. Just make sure that both remote units maintain line of sight with the on-camera flash. To be certain, use the test fire procedure.

Note: When you return to conventional flash photography, do not use the camera's wireless flash mode. Select one of the other flash modes in the camera's Recording menu 2 📷2 . If you forget to do so, flash exposures may be incorrect.

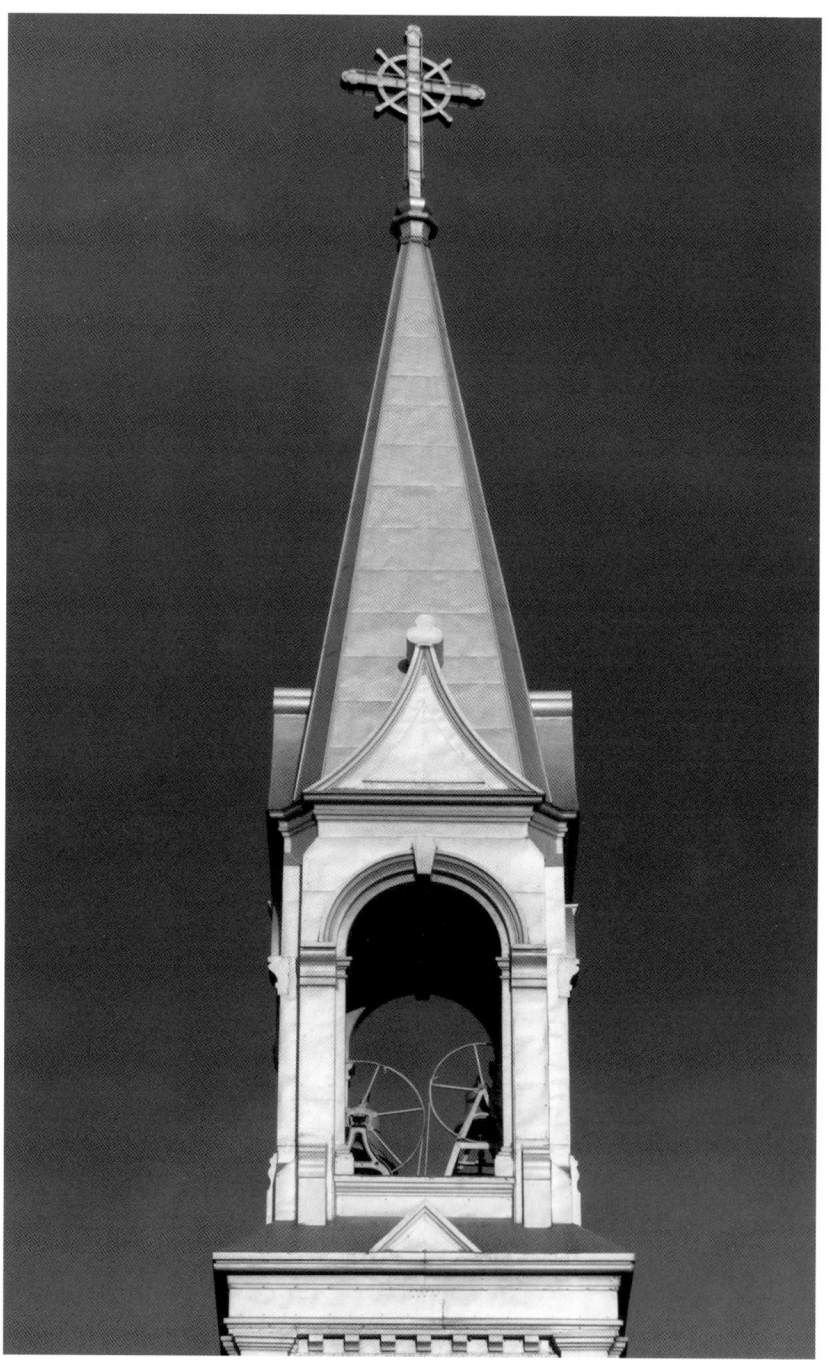

Lenses and Accessories

The first commercially viable 35mm autofocus SLR camera, the Maxxum/Dynax 7000, was introduced in 1985 with several autofocus lenses. Since that time, the company has released numerous other lenses. Every one of the current and discontinued Maxxum/Dynax lenses are fully compatible with the digital 5D. (The Anti-Shake function will not operate with the 16mm f/2.8 Fisheye and the 3x–1x Zoom f/1.7–2.8 Macro, but they're compatible with the camera in other respects.) Over 40 lenses are currently available, including many in the D-type series. The D denotes a distance-encoding device (in the lens barrel) that allows the camera to make improved calculation for flash exposure (ADI) when using the built-in flash or an accessory D-series Program flash.

Effective Focal Lengths

Because the 5D's CCD sensor is smaller than a 35mm film frame, the effective focal length of any lens used on the 5D is increased by 1.5x when compared to the same lens used on a 35mm camera. (The sensor measures 23.5 x 15.7 mm, while a 35mm film frame is 24 x 36 mm in size.) The smaller sensor actually produces a field-of-view crop: any lens used with a smaller sensor produces a narrower field of view than it does with a 35mm camera.

A telephoto zoom allows you to crop tightly without moving. This image was made at a 200mm zoom setting, providing a 35mm format effective focal length of 300mm.

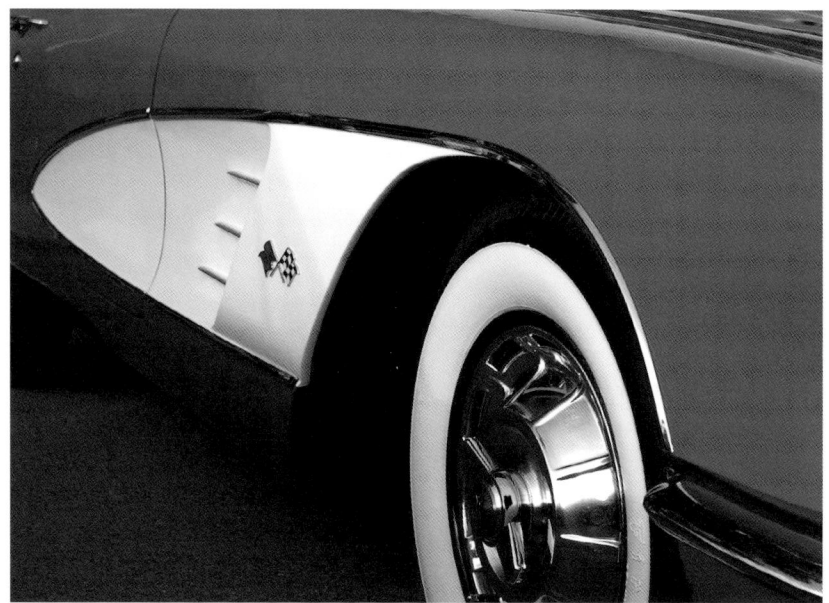

Even a modest zoom, such as the 18-70mm DT lens, provides versatility and is useful for filling the frame with a small subject area.

If you are used to shooting with a 35mm SLR, to get an idea of the field of view a lens will produce, simply multiply the focal length by 1.5. For example, images made with a 20mm lens on the 5D will look like images made with a 30mm focal length on a 35mm camera. A 300mm telephoto produces the view that we would expect from a 450mm lens.

That's great news if you appreciate sports and wildlife photography, where even a moderate telephoto lens can produce frame-filling images of distant subjects. But it's less than ideal if you prefer ultra wide-angle landscape or travel photography, with images that include vast scenic vistas. Fortunately, Konica Minolta has started making lenses with shorter focal lengths, such as the AF DT 11–18mm f/4.5–5.6

D zoom, that produces the view that 35mm film photographers would expect from a 16.5–27mm zoom. In future, expect to see additional lenses with short focal lengths for ultra wide-angle photography with the 5D.

The following discussion of different focal-lengths will tell you what to expect on your 5D camera.

Normal Lenses

Technically, the focal length of a normal lens corresponds to the diagonal of the format. With 35mm film, this measurement would be exactly 43.3 mm, but, for design reasons, most normal lenses for 35mm SLRs are about 50mm. With the 5D, a focal length of about 35mm would generally be considered a normal lens.

Subjects in the camera's viewfinder, with a normal lens mounted, usually appear about the same size as they appear to the naked eye. For most amateur photographers, a normal lens is adequate for many subjects, as long as you can get close enough to (or far enough away from) your subject. However, if you want to achieve a closer view without moving physically closer to your subject, for example for a portrait or to photograph a horse in a field, you will need to use longer lenses. Conversely, if you want to photograph a sweeping vista or a group of people inside a small room, a shorter focal length will give you a wider field of view.

Telephoto Lenses

Lenses with focal lengths that are greater than a normal lens are called telephotos. In the case of the 5D, this would be any lens with a focal length greater than the 35mm. These lenses, often referred to as "long lenses,"allow us to bring a distant subject "closer," which is great for sports and wildlife photography.

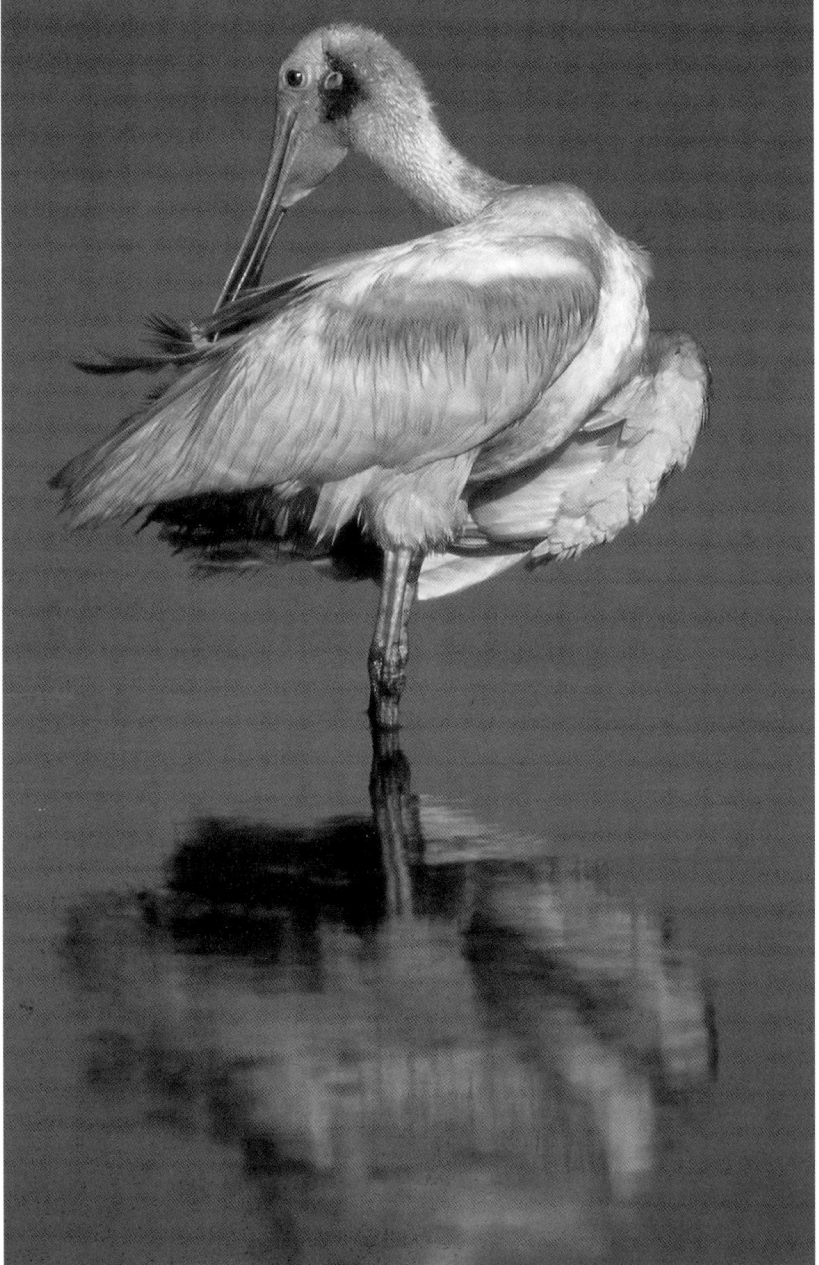

Telephoto lenses have some other interesting characteristics. The longer the focal length, the more obvious these characteristics are. Long lenses compress perspective, reducing the apparent distance between objects in a scene. This is useful for creating interesting effects such as compressing many blossoms into a single frame for a unity of design, stacking near and distant hills in haze, or making a traffic-filled city street look especially congested.

The narrow angle of view of a telephoto lens often limits the number of components that will be included in the image, eliminating clutter. In high magnification photography, depth of field is very shallow, so only the focused plane is sharp; that's useful for blurring away a distracting background. This makes a telephoto lens an excellent tool for making a subject "pop."

Short Telephoto Lenses
Short telephoto lenses (from 35mm through about 80mm on the 5D) are less expensive, faster, and lighter than longer ones. With the 5D's smaller sensor, they will give you quite a bit of reach. This type of lens allows you to capture a subject from a certain distance and, due to its often faster speed (wider maximum aperture), can be useful in low light. In fact, if you own a collection of lenses from the Maxxum 35mm camera series, a normal 50mm lens placed on the 5D will be a good portrait lens (short telephoto) because it is fast and has an effective focal length of 75mm. This is a suitable focal length for a head-and-shoulders portrait and the wide maximum aperture (often f/1.7) will be a benefit in existing-light portraiture.

Long focal lengths (400mm equivalent in this case) provide a narrow angle of view that can be used to isolate your subject in a scene, such as this Roseatte Spoonbill preening in a nesting area.

In any event, these shorter lenses remain the most universally used telephotos. They are recommended for portraits because they deliver a sharp image of a person from 6-12 feet away. By focusing on the eyes, you can take maximum advantage of the shallow depth of field at larger apertures. This brings the focus of attention to the face and head.

These lenses are also useful for some sporting and school events, for street and travel photography, and for photographing artworks in your home. They effectively magnify your subject while offering the ability to take handheld shots.

Classic Telephoto Focal Lengths

This classic range is from about 90mm to 200mm, equivalent to the popular 35mm telephoto lens range of 135mm to 300mm. The wide apertures (available on many telephotos in this range) are great for fast autofocus (with lots of light to the sensor) and for making images with shallow depth of field.

Such focal lengths are ideal for candid shots of children and render excellent compressed portraits. If you can get physically close to animals (at the zoo or around the house), a 200mm or 300mm focal length will work well. However, compared to super telephoto lenses, they are not recommended for wildlife and sporting events where you will be at a substantial distance from your subjects.

Lenses of 300mm or longer on the 5D are recommended for photographers specializing in sports or wildlife photography and shooting from a distance. These lenses effectively move your view much closer to your subjects and allow for creative shots, using the compressed perspective. The increased subject magnification and size of these lenses can often lead to camera shake, but the 5D's Anti-Shake system can be helpful in reducing this risk.

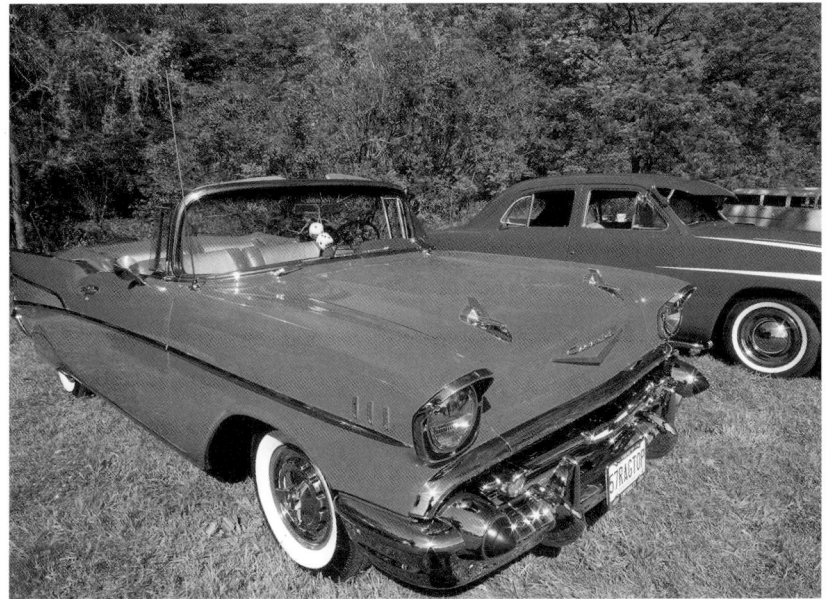

With up to a 104° field of view, Konica Minolta's AF DT 11-18mm f/4.5-5.6 zoom is the perfect choice for wide-angle shots such as this study of a 1957 Chevy.

Wide-Angle Lenses

Wide-angle lenses produce a wide field of view and "expanded spatial perspective." Foreground elements become prominent while more distant objects are "pushed back," rendered smaller than the eye perceives. You can exploit this trait with a variety of subject matter, including cramped interiors, yachts at a marina, or land and cityscapes. Depth of field is also extensive, so an entire vista can be rendered in reasonably sharp focus at any aperture.

If you own a lens around 18–20mm, it will offer a wide, but not extreme, view of your subject, which is often ideal for point-and-shoot photography. This lens will also produce greater depth of field than a 35mm "normal" lens.

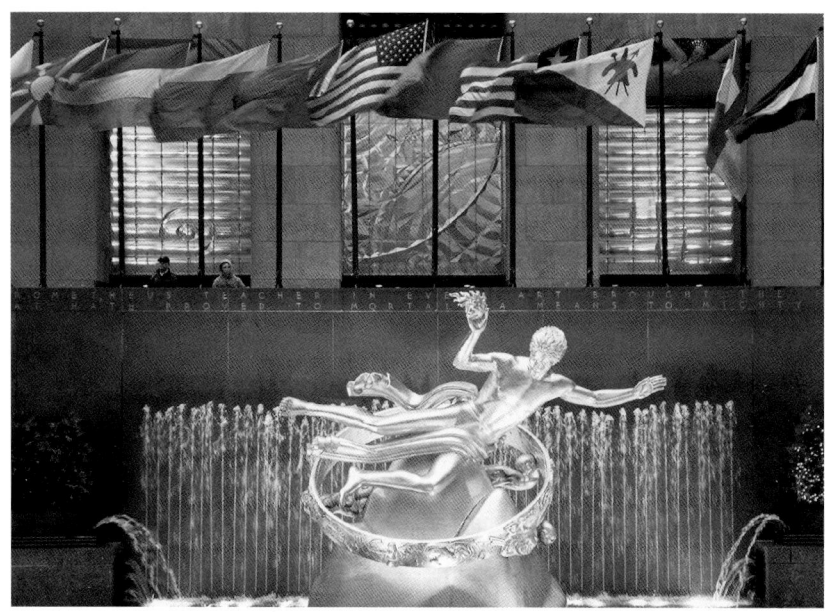

A lens with a very wide maximum aperture (such as f/1.7 or f/2.8) can be valuable in low light for faster shutter speeds without the need to use a tripod, electronic flash, or extremely high ISO levels.

Compared to normal lenses, wide angles offer greater depth of field, which enhances perceived sharpness throughout the scene. For instance, since the depth of field with a 28mm lens is 6.6 feet to infinity at f/8, you will rarely need to pause to focus your shots. (This depends on the focused distance, so refer to the lens' depth-of-field table, or scale, to set the distance to maximize this feature.) So, if you are in a situation where you want to quickly shoot spontaneous shots, such as a sporting event, you can turn off the AF feature and shoot faster using the 28mm lens. This lens, with its long depth of field, is also ideal for landscapes and architectural shots.

When trying to fit as much of a scene into your picture as possible, or while working in limited space, an even wider angle may be a better choice. That's why Konica Minolta developed the 11–18mm zoom, providing a 16.5–27mm equivalent focal length.

Understanding the Fine Points of Lenses

Composed of various types of multiple elements, lenses focus light rays on a common point: a sensor in a digital camera or film in a conventional camera. But lenses have several other essential functions. They control the amount of light that will make an exposure (depending on f/stop selected), the range of acceptable sharpness within a scene (depth of field), the exact point in sharpest focus, the subject magnification, the angle of view (the amount of any scene which will be included in the image) and the apparent perspective.

Large vs. Small Maximum Apertures

Some lenses feature a large maximum aperture such as f/2.8, while others have smaller maximum apertures such as f/5.6. Many zoom lenses have variable maximum apertures. For example, the AF 100–400mm f/4.5–6.7 zoom has a fairly large maximum aperture of f/4.5 at its short end that diminishes gradually as you zoom to longer focal lengths. By about the 320mm setting, the maximum aperture is a mere f/6.7.

A lens with a large maximum aperture (called a "fast" lens) such as f/2.8 has benefits over one with a small maximum aperture (called a "slow" lens) such as f/5.6. Most importantly, a large aperture allows the camera to set a faster shutter speed. That can reduce the risk of blur from camera shake or subject movement. With a fast lens, there's less need to use high ISO settings to get the faster shutter speeds, so digital noise will be less prominent in the images.

The trade-off however is significant: a fast lens is much larger and heavier than a slow lens and it's also a lot more expensive. That's why most lenses (in all brands of camera systems) feature moderately small to very small maximum apertures; these types outsell large aperture lenses by a very wide margin.

Hint: If you want a compact, lightweight and affordable "fast" lens, check out the Konica Minolta AF 50mm f/1.7. (In most countries, it sells for less than the equivalent of $100(US) or 100 Euros.) The incredibly large maximum aperture of f/1.7 will allow you to shoot in low light and its 75mm effective focal length is great for portraits.

When zoom lenses first came on the market, they were not close to a single-focal-length lens in sharpness, color rendition, or contrast. Today, you can get superb image quality from either type. Zooms are certainly versatile, but they do have some limitations when compared to lenses with a single focal length.

The most important drawback to zoom lenses is smaller maximum aperture(s). Except for a few "fast" (f/2.8) professional models, most zooms are "slow" , featuring small maximum apertures. Consequently, you'll need to use a higher ISO setting for a fast shutter speed, and the images may exhibit more visible digital noise.

Note: Small maximum aperture is less relevant when shooting with the 5D, at least in terms of the shutter speeds required to prevent blur from camera shake. When using the Anti-Shake function, there is less need for fast shutter speeds than with other cameras. Still, in dark locations, and in action photography, the faster shutter speeds available when using a "fast" lens are certainly beneficial.

A few zooms do feature a large maximum aperture of f/2.8, but the longest focal length available is 200mm (the AF D 70–200mm f/2.8 APO G SSM zoom). If you need a longer lens with a large maximum aperture, you would need to buy one with a fixed focal length such as 200mm or 300mm (both available in f/2.8 and f/4 versions) or a 600mm (f/4) super telephoto. For most photo enthusiast, such lenses are prohibitively expensive and excessively large and heavy. Consequently, the "slower" zoom lenses (such as the f/4.5–5.6 models) are most popular.

The best feature of a zoom lens is versatility. A single zoom can replace four or five other lenses, making for greater convenience and portability. While a fixed focal length lens may produce higher optical quality, the mid to higher priced Konica Minolta Maxxum/Dynax zooms also produce images with very high resolution and sharpness. If you must have a fast zoom, check out one of the f/2.8 models. Granted, their price, size, and weight will be higher. And if you decide to stick with single-focal-length lenses, do so as an educated consumer and not because of some old horror stories about the inherently poor quality of zoom lenses.

High Tech Glass
Some telephoto and zoom lenses are designated as APO (apochromatic), indicating that they incorporate special glass elements ("low dispersion" or "anomalous dispersion"). These modify the way that light rays are bent, producing superior color rendition as well as higher sharpness across the entire image frame. The benefits are most obvious in images made at large apertures and long focal lengths.

An increasing number of wide-angle lenses (primarily zooms) incorporate element(s) with a non-spherical surface. Such "Aspherical" lenses boast reduced flare, more consistent sharpness across the frame at large apertures, and less bending of straight lines near the edges of the image. A single aspherical element can take the place of two conventional elements, reducing size and weight of the lens.

Ultrasonic Focusing Motor
Konica Minolta lenses designated as SSM incorporate an ultrasonic focus motor, called Supersonic-Wave by the company. The primary advantages are quieter operation and excellent starting/stopping response. The SSM lenses also include two Direct Manual Focus (DMF) modes useful with other Maxxum/Dynax cameras: Standard DMF and the newer full-time DMF. That feature allows for manual focus adjustment (while in autofocus mode) at any time, with any Maxxum/Dynax camera, even if the AF system has not yet acquired focus.

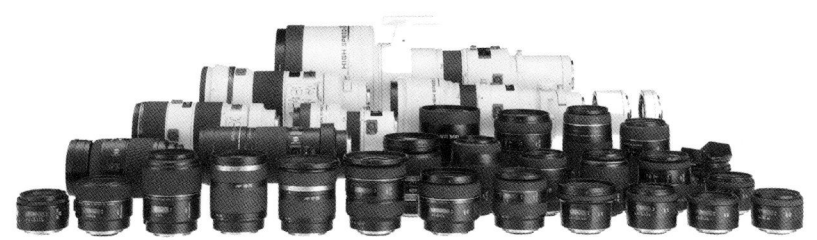

The 5D is compatible with every Konica Minolta autofocus lens (in Maxxum/Dynax mount) ever made. Photo © Konica Minolta.

ADI Compatibility

The D-series Konica Minolta lenses incorporate a distance encoding chip that is required for full compatibility with ADI (Advanced Distance Integration) flash metering. This metering system is less influenced by subjects of high reflectance (such as a bride in a white gown) or low reflectance (such as groomsmen in black tuxedos). By combining subject distance into the equation for a correct flash exposure, the ADI system can produce better results when using the built-in flash or a D-series Program flash. (When a conventional Konica Minolta lens is used, the camera employs the older, conventional Pre-Flash TTL flash metering system.)

Close Focusing

Many Konica Minolta telephoto zoom lenses allow for close focusing in order to render a small subject about 1/4 life-size on the image sensor, also called 0.25x magnification or a 1:4 reproduction ratio. The true macro lenses in the line provide a full life-size rendition (1x magnification, or 1:1 reproduction ratio) at the closest focusing distance. At 1x magnification, a honey bee will be exactly bee sized in the digital image, without the need for magnification on a monitor.

The macro lenses are available in 50mm, 100mm, and 200mm focal lengths. The longer Macro lenses are most useful in nature photography because they provide high magnification without the need to move extremely close to a skittish subject, such as a butterfly. For extremely high magnifi-

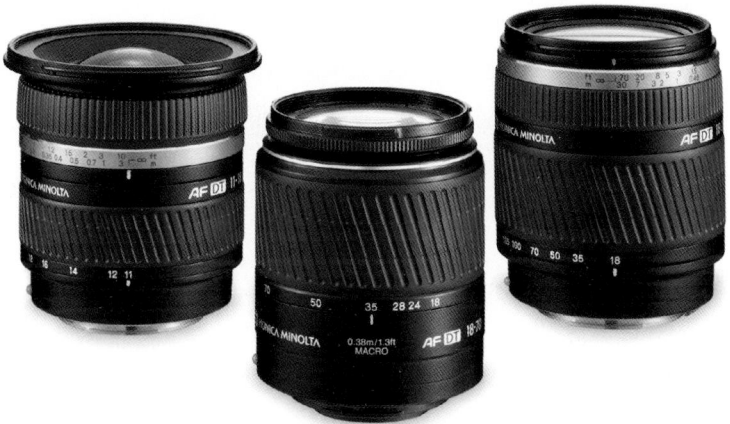

The DT series Maxxum/Dynax, lenses were designed exclusively for use with the Konica Minolta digital SLR cameras' smaller sensor. They are compact and are optimized for digital photography. Photo © Konica Minolta.

cation photography of inanimate objects, Konica Minolta makes the 3x–1x Zoom f/1.7–2.8; it's capable of any magnification from 1x to a full 3x; this is an expensive accessory intended for scientific applications.

Digital Optimization
Until 2004, all of the Konica Minolta lenses were designed for 35mm cameras. Although they are fully compatible with the digital camera, Konica Minolta has started optimizing their newest, short focal length lenses, for digital capture. The first zooms optimized for digital capture were the AF 17–35mm f/2.8–4 D and the 28–75mm f/2.8 D; since then, other "digitally optimized" lenses have been designed. These include three in the DT series, exclusively for use with Maxxum/Dynax D-SLR's: the 11–18mm, 18–70mm and 18–200mm zooms. (If a DT series zoom were used with a 35mm camera, the corners of the image would be black; that's because the smaller lenses do not project an adequately large image circle to fill the larger 35mm film frame.)

Digital optimization includes technology to minimize vignetting (darkening at the corners), maximize sharpness near the edges of the frame, and prevent internal reflections that can cause flare. Such steps are definitely valuable with wide-angle lenses used with digital cameras, especially at apertures larger than f/8. In future, expect to see a great emphasis on digital optimization—and an increasing number of "digital only" DT lenses—in news items about Konica Minolta products.

Selecting a Lens

Think hard about your specific photographic needs before spending money on lenses, and then choose ones that meet those needs. This seems obvious, but many enthusiasts will buy a lens based on what they see a professional using, or what their friends have. The focal length and design of a lens will have a huge affect on how you photograph. The right lens will make photography a joy; the wrong one will make you leave the camera at home.

One approach for choosing a lens is to determine if you are frustrated with your current lenses. Do you constantly want to see more of the scene than the lens will allow? Then consider a wider-angle lens. Or maybe the subject is too small in your photos. Then look into acquiring a zoom or telephoto lens.

If you used your lenses on a Maxxum 35mm camera, you will quickly discover that these same lenses will have a different view on the 5D. Certain subjects lend themselves to specific focal lengths when using the 5D with 1.5x "extended lens focal length." Wildlife and sports action are best photographed using focal lengths of 300mm or more, although nearby action can be managed with 200mm. Portraits look great when shot with focal lengths between 60 and 90mm. Interiors often demand wide-angle lenses such as a 17–35mm zoom or a 20mm or 24mm lens. Many people also like wide-angles for landscapes, but telephotos can come in handy for distant scenes.

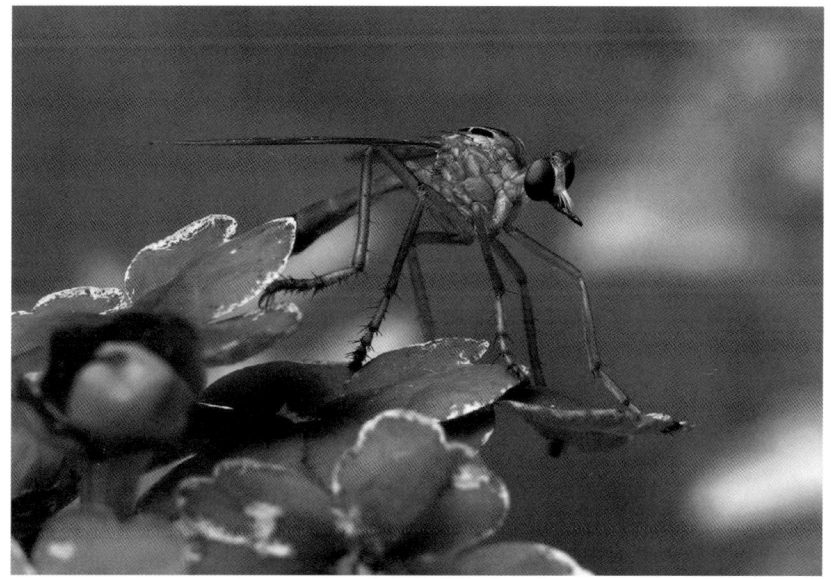

Getting close-up shots of insects and other subjects is a lot of fun. A number of lenses and accessories are available for close-up photography, including telephoto zooms, macro lenses, diopters, and extension tubes. Photo © David B. Williams.

Macro Accessories for Lenses

If you own a lens that does not allow for extremely close focusing, but you cannot justify the cost of a true Macro lens, check out two types of devices that are available.

Magnifying Filters

Resembling magnifying glass in a filter mount, a "close-up filter" or "plus diopter" is ideal for use with telephoto zoom lenses. Simply screw it into the front threads of the lens as you would with any type of filter. This type of accessory is not available from Konica Minolta but is sold under various names by manufacturers such as Raynox, Canon, and Nikon. For the best image quality, look for models that are "achromatic" (highly-corrected, multi-element lenses). Naturally, the better the zoom lens that you use, the higher the image quality will be in extremely close focusing.

Extension Tubes

Available from aftermarket manufacturers, extension tubes are mechanical devices without any optical elements. They fit between the lens and the SLR camera body, allowing a lens to focus much closer than it could normally. Automatic extension tubes (dedicated to Maxxum/Dynax cameras) are designed to work with all lenses for your 5D, but are most suitable for fixed focal length lenses.

Be aware that extension tubes do cause a light loss. The camera's light metering system compensates for this loss of light by selecting a longer shutter speed, but that can mean that you'll need to use a higher ISO setting for sharp pictures. Otherwise, you may get images that are blurred by camera shake or by subject motion. Remember that you need to use a shutter speed of at least 1/250 second to "freeze" the swaying of a flower moved by a light breeze.

Hint: Though relatively expensive, true macro lenses are a good investment for anyone who often needs extremely close focusing capability. Such lenses are designed for superb sharpness at all distances and will focus from mere inches to infinity. In addition, they are typically very sharp at all f/stops. If you do not often need that capability, buy a top quality close-up filter for a zoom lens or a 50mm extension tube for a fixed focal length lens.

Whether using a macro lens or accessories, depth of field is extremely shallow in close focusing. The range of acceptable sharpness may be only a centimeter or two. Anything outside the depth of field will be unsharp to some extent. Do not confuse this effect with poor optical quality. For greater depth of field, use a small aperture such as f/16. Focus manually, with extreme care, on the most important subject element: the eyes of an insect, for example. After taking a shot, review it on the LCD monitor, using the magnify feature; if the focus or depth of field is not correct, re-shoot after modifying focus or selecting a smaller aperture, such as f/22.

At extremely close focus, even the slightest camera movement or subject movement will produce an unsharp image, due to the higher magnification. Use a tripod and an ISO setting that will provide a moderately fast shutter speed of at least 1/125 second, or 1/250 second if a breeze is blowing the subject. Or shoot early in the morning, before the wind picks up.

Other Lens Accessories

Several other types of lens accessories are available, and each type can be useful for specific purposes.

Teleconverters
A small optical device that fits between the camera and a lens, a teleconverter increases the effective focal length of a telephoto lens. The current Konica Minolta 1.4x II APO[HS] and 2x II APO[HS] converters are compatible with all Konica Minolta single focal length APO G lenses from 200mm to 600mm, increasing their effective focal length by 1.4x and 2x, respectively. Do note however that these accessories are not compatible with zoom lenses. A teleconverter is not inexpensive, but if you already own one of the compatible lenses, it can allow you to take frame-filling shots of more distant subject without the massive investment that would be required to buy a super telephoto lens.

Any teleconverter causes some loss of light. Less light will reach the camera's CCD sensor. The camera's light metering system compensates for this loss of light, but you may need to use a higher ISO setting for sharp pictures. Otherwise, you may get images that have less depth of field, are blurred by camera shake, or by subject motion.

Protective Filters
Many amateur photographers buy haze or skylight filters to protect the front lens element from scratches. After all, a filter is a lot less expensive to replace than a damaged lens element. A protective filter can also be useful when photo-

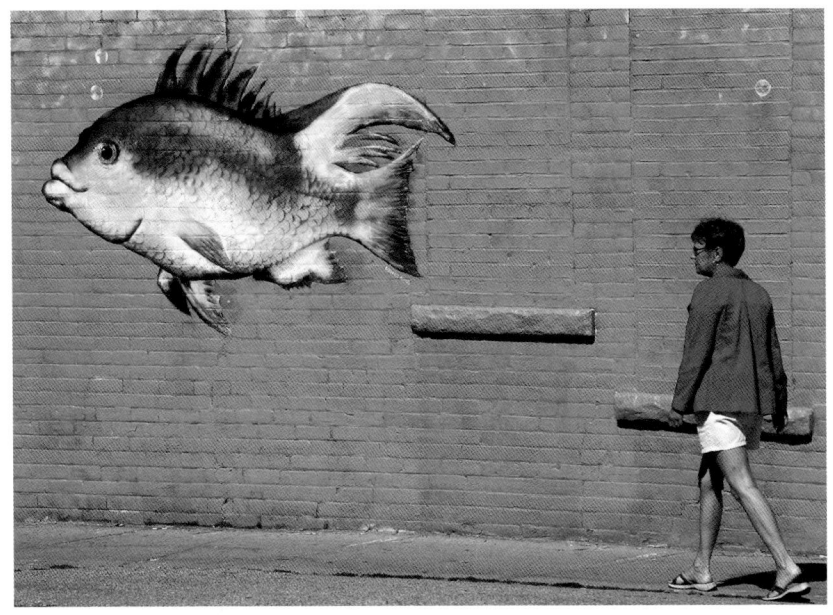

Polarizers are useful in outdoor photography anytime you want to reduce glare and reflections from non-metallic subjects.

graphing under such conditions as strong wind, rain, blowing sand, or going through brush. If you do use a filter for lens protection, a high quality filter is best, preferably one that is multi-coated to reduce light loss and flare. An inexpensive filter can degrade the image quality. Remember that the manufacturer made the lens/sensor combination with very strict tolerances. Remove any filter when shooting toward the sun to minimize the risk of flare.

Graduated Filters

Because the color balance of an image can be adjusted in camera and fine-tuned afterwards in a computer, digital camera owners rarely need the color balancing filters used by film photographers. There is one useful filter however, called a graduated neutral density filter, or ND grad. Half of the glass is clear while the other half is dark (gray.) It is used especially in landscape or cityscape photography to reduce bright areas (such as sky) in tone, while not affecting darker areas (such as the ground).

Some computer software program's can mimic the filter's affects, but you may not be able to recreate the scene you wanted. An ND grad filter is most convenient to use when it comes in a rectangular sheet; mount it in a filter holder designed for such filters and you can move it up and down until the center lines up with the horizon in the scene.

Polarizing Filters

I strongly recommend one filter for every photographer: the circular polarizer, preferably a multi-coated model of high optical quality. By blocking polarized light that's reflected from water droplets and particles in the air, this accessory can deepen the tone of a blue sky for more pleasing photos. But a polarizer can also reduce glare from non-metallic subject surfaces for richer, more saturated colors.

Note: There are two types of polarizers, "circular" and "linear." They look identical and produce the same result but use different technology. The 5D requires a circular polarizer for correct exposure and accurate autofocus.

As you rotate the polarizer, watch the effect—richer sky colors for example—through the camera's viewfinder. A polarizer is not always effective because it works best when the sun is at a 90 degree angle to your position. If the sun is directly behind you, or if you are shooting directly into the light, a polarizer won't have any effect. But if the sun is to the side, or directly overhead, the filter will work its magic effectively. It will remove annoying glare, make pale blue skies an azure blue, cut through haze for sharper pictures, and saturate colors for a rich, striking effect

While a polarizer cannot turn a grey sky blue, this filter is useful even on overcast days. In such conditions, every leaf, blade of grass, and wet stone reflects some dull, grey light from the overcast sky. These reflections mute the colors significantly, producing a "muddy" effect. Try shooting a scene with and without the polarizer and you will often see an amazing difference in the images.

Camera Support Accessories

If you want to get the most from your Maxxum/Dynax camera and lenses, be aware that camera movement can affect sharpness significantly, causing image blurring. While the Anti-Shake system allows us to use longer shutter speeds in hand-held shooting, it cannot perform miracles. Especially with telephoto lenses and in macro focusing, a rigid tripod can be an essential accessory when you cannot use very fast shutter speeds. By holding the camera/lens rock steady, it can assure razor sharp images, an important consideration especially if you want to print your images in large sizes.

Hint: When the camera is mounted on a tripod, consider using an accessory cable release to trip the shutter without jarring the camera. Two Konica Minolta accessories are available: Remote Cord RC-1000S and Remote Cord RC-1000L. You can also prevent blur from camera shake by using the camera's self-timer with the 2-second delay, although that technique does not allow for taking a shot at the perfect instant in sports and wildlife photography.

Tripods are the best known aid, but beanbags, monopods, mini-tripods, shoulder stocks, and clamps can be useful too. Many photographers carry a small beanbag or a clamp pod with their camera equipment for those situations where the camera needs support but a tripod isn't practical. Check your local camera store for the variety of equipment available. A good tripod is an excellent investment. A cheap tripod can actually be wobbly and cause more problems than it solves. When buying a tripod, extend it all the way to see how easy it is to open, then lean on it to see how stiff it is. Both aluminum and carbon-fiber tripods offer great rigidity. Carbon-fiber is much lighter, but also a lot more expensive.

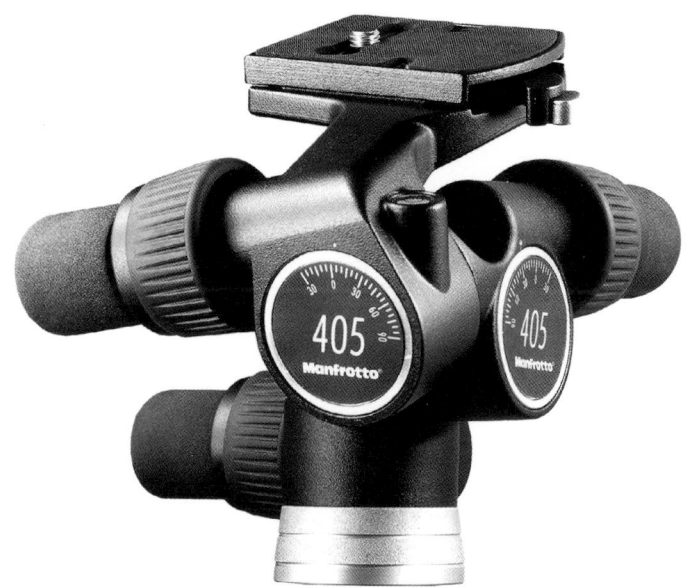

A rigid tripod deserves a solid head that will maintain stability while providing full versatility in camera positioning. This is a high-quality head that offers gear-controlled movement and a quick release feature that lets you easily secure and remove the camera. Photo © Bogen Imaging.

The tripod head is an important consideration and may be sold separately. There are two basic types for still photography: the ball head (my favorite) and the pan-and-tilt head. Both designs are capable of solid support. The biggest difference between them is how you loosen the controls and adjust the camera. Try both and see which seems to work better for you. Be sure to do this with a camera on the tripod because that added weight changes how the head works.

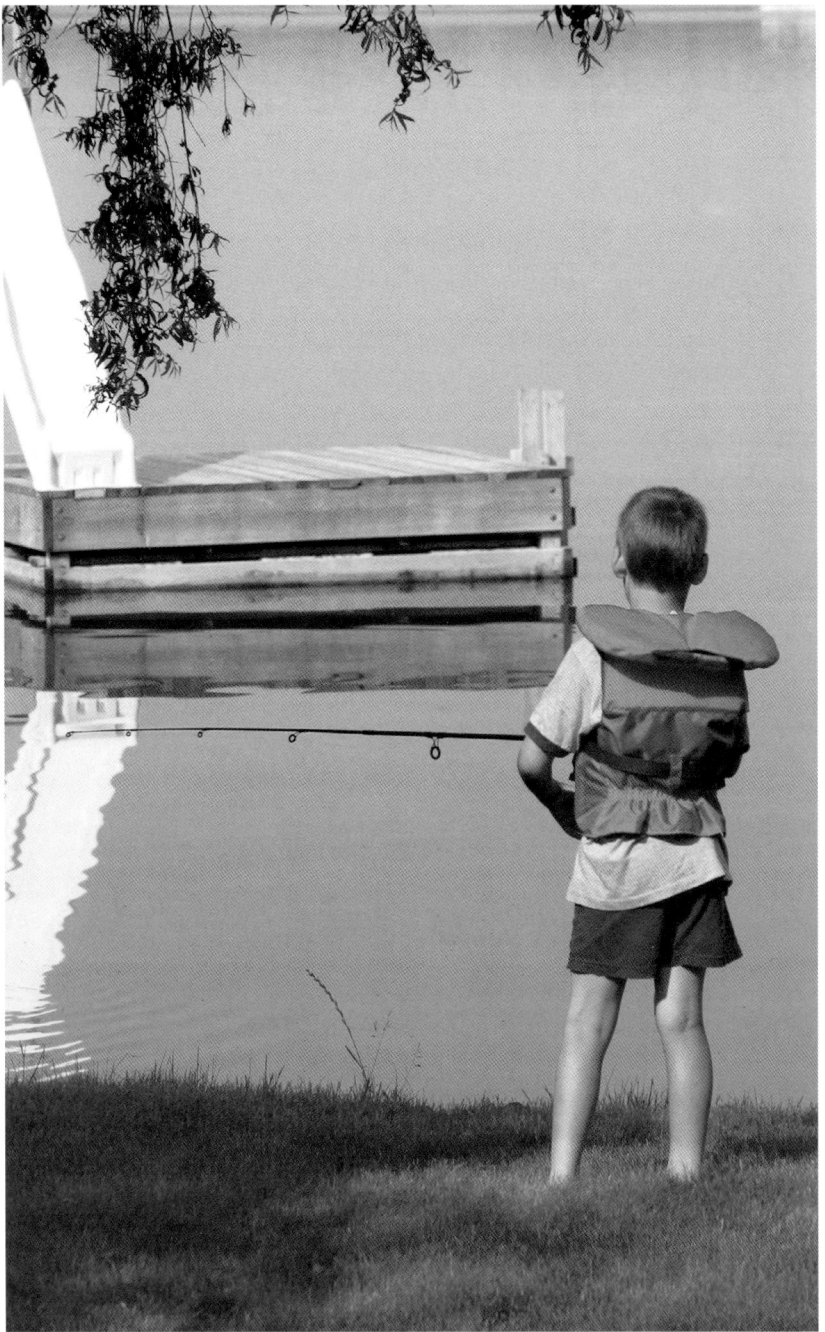

Working With Images

Taking great pictures with your Maxxum 5D/Dynax 5D is only the first part of the digital photography and imaging process. Subsequent parts include downloading the images to a computer, converting/enhancing RAW files with special software, filing your photos for easy recovery, enhancing them with image-processing programs, making prints, and so on.

Image Data

In addition to the photos that are captured by the camera, a wealth of other information is recorded, including the camera settings that were used as well as instructions for printing pictures. This data is stored in the Exchangeable Image File Format (EXIF—often called Metadata, a generic term). Some of this data will be used by the printer in direct printing, as discussed on pages 226-228.

The information that's embedded with the image file includes: date and time of recording, aperture, shutter speed, ISO, operating mode, exposure metering mode, lens focal length, white balance setting, color mode, exposure compensation or flash exposure compensation that was used, overrides for color saturation, contrast, hue, or sharpness, and so on.

◁ *The 5D records a wealth of image information, including the date and time the picture was taken as well as such camera settings as f/stop, shutter speed, ISO, white balance, and focal length. This data can be extremely useful in helping you understand the photographic results you get with your 5D.*

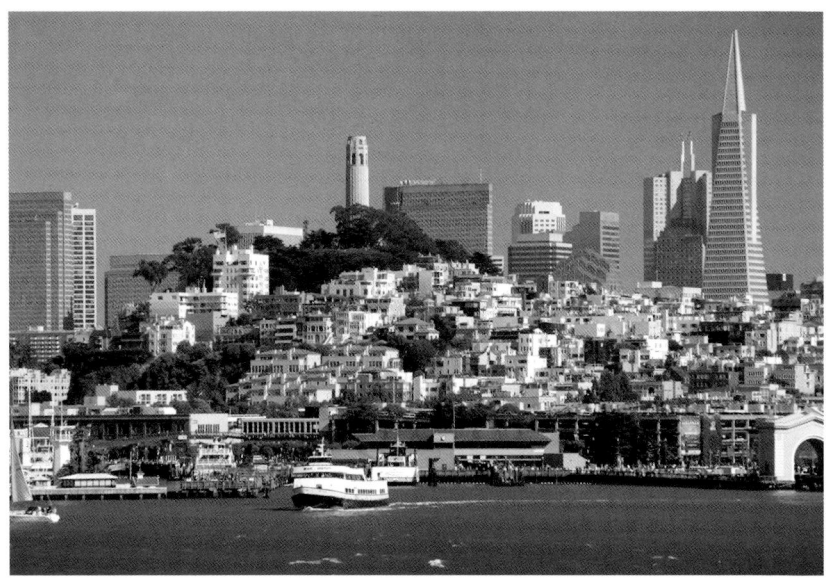

You can use a card reader to download image files from your memory card, or you can download and even print photos directly from your 5D by plugging the camera into your computer's or printer's USB port with the cord supplied with the camera.

You can examine some of the EXIF data on the LCD monitor, or you can review all of it using the DiMAGE MasterLite or other image-browsing or enhancing software in your computer. It's worth occasionally checking all of the data as a reminder of the camera settings that you used. Compare pictures and data to learn more about exposure, depth of field, the depiction of motion, flash exposure, and so on.

Downloading Images

There are two main ways of getting digital files off the memory card and into your computer. One is to use an accessory called a card reader that reads and copies the data on the card. Another is to download images directly from the memory card in the camera using a USB cable (included when you purchased the 5D). Direct downloading eliminates the need to buy a card reader but it has several disadvantages. For one, the camera generally downloads slowly. Plus, the camera has to be unplugged after each use, while you leave a card reader attached all the time. Finally, downloading directly from the camera also consumes a great deal of battery power, which is one argument for using optional AC Adapter AC-11.

Memory Card Reader
A memory card reader is a simple desktop device that plugs into your computer either using USB or FireWire connection. This accessory can be purchased for use with only one particular type of memory card, or as a multi-format reader that is able to accept several different kinds of cards. The latter can be useful if you own another digital camera that uses a memory card different than CF, or if you also use SD memory cards in your 5D, employing the SD to Compact-Flash Adapter SD-CF 1 available from Konica Minolta.

After you have plugged the card reader into your computer, remove the memory card from your camera and put it into the appropriate slot. The card will often appear as an additional drive on Windows XP and Mac OS IX and X operating systems (for other operating systems you will have to install the drivers that come with the card reader). Select your files from the card reader and drag them to a preferred computer drive and folder.

PCMCIA Card
If you use a laptop computer, you may prefer an alternative to the card reader, especially when traveling. Buy a Compact-Flash PC card adapter, also called PCMCIA card (Personal Computer Memory Card International Association). This device is compatible with any laptop's PC card slot. Insert the memory card into the CompactFlash PC card adapter. Then, insert the adapter into your laptop's PC card slot. The computer will recognize this as a new drive, and then you can drag and drop images from the card to the desired folder in your computer's hard drive.

Hint: Most PC card adapters use the 16-bit standard, but several companies make 32-bit PC card adapters, sometimes called Cardbus 32 Adapters. These can take advantage of internal bus speeds that can be four-to-six times faster. The 32-bit accessory costs three or four times more, but it's great when you have large image files to download to a laptop computer.

Direct from the Camera

To download from the camera, instead of using a card reader or PCMCIA card accessory, proceed as follows:

Make sure to use a fully charged battery or plug in the optional AC Adapter AC-11. While the 5D is off, insert the memory card into its slot. Turn the camera on to make sure that the *Transfer Mode* option in Setup Menu 1 is set for *Data storage* (see page 116). Now, be sure to turn the camera off before taking the next steps.

You must use a computer with a USB port and USB interface support. If your computer does not include USB connectivity, one must be installed; discuss this with a computer accessories retailer. For the latest computer operating system compatibility information, check www.konicaminolta.com, or www.konicaminoltasupport.com. If your computer uses Windows 98, you'll need to install the driver software that came with the camera; do this even if you have some other version of the camera software (from a DiMAGE camera kit) already installed.

Start the computer. Connect the small end of the USB cable that came with the 5D to the camera's USB port (under a cover at the top of the memory card-slot door on the right side of the camera). Attach the other (larger) end of the cable to the computer's USB port. (To prevent possible problems, do not attach to a USB hub.) Turn the camera on. A screen will appear on the LCD monitor confirming connection. Data transfer will then begin.

If you're using Windows XP or Mac OS X, a window may appear on your computer monitor; follow the instructions it provides. An icon should also appear designating the camera as a drive, for example, "Removable Disk (D:)." If the latter does not appear, disconnect the camera and start the process over.

Images are located in the DCIM folder. Double click on that to reveal the specific files in the folder. (The "Misc" folder contains data that may be required for DPOF printing, discussed later in this chapter.) Do not change the names of any folder or file. To copy images simply drag and drop the file icons to a location in your computer, such as "C: My Pictures." Be sure to specify *Copy* instead of *Move*.

Note: Image file names with an MRW suffix indicate RAW files. You can download these, but later you'll need to convert them to JPEG or (preferably) to TIFF using special software. (You can use the DiMAGE MasterLite that came with the camera, the optional DiMAGE Master, or another MRW-compatible RAW converter program.) A JPE or JPEG suffix indicates a JPEG image, which can be read by any imaging software. The suffix THM denotes small thumbnails of images generated by the camera.

Caution: *Never disconnect the camera or switch to a different memory car while the camera's red access lamp is lit. If you do, data will be lost and the memory card may be permanently damaged.*

After downloading is complete, the red lamp on the 5D stops lighting. Turn the camera off and disconnect the USB cable. If your Windows system requires that you first "*Stop Mass Storage Device,*" be sure to follow the "*Unplug*" or "*Eject*" hardware routine before unplugging the camera or switching to a new memory card. Start by clicking on the unplug or eject icon located in the task bar. Follow the procedure required to unplug or eject the pertinent device (camera) before unplugging it or removing the memory card and inserting a new card. If using a Mac computer, drag the mass storage device icon for the camera into the trash.

After that routine is completed, turn off the camera and unplug it. If you only want to switch to a new memory card, turn off the camera, change memory cards, and turn the camera on again to reestablish the USB connection.

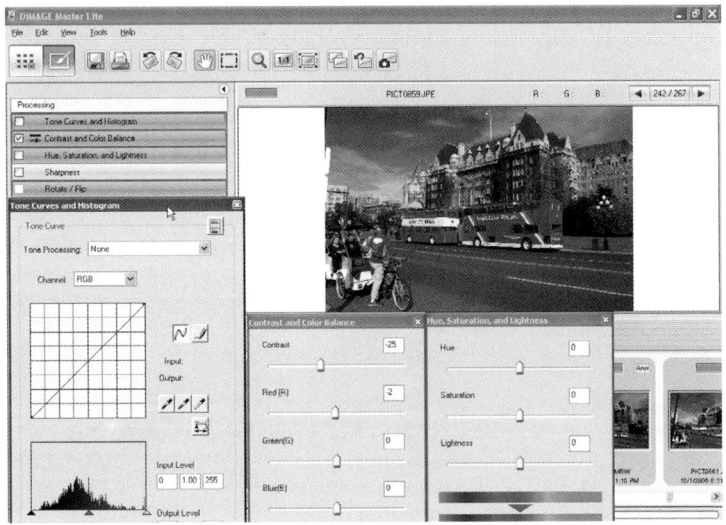

The DiMAGE MasterLite software is useful for adjusting your images and also allows you to convert MRW format files to JPEG or TIFF.

DiMAGE MasterLite Software

This is an uncomplicated program that includes a basic browser and a wide range of image adjustment options. (An instruction manual is included when you download the software to your computer from the Konica Minolta CD-ROM disc.) Full (EXIF) shooting data is displayed and a histogram display is available.

The software allows you to adjust, rotate, crop, and print your JPEG images. It's also designed for adjusting MRW files and converting them to JPEG or TIFF. DiMAGE MasterLite possesses a variety of tools for adjusting attributes such as sharpness, tone curves, brightness, contrast, color balance, hue, and saturation.

Converting RAW/MRW Files

Use DiMAGE MasterLite to enhance and convert your MRW file(s) to JPEG or TIFF (the usually preferred format). Important adjustments include color temperature (white balance), color balance, and exposure. Select the Preview option so you can see the effect of any changes that you make. Then experiment with the various tools until you get the color and exposure adjusted to your liking before converting the MRW file. Be aware that extensive adjustment is a slow process, because it takes several seconds for each change to be applied to the image.

Take care to avoid loss of important highlight or shadow detail. Set contrast, color saturation, and sharpness at fairly low levels because it's easier to boost these factors using image-processing software after you've converted from MRW than it is to tone down excessively high levels.

After the enhancement is finished, use DIMAGE MasterLite to convert the MRW file to TIFF (or JPEG) and save it in an appropriate file folder in your computer. Be sure to give each image a unique name, such as New_York_Dec_06 instead of using the camera assigned file name such as PICT0811. You can further process this newly converted image using your image-processing software. Select the 8-bit option unless you own a program with full support for 16-bit TIFF files.

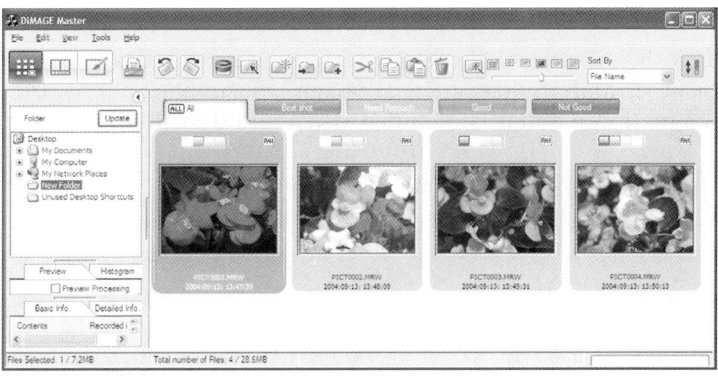

Available as an accessory, the DiMAGE Master software includes more options for adjusting MRW format files before conversion.

Note: Konica Minolta also offers an optional program, DiMAGE Master, designed to improve creative workflow for professional and advanced digital camera users. It's faster and provides extra functions, including advanced image adjustment and color management features.

Some other image-processing programs—including Adobe Photoshop CS2 and Elements 3.0 or 4.0—include MRW-format converters. These Adobe products are faster than DiMAGE MasterLite (adjustments take about one second. Before considering any aftermarket software, be sure to check that it is MRW compatible.

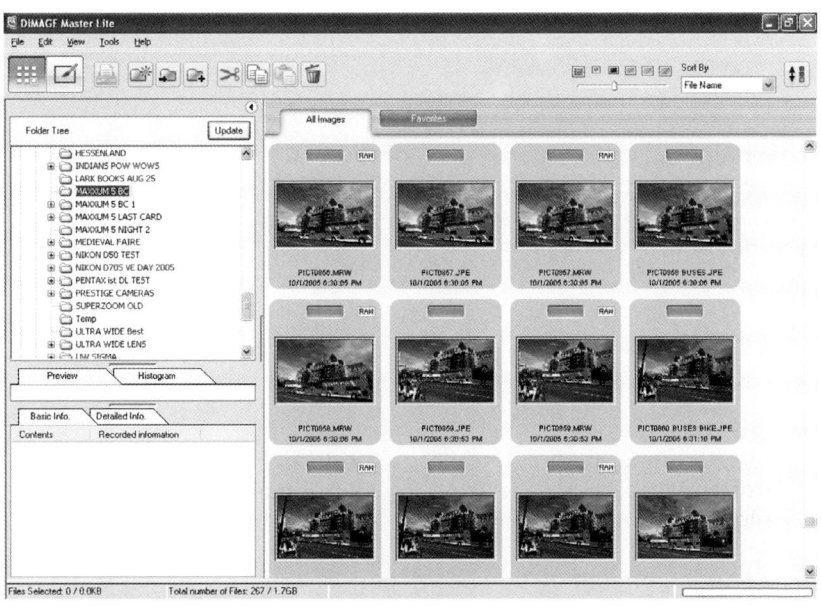

Though the browser in DiMAGE MasterLite software is not as versatile as many programs dedicated to browsing, it is compatible with MRW files.

Browser Programs

While DiMAGE MasterLite has a basic browser that can help organize photos, it's not as versatile as software specifically made for this purpose. The latest version of ACDSee is a superb program with a customizable interface and some unique characteristics, such as a calendar feature that lets you find photos by date. Another very good program with similar capabilities is CompuPic. And Digital PhotoPro was designed by professional photographers and includes some interesting pro features, like a magnifying digital "loupe."

Note: Not all browsers are compatible with MRW format and therefore may not allow you to view MRW files. Check the software distributor's web site for information about MRW file compatibility with the most recent version of their programs. Some of the latest browser programs may allow you to view MRW images made with your Maxxum 5D/Dynax 5D. However, they cannot convert the raw data. Do not attempt to open or to modify MRW-format files with any software that was not specifically designed for that purpose.

Most browser programs include some database functions (such as keyword searches) and work on both Windows and Mac platforms (although a recent version of ACDSee is only available for Windows). These programs allow you to quickly look at photos on your computer, rename photos one at a time or all at once, read all JPEG files, move photos from folder to folder, resize photos for e-mailing, create simple slideshows, and more.

An important function of a superior browser program is its ability to print customized index prints. You can then give a title to each of these index prints, and also list additional information such as the photographer's name and address, as well as the photo's file location. The index print serves as a hardcopy that can be used for easy reference (and visual searches). You might want to include an index print with every CD you burn so you can quickly reference what is on the CD and easily find the file you need. A combination of

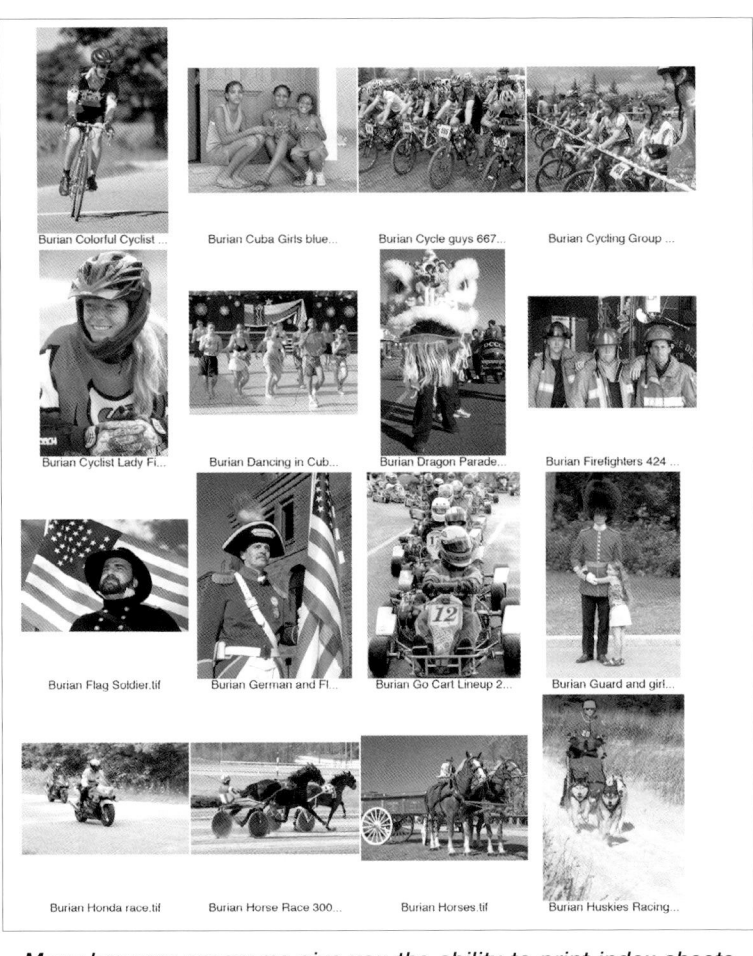

Burian Colorful Cyclist ...   Burian Cuba Girls blue...   Burian Cycle guys 667...   Burian Cycling Group ...

Burian Cyclist Lady Fi...   Burian Dancing in Cub...   Burian Dragon Parade...   Burian Firefighters 424 ...

Burian Flag Soldier.tif   Burian German and Fl...   Burian Go Cart Lineup 2...   Burian Guard and girl...

Burian Honda race.tif   Burian Horse Race 300...   Burian Horses.tif   Burian Huskies Racing...

Many browser programs give you the ability to print index sheets that show small-sized images of what is in a file or on a CD. These can be handy when you have a number of CDs or DVDs to sort through.

uniquely labeled file folders on your hard drive, a browser program, and index prints will help you to maintain a fast and easy way of finding and sorting images.

Enhancing Your Images

In addition to features for MRW file adjustment, the DiMAGE MasterLite software includes some image-enhancing tools for use on photos captured as JPEGs. After you become skilled at working with this easy-to-use software, consider upgrading to a full-featured program such as DiMAGE Master, or even a recent edition of Adobe Photoshop, Adobe Photoshop Elements, Jasc Paint Shop Pro, Microsoft Digital Image Suite, or Ulead PhotoImpact, to name a few.

The Adobe series of image-processing programs is the most popular among serious photo enthusiasts. If you believe that you'll want a professional version of Photoshop someday, you may want to start with Photoshop Elements. Many of the tools available in this user-friendly program are similar to those you'll find in the more expensive professional version, Photoshop CS2.

Image Cataloging

How do you edit and file your digital images so that they are accessible and easy to use? To start, it helps to create folders specific to groups of images in your computer's hard drive. For example, in "C:MyPictures," you might want to create a variety of folders, titled *Vacation 2006*, *Katie's Graduation*, *Julie's Birthday 2006*, and so on. Create new folders frequently for new events or new subject matter such as *Trip to Hawaii* or *Robbie's Florida Birds*. You can organize your photo folders alphabetically or by date inside a "parent" folder.

Be sure to edit your photos, keeping those you want to look at more closely while erasing extraneous shots. Before downloading any images, take a few minutes to review them on the camera's LCD monitor. Delete any that are obviously unacceptable. After downloading the remaining photos, check them on your computer monitor; delete those that you don't want in order to avoid squandering precious hard drive space.

Rename the images, selecting more logical file names than those that were assigned by the camera. You'll probably agree that "Julie_BDay_Candles.jpg" makes more sense as a file name than "PICT0289.JPG," for example. Later, be sure to convert JPEG files to TIFF before commencing any enhancement in image-processing software. Working on TIFF files will preclude the loss of data that is common when working with JPEGs.

Hint: After shooting an event, you may want to set up one folder for isolating the images: *Bob and Joan's Wedding*, for example. After you adjust a photo using image-processing software, save it using a different file name. If the file name was "Bridesmaids_4.tif," for example, you might save the enhanced file as "Bridesmaids_4B.tif." This step will prevent overwriting the original image so you can later return to it and try entirely different enhancing effects, or use more sophisticated image-processing software.

Image Storage

Although your images are stored as digital files, they can still be lost or destroyed without proper care. Many photographers use two hard drives, either adding a second one to the inside of the computer or using an external USB or FireWire drive. This allows you to immediately and easily back up photos on the second drive. It is very rare for two drives to fail at once (though it is still highly recommended that you burn your images to CD).

Hard drives, Zip discs, and memory cards are certainly useful devices, but they are not ideal for long-term storage. Magnetic media such as Zip discs have a limited life; most manufacturers won't rate such storage devices beyond 5 or 10 years. This is a conservative number, to be sure, but this type of media has been known to lose data in that time span. The life of a hard drive is unknown; but hard drive failures can occur after a couple of years.

A number of malicious computer viruses can wipe out image files from a hard drive (especially JPEGs). Even the best drives can crash, rendering them unusable. Plus, we are all capable of accidentally erasing or saving over an important photo.

The answer to these storage problems is optical media. A CD-writer (or "burner") is a necessity for the digital photographer. DVD-writers work extremely well, too, and DVDs can handle about eight times the data that can be saved on a CD. Either option allows you to back up photo files and store images safely.

There are two types of disc media that can be used for recording data: R designated (i.e. CD-R, DVD-R) recordable discs, and RW designated (i.e. C-RW, DVD-RW) re-writable discs. You can record to CD-R and/or DVD-R discs, but you cannot delete data to re-use the disc to add new images. The RW discs, on the other hand, can be recorded on and then erased and reused later, and you can add more data to them (to the point that the disc space allows).

Hint: For long-term storage of images, only use R discs and not RWs. (The latter are fine for temporary storage, as when transporting images to a new location.) The storage medium used for CD-R and DVD-R discs is more stable than that of RWs which makes sense since the RW discs are designed to be erasable.

Buy discs of the highest quality from well-known manufacturers. Inexpensive discs may not preserve your photo-image files as long as you would like. Read the box. Look for information about the life of the disc. Most long-lived discs are labeled as such, sometimes with terms like "archival," and they cost a little more.

Video Output

The 5D can also be connected to a television set, allowing you to show JPEG images to friends and family in a convenient manner. If you decide to try this feature, start by making sure that the *Video output* option in Setup Menu 1 is set for the correct standard, *NTSC* for North America or *PAL* for Europe and most other regions of the world.

Turn off the television or the VCR as well as the camera. Insert one end of the video cable (provided in the camera kit) to the Video Out terminal behind the small door at the top of the memory card-slot cover. (It's the same port that's used for USB.) Plug the other end into the video input terminal of the TV set or VCR. Turn the video device(s) on and select the video channel. Turn the camera on and press the playback button.

No images or data are displayed on the LCD monitor, but they are displayed on the television screen. Now you can begin viewing JPEG images as you would in conventional camera Playback mode, but using the larger television screen. The image quality and resolution will be lower because of the broadcast standard that's used for the display, but the quality should be adequate for a quick slide show of snapshots.

Direct Printing

The 5D offers a useful amenity—direct printing without using a computer. This feature is available when you connect the camera to any brand of PictBridge compatible photo printer using a USB cable (one is provided with the camera). It works only with JPEG images and only those made in one of the many sRGB Color Modes (see pages 86-88). You cannot use direct printing with MRW-format files, or any image that was made using one of the Adobe RGB color mode options.

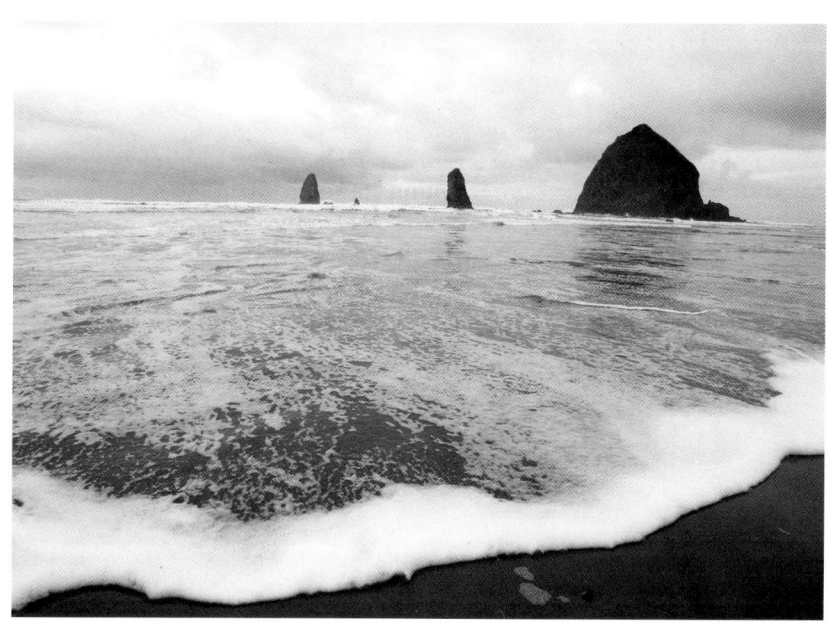

Part of the fun of digital photography is having prints of that memorable vacation or family outing. There are many options for printing: sending files to on-line web services; taking memory cards to kiosks; giving a CD to a minilab; or printing at home.

Note: PictBridge is a technology that allows for direct printing between any brand of digital camera and printer as long as both are PictBridge compliant. The Maxxum 5D/Dynax 5D is PictBridge compatible, as are most Epson, Canon, and HP photo printers released since early 2004. Look for the PictBridge logo on the box when shopping for a printer. Of course, some photo printers also include slots for memory cards, allowing you to print JPEG's directly from the camera's CompactFlash card; this method does not require a PictBridge compliant printer.

Start with a fully charged camera battery or use the optional AC Adapter AC-11. Make sure that the *Transfer Mode* option in Setup Menu 1 is set to *PTP*. Turn the camera off and connect the USB cable from the camera to the printer. Then turn the camera on. The PictBridge screen appears on the LCD monitor. Use the controller keys to scroll and identify the image to be printed and to select the number of copies to be made. You can also activate or close the PictBridge menu using the camera's MENU button.

Using the controller keys, you can control the entire printing process: make an index print of all images on the memory card, select the paper size, layout, and print quality, make printer setup changes, and so on.

Direct printing will not give you the same results as printing from images that have been enhanced in a computer using image-processing software. You have little to no control over aspects such as color and brightness. The amount of control you have over the image is limited entirely by the printer. Some printers do allow minimal image enhancement during direct printing, while others offer none at all.

Digital Print Order Format (DPOF)

Another printing feature of the 5D is DPOF: Digital Print Order Format. This allows you to decide which images to print before you actually do any printing. Then, if you (or your photo lab) have a DPOF compliant printer, it will print those specifically chosen images after you make the USB connection. The DPOF options are available in Playback Menu 2 (see page 107).

The DPOF feature is also useful for selecting images on a memory card for printing at a photo lab that uses DPOF compliant equipment. (Ask about that before leaving your memory card.)

Digital Prints

Unless they own a fully equipped darkroom, photographers who still use 35mm must leave their film at a photofinisher for processing and printing. After a period of time passes, they must return to the store to pick up the order.

With digital capture, images can be printed immediately after taking the picture. There are multiple choices for printing. The following are most common:

Computer Download
After downloading images to a computer, use your own photo printer to make prints of any desired image.

Direct-Print Printers
Use a photo printer with a card reader (slots for memory cards) to make prints direct from the JPEGs on your card. Many such machines provide some control over exposure, color rendition, and cropping. Or, hook up your camera to a PictBridge compliant printer to make prints from the memory card in the camera.

Kiosks
Many stores offer self-service photo kiosks. Plug your memory card into the slot. Use the kiosk's controls to crop and enhance JPEG images from your memory card; specify the desired size and quantity.

Photofinishers and Mini-Labs
Most photo labs now have the capability to take your memory card and make prints or CDs from the image files.

On-Line Services
There are many photofinishers that offer their services through websites. Prices are reasonable and your prints are delivered by mail in less than a week. Once you start an online album on a company's website, you can invite friends and relatives to view images and order prints.

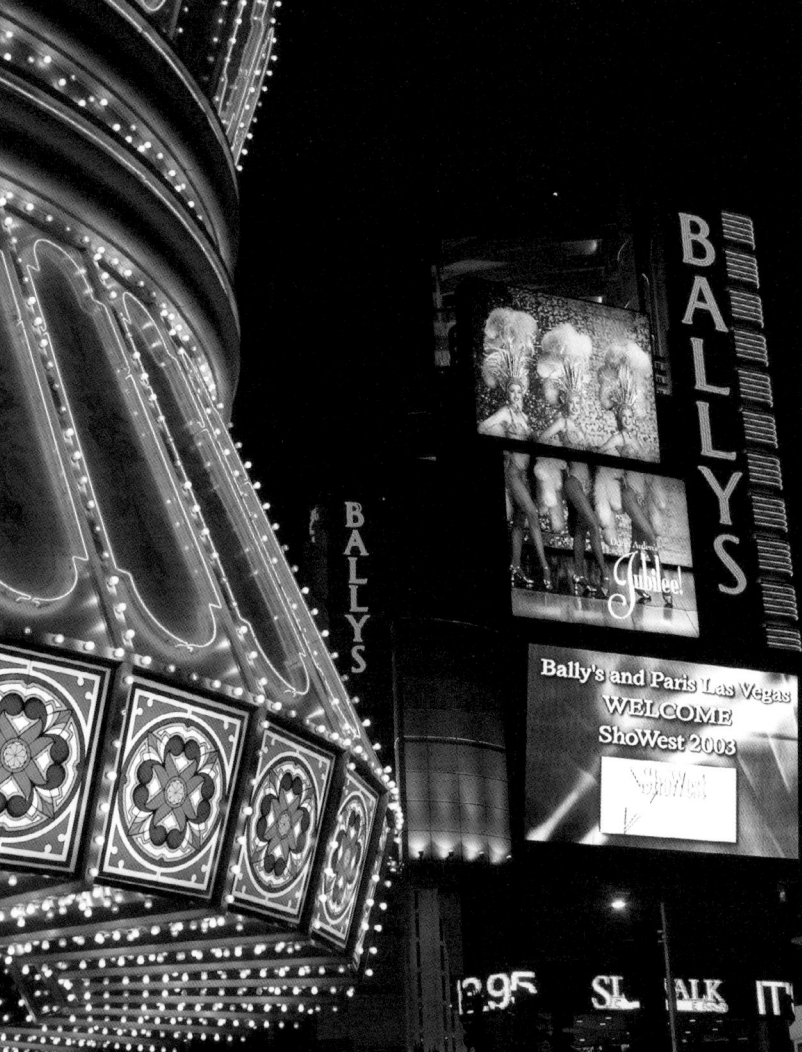

Troubleshooting Guide

The Maxxum 5D/Dynax 5D is a sophisticated high-tech device that provides reliable service. Although rare, a malfunction can occur as with any electronic device. And occasionally, a technical problem will occur due to inappropriate camera settings. The following chart provides steps you can take in these cases.

Note: Unlike some cameras, the 5D does not include a reset button for use in case of some electronic malfunction. However, removing the battery (or unplugging the optional AC adapter) for 30 seconds achieves the same purpose. Do not remove the battery (or disconnect the AC adapter) when the red recording lamp on the camera back is lit; if you do so, the images may be corrupted and, in a worst-case scenario, the memory card may be damaged.

Web Support

Check the Konica Minolta Web site occasionally for updates to firmware (in-camera software), new tips on problem-solving, or information on company authorized service centers in your area: www.konicaminolta.com. The solutions recommended below should solve most problems; however, if you experience camera malfunction—especially one that cannot be solved by removing the battery for 30 seconds—contact an authorized service center.

↩ *The 5D is a reliable camera that is sturdy enough to travel anywhere with you. Technical support is offered by Konica Minolta through their website, www.konicaminolta.com.*

Problem	Possible Cause	Solution
The camera does not operate	Camera is off	Turn camera on
	Battery is dead	Recharge battery
	AC adapter not properly connected	Re-connect AC adapter
No data or image display on LCD monitor	Display mode is set to Off	Press Display button
Overheating message is displayed	Camera is stored in hot environment	Move camera to a cooler location
		Turn camera off until it cools
Camera is on but will not take a photo	Memory card not installed	Install memory card
	Memory card full	Delete images on card to make space for new images
Focus signal blinks and camera cannot focus	Subject is too close	Move farther back
	Subject in low light	Pull flash up for focus-assist pre-flash
	Unusual subject type causing difficulty for AF system	Turn camera on a slight angle and try AF again or switch to manual focus
Pictures are blurry	Camera shake during long shutter speeds	Turn Anti-Shake On
		Use higher ISO
		Activate flash for nearby subjects
		Use a tripod
Action photos are not sharp	Single-shot AF selected or subject movement from long shutter speeds	Select AF-C (Continuous AF)
		For faster shutter speeds, set higher ISO level

Problem	Possible Cause	Solution
Anti-Shake system does not work (viewfinder scale blinks)	Internal electronic error	Remove battery for 30 seconds and re-install
Flash photos in low light are too dark	Subject is beyond range of flash	Move closer to subject
		Set higher ISO or longer shutter speed
	Small subject against bright backlighting	Set a +1 Flash Exposure Compensation in backlighting
Bottom of image is dark in flash photos	Lens hood or large lens barrel is blocking some of the light	Remove lens hood
		Use accessory flash when shooting with large lenses
Unable to find desired image in Playback mode	Appropriate folder has not been selected	Select *All folders* in Playback Menu 2
		Check each folder in Playback for desired image

Index